MW00593345

ALSO BY ABI MAXWELL

Lake People

The Den

ONE DAY I'LL GROW UP
AND BE A BEAUTIFUL WOMAN

ONE DAY
I'LL GROW UP
AND BE A
BEAUTIFUL WOMAN

A MOTHER'S STORY

ABI MAXWELL

ALFRED A. KNOPF

NEW YORK

2024

THIS IS A BORZOI BOOK PUBLISHED BY ALFRED A. KNOPF

Copyright © 2024 by Abi Maxwell

All rights reserved. Published in the United States by Alfred A. Knopf,
a division of Penguin Random House LLC, New York, and distributed in Canada
by Penguin Random House Canada Limited, Toronto.

www.aaknopf.com

Knopf, Borzoi Books, and the colophon are registered trademarks of
Penguin Random House LLC.

Library of Congress Cataloging-in-Publication Data
Names: Maxwell, Abi, author.
Title: One day I'll grow up and be a beautiful woman : a mother's story /
Abi Maxwell.
Description: First United States edition. | New York : Alfred A. Knopf, 2024.
Identifiers: LCCN 2023050370 | ISBN 9780593535844 (hardcover) |
ISBN 9780593535851 (ebook)
Subjects: LCSH: Parents of transgender children—United States—Biography. |
Mothers—United States—Biography. | Transgender children—United States. |
Gender identity—United States.
Classification: LCC HQ1075.5.U6 M399 2024 |
DDC 306.874086/7—dc23/eng/20240223
LC record available at https://lccn.loc.gov/2023050370

Jacket design by Janet Hansen

Manufactured in the United States of America

FIRST EDITION

For O, for F

PART ONE

1

As a child, I spent countless hours staring at other people's houses and imagining life inside. Not their life but mine, if only I lived there. I could slip into it so easily. One cold winter morning while delivering newspapers with my older stepsister Courtney: *If I lived in that house I would still be asleep. If I lived in that house I would be warm. If I lived there and still had to deliver papers, I would have winter socks and good mittens.* I especially remember staring in this way while riding in my father's van. My understanding is that my father never wanted children and that my parents' divorce before I was two had something to do with this. But he remarried almost immediately, and between two marriages, he ended up with eight children—three with my mother, three stepchildren, and two with his new wife. Almost all of us attended different schools, which meant there was a lot of time spent riding in his blue van to drop us off and pick us up. He always took the back roads, and in my memory it's all trees and silence, save for his NPR. I stared out the window, watching stone walls give way to houses. *If I lived there, I wouldn't have to go back and forth between parents. There, clean clothes and a toothbrush no matter whose house I'm at. There, there, there.* It could be a farmhouse or trailer, it could be anything. All these New Hampshire visions, and I sank right down into them.

I was fifteen years old the first time I traveled away from the east. My older brother Henry had moved to Montana for college, and my mother and I flew out to visit him. As the plane lowered toward Missoula, I could see the city, the entire stretch of it, and beyond that the open land. It didn't make sense to me. How could a person live in a place so exposed, the view so relentlessly expansive? Day after day we drove that city in a borrowed Bronco looking for a new vehicle and an apartment for my brother. I remember how odd it all was to me, the people in their cowboy hats and boots with the gall to say hello to strangers on the streets, the jukeboxes and bars in all the restaurants, and that space, open, unprotected, the wind surging through. But mostly I remember that my game didn't work. *There,* I would say. *There, there, there.* But I could not imagine living in a single house.

I grew up, went to college in Wisconsin. *There. There.* Nothing worked, none of it felt real. I moved west, following my brother, and began to stare at the actual houses I lived in. *Here,* I would say to myself instead. *I live here.* Sometimes I had to shake myself. *Real life.* I'd felt detached from my body for as far back as I could remember, felt I watched it from above, but in those places that were not my childhood home, that sense felt extreme.

I spent the end of my twenties and nearly all of my thirties in a small brown ranch house that my grandparents had purchased my final year in college, when they'd had to downsize. My husband and I moved into it after my grandfather passed, to help care for my grandmother, and after she passed, we bought the house. It sits in the center—known as the village—of the small, wealthy, lakeside New Hampshire town of Gilford, where my grandparents had attended church since 1940, the year they got married. Back then, Gilford was a farmers' community, and my grandparents were business owners who lived a few miles down the hill in the small mill city of Laconia; but after the war they, like many others, moved up to the nearby country town that bordered the mountains and lake. They gave their lives to Gilford, volunteering, playing the organ for the church, organizing community plays and outings, showing up for those *less fortunate,* raising four children and then burying one. Now, though they have been gone over a decade, their names continue to be well known in that area.

I don't love that house I lived in, or that neighborhood. The house itself is somewhat shabby, and it's also surrounded by large, expensive homes with professional lawncare, and this always made me feel out of place. I don't love that town, either, though I used to, for it is idyllic. There are mountains crisscrossed with hiking trails, there's the largest lake in the state, and there's a ski area. The library is well funded, and so is the school—so well funded, in fact, that there's even a sap house so children can tap the maple trees and learn to make syrup in March. On Halloween, the village street where I lived is closed off, and the scene of families walking up and down the block at the base of the mountains beneath the red maples is picture-perfect, out of a children's book. Same at Christmastime, when the street is shut down again for a candlelight stroll of caroling, warm treats in neighbors' yards, and open tours of the village's oldest buildings.

Though I went back and forth between parents, my primary childhood home was my mother's old farmhouse, in a poor mill town some ten miles to the west. Growing up, we would play against this wealthy lake-and-mountain town in school sports, always painfully aware of what they had and we lacked: good uniforms, school ski teams, photography and creative writing classes, an auditorium so school plays could be performed on a real stage instead of in the cafeteria. So, even though Gilford was where my father had come from, and where my grandparents had lived, when I moved there as an adult it felt like an acute betrayal.

"I had a wonderful childhood in that town," my father tells me. He tells me stories about trick-or-treating on my street, which was closed off back then in just the same way. He tells me about the family who managed to raise five children in my very small Gilford house when he was a boy. When he hears what my daughter had to endure in that town, he says, "I just can't imagine it. Elementary school should be a time of pure happiness."

Does he have amnesia? Is it possible that he has entirely forgotten the landscape of my own childhood?

2

was born in Laconia, that small mill city my grandparents first lived in together. Today, it has all the markings of an East Coast city plagued by the opioid crisis: empty mills, boarded-up storefronts, pharmacies on what feels like every corner. But of course it wasn't always like that. My paternal grandfather grew up in that city during its heyday, when it had working mills, trolley cars, a train to Boston, and thriving businesses. One was my family's—an ice cream and candy shop passed down to my grandfather from his father, a German man who had moved to the area from the southern part of the state at fifteen to escape a life on the family farm. He must have been a good businessman—he'd bought that shop after working just one year in it, and he eventually came to own the entire city block the shop was in. But he had also married into the wealth of my great-grandmother's family. She was a proud Daughter of the American Revolution who had grown up in Laconia, in her mill-owner parents' mansion; and her parents, her grandparents, and at least one branch of her great-grandparents were also born in that city—or at least that county—dating all the way back to 1775. Before that, they'd lived on the coast of New Hampshire since the first Pilgrim ships arrived.

"Why didn't they stay on the coast?" I asked my father the moment I realized this. The reason was almost surely the mills, though I like to imagine they came for the lake that would hold the heart of so many of their descendants. My father understood the meaning behind my question: If our ancestors had stayed on the coast rather than move inland, maybe my daughter would have been born there, in a decidedly more accepting place. If they had stayed there, and we had, we could have avoided so much suffering.

But no matter. I talk about my ancestors as though these people have something to do with who I am, as though they, by virtue of a speck of blood, would accept and love not only me but also my daughter. But of course I have no idea, and anyway, this proud New Hampshire history is so terribly fraught. I used to say that I wondered what my ancestors had to do with the colonizing of this country, but the truth is that I do not need to wonder. They were some of the very first white people to settle in this state, so it seems they must have stolen the land with their own hands. And for all the pride of our family history, there are no stories of abolitionists. Surely, if they had been present, their stories would have been passed down. Instead, this, a story from my aunt, given to me one January evening as I put my coat on to leave her grandson's birthday party: "When your grandparents sold the Gilford house up on the hill, they told the real estate agent to find any good family, so long as they were white. They'd bought the land from the Carsons," she explained, "who still lived there. They felt it would have been impolite to give them Black neighbors."

I didn't know this growing up, would never have imagined it.

3

·························

There's a large cemetery in Laconia, where so much of my family history resides, and I used to like to go there and walk the grounds, to see my family's plot. There are my grandparents, and my uncle who died at twenty when his car slipped on wet leaves and hit a tree out on the main road just down the street from the house I would live in. There are names I know but cannot place. I suspect my father will have his own stone there one day, but I will not. I do not love that area anymore; in fact, I think I hate it.

That plot of more recent family is deep in the cemetery, but at the entrance is my ancestors' plot, which is where my great-grandmother and her family are buried. Being mill owners, they were rich enough to have a large statue of a robed figure holding a scroll. The base of the statue reads: *And I heard a voice from heaven saying unto me, Write. Blessed are the dead which die in the Lord from henceforth.*

There's a lot I don't understand about that quote. I have no religious upbringing whatsoever. But what I do understand is that, of all the thousands of biblical quotes my ancestors could have chosen to emblemize them for eternity, this is what they chose: *Write.*

I'm trying to listen. I'm trying to describe what it felt like to be raised to believe that, despite what I had—love, but also neglect, parents entangled in a vicious divorce that resulted in a dark childhood and a mess of a family that was in and out of court—I still had reason to be proud, to know that my family came from here, that we had history. That above all else, I was of and from this New Hampshire land. I'm trying to say what it felt like, then, to have this place and its people stand up and say to me, *No, we are from here, we were raised here,* as though they had been here any longer than I, but also as though such a statement could or should ever lay claim to who is and is not allowed to occupy this land. To have my town look at my daughter and stand up and say, *No, we will not make a safe space for her here.* To have it say, *No, she does not belong, she is not what we believe a child should be.* I'm trying to describe the depth to which that broke my heart, and woke me up to the truth of this rural landscape I was raised to love.

4

....

When I first discovered I was pregnant, I went for a walk alone in the woods. I remember holding my hand to my belly as I walked, speaking to the child I had never planned for. I believed she would be a girl. I named her on that walk, Clementine Eleanor. I felt sick with anxiety, afraid of how I would care for another human—not whether or not I could, but how much of myself it would take. I had just sold my first novel. My husband and I were training for a cross-country ski marathon, and in the best shape of our lives. Finally, I had what I'd worked so hard to create: a New Hampshire life of writing and reading and skiing, and hanging out with my husband on weekends. Where would that life go?

We had an old, needy dog at that point. I fed him by hand, and even though he was relatively large, I let him crawl onto my lap. On walks, when he would suddenly get afraid and refuse to move, I would lift him up, all fifty pounds, and carry him home, my exhaustion masked by pure love for that helpless creature.

"Look at how I parent a dog," I remember saying to my oldest friend. "A baby will ruin me."

That friend, Ingrid, had just a year previously given birth to her first child, so throughout the process she guided me. When the time came, she asked me why I would bother finding out the sex of the baby. I can still remember my precise answer to her: "I want to know who I'm talking to in there."

So there it is: the moment my child's anatomy flickered on the screen, my relationship to her, the way I thought of and spoke to her, shifted. And she still had months left in the womb.

The technician that day said that it had been almost all boys all year. She covered my growing belly in a cold gel and ran her wand across, eyes on the screen, and when she was done she printed out a string of black-and-white photos in which I believed I could see that same upper shelf of a top lip so reminiscent of my husband's family line. Two of the photos were of my baby's entire body, large head followed by curved back and kicking feet. Five were of her genitalia. *It's a boy!* the technician scrawled across the top.

We had to choose a new name, and the first one we settled briefly on together was Orlando. My husband had no association, but I did to a certain degree. At that point I knew no transgender people—or more accurately believed I knew none—and could not even define the word correctly. But I had read and loved Virginia Woolf's *Orlando,* the wild novel of that brave, gentle, gender-bending being who reminded me of my little brother, Noah—half brother, technically—who loved dresses and wigs, high heels, Broadway shows, and who grew up to be a proud gay man. I think of that initial name choice now, and though I believe the universe has no order, though I cannot subscribe to a doctrine that suggests anything happens for a reason, I do wonder about the future signaling itself. How odd it would have been had we stuck with that name. *Same person, different sex.*

When my baby was born, they put her on the scale and called out that she was a boy and my husband named her while I blinked in and out of consciousness. She was big, nearly ten pounds, and when the doctors asked my husband to read her weight he misplaced the decimal point and yelled out "13.7!" instead of the correct 9.137. They put her body on mine and wheeled us out. My mother was waiting in the hallway, desperate to behold us. She leaned over and asked me if I could feel the love, if I could finally understand. But labor had been long and had ended in an emergency cesarean, and I could not feel the love. I could feel nothing.

"We are connected," my mother was saying earnestly to my baby. "We are connected."

The nurses had me sleep with my baby that night, her body tucked beneath my arm, and my arm held in place by the armrest of the hospital bed. I remember the fever dreams of that night like they were yesterday. All night, I was searching the halls. I could not find my child, had lost her, but it wasn't just a physical loss. There was a confusion to the dream, some insurmountable wall between my child's actual existence and where she had disappeared to.

I think of that dream now, too. Up until somewhat recently, I kept a school photograph of my daughter's first-grade year on my dresser. I don't know how she would have reacted if she noticed the photo there. In it she looks proud but awkward, somehow physically uncomfortable, as she often did back then. She is just barely six years old, and she's wearing the blue plaid button-up shirt that I forced her to wear. Her hair is cut into the short, little-boy cut that I forced her to get so that she looked like the cute little boy that I believed her to be. She was still known to the world as a boy at that point, still the wearer of her former name, the name she complained about for some three years before I listened. I look at that photo and I think of that dream. I want the child I have, the current one. I want her one million times over. And I understand, of course I understand, that despite a change in name and pronouns and wardrobe, my child is the same exact person she has always been. But the person in that photo, she was also not the same. We knew her as brilliant but angry. Our current child is happy and fierce. I look at that photo and think of that dream and I wonder where that other child went. That child is gone, vanished, and I can scarcely remember them.

5

first met my husband, Paul, on the sidewalk in Missoula, Montana. I had just finished college and was headed to Idaho with my brother Henry, who would attend graduate school there, and Paul was just about to leave Missoula for culinary school in Vancouver, Canada. It was morning, June, hot and sunny. My brother and I had stopped in Montana to visit friends for a few days. It felt like the entire town was out for the Saturday market, and Henry and I were weaving through the crowd when we ran into Paul—the younger brother of my brother's good friend. He introduced us. Paul was stoned and smiling wide, looking like he'd never had a care in the world. He held out a bag of Sour Patch Kids and Swedish Fish and asked if I wanted some.

"I'm in love with Paul Maxwell," I said to my brother as we walked away.

A year later, I returned to Missoula to live, and so did Paul, and through mutual friends we met again at a bar. He had thick blond hair and button-down shirts, and when I first laid eyes on him I told my friend that he was too clean-cut to ever be interested in me, a girl who worked for a wilderness trail crew and did not shave. But when I heard he'd said I was cute, I found out his address and left wildflowers in an empty beer can on his porch, along with my phone number.

On our first date, we drank a pitcher of beer and played pool in a western bar, and after midnight we walked across town, toward the house he lived in with friends. I still remember the glow of the neighborhood street, the whistle of the trains through the valley, and the feeling that he and I were contained in a bubble with nothing and no one else. I told him I would be a writer. He told me he loved fishing on the Encampment River in southern Wyoming. He'd been born in Colorado, but when his parents divorced he'd eventually left the west with his mother, and we realized the small town where I'd camped every summer of my childhood was the same coastal Maine town he'd ended up in as a teen. That night, we discovered other ways we'd circled each other over the years, other places we'd unknowingly been within an arm's reach of each other.

In our first days together, I learned that my initial impression of a clean-cut man had been off; Paul rented an attic bedroom with only trapdoor access in a small house on the railroad tracks, and he washed his clothes in the river because he enjoyed the slowness of it. All his belongings fit into an old camp trunk—a pair of wool pants, a wool jacket, fishing clothes and equipment, a set of chef's knives his grandmother had gifted him, and a collection of CDs. A few weeks into our relationship, when I picked him up at his house—because he had no car or driver's license, and instead preferred to walk or ride his bike—he put that trunk into the back of my car without a word. I lived in a cabin thirty minutes outside the city, and as we drove along the Blackfoot River I asked him why he'd brought the trunk.

"You said you needed a new roommate," he said simply.

It was true—my college friend had decided to return home to Alaska, and I wouldn't be able to cover rent myself. I didn't know how to respond, so I said nothing, and in this way my husband moved in with me that day, and he never left my side again.

. . .

Sometime in that first month together we were once again out late at a bar where a western cover band played. We were among many friends, his older brother included, and when we leaned in close to reach our drinks his brother said to me, "Where will you get married? Montana or New Hampshire?"

I didn't miss a beat. Didn't think, *We won't get married.* Didn't think, *We've known each other scarcely a month.* I just answered the question. "New Hampshire."

It didn't happen for another seven years, but it did happen eventually, just as I'd said it would. One summer we packed our belongings, our cat, and even our fish, and we left that western city for my home. We got married a few weeks later, on the lake island of my childhood.

Now I sometimes look back on those first days and try to implant the knowledge of the future into those young selves of ours. I think of all the decisions that might have been altered, had we known where they would lead. Recently, my brother-in-law asked me if I remembered why we had ever left the west all those years ago. I do, and a part of it is so easy to explain—I had wanted to be closer to my aging grandmother, and to hear her stories before she passed. But the other part is so much harder.

My paternal grandmother was the daughter of Swedish immigrants, and she grew up first in tenement housing and then in a small home her father had built on the outskirts of Boston. She could play the piano by ear, and she loved to read Keats and Tennyson, and to ponder her deep spirituality. Her father was a millworker, her mother stayed at home, and her spinster maternal aunts were maids for a wealthy man on the Boston shore who shot himself in the head the day the stock market crashed. There would be no money for her to go to college. She had a paternal aunt, though, who lived in Wellesley, where the public school awarded its top student a full scholarship to attend Wellesley College. My grandmother moved in with her aunt for her senior year of high school and worked hard and won that scholarship. She continued living with her aunt during her four years of college, and every summer she found a job to help pay for expenses. One year, that job was as a waitress at a lakeside resort in New Hampshire.

My grandfather loved to tell the story of meeting my grandmother, which was simply that he had gone for dinner with a friend and been introduced to her and it had been love at first sight. After that he transferred from the University of Vermont to Babson College in Wellesley while my grandmother finished her studies, and then they married and settled in my grandfather's hometown of Laconia, and within a year they moved up the road to Gilford.

My grandfather's studies combined with his natural talents made him an excellent businessman, and with the help of my grandmother, the candy and ice cream shop he had inherited from his father flourished. They had children, built a house in Gilford that overlooked the lake, and in the 1950s bought a boat, a boathouse, and the island property that would become our family's sanctuary. When the local Boy Scout camp had an old cabin they wanted to get rid of, my grandfather bought it, put it on runners, towed it out across the water, and repurposed it for a family cabin. His own father, around this time, was a state senator who also loved the lake and hated to see the development occurring on its shores. He spent his time in office advocating for public parks on the water, which today—according to the way my father tells it—is the reason for the one and only state park on that entire lake.

The land my grandfather purchased faces directly east, so that the sun beams straight on in the early morning and disappears by four o'clock even in the height of summer. My father spent his childhood summers there, while my grandfather commuted by boat back and forth to the store. My grandmother, unaccustomed to the wealth my grandfather had grown up in, was committed to sharing their good fortune, and always encouraged guests to join them on the lake. One of these was a friend in Boston, who now had a husband and five children. She and her family would travel up to New Hampshire to join my father's family for two weeks every summer, and she would turn out to be my maternal grandmother, which means that my mother and father—destined for a bitter divorce—would swim and play in the sand together for years as children.

By the time I was a child, the cabin was mouse- and spider-infested, with floors sagging and moss growing on the roof. Going out there was always an unplanned surprise, at least from my perspective; my father and stepmother would come home to the house full of kids and tell us to find our swimsuits and get in the van. They'd drive to the grocery store, and they'd go in while we waited in the parking lot. In the van, we would fight and yell and throw things out the windows at strangers. We were a pack of wolves, and occasionally we were reprimanded by adults walking past. Eventually my father and stepmother would return to us with loads of paper shopping bags, and we would drive to the Gilford boathouse my grandfather had bought all those years ago. My father still keeps that boathouse, and sometimes, on our hardest days in Gilford, I would go there just for the feeling it gave me, that an entrance to some other world was still possible.

Back then, the family boat was for the whole family—my grandparents, my aunt and uncle, my father. We had a few different ones over the years. They were always clunky and used, the kind that required my father to spend a lot of time looking the motor over and tinkering with the various pumps. They also frequently broke down in the middle of the lake, and one of them even caught fire and sank. I never quite knew when we'd gotten a replacement, but they were all essentially the same: old and blue, with a flat, seatless bow encircled by a low, weak metal bar at its perimeter and an echoey crawl chamber below, ripped-up driver and passenger seats, plus a few more seats in the stern. My stepsister and I would ride on the bow, clinging for our lives to a rope while my father gunned it across the dark water.

A few things are true about our time out there as children: We were hungry, and generally not allowed to enter the kitchen to find food, so my memories are clouded with stolen, unripe plums. We were thirsty, sunburned, and unsupervised. But also, we were the luckiest children in the entire world. Lucky—for we had no concept of the privilege that got us to this place—to not only have landed here but to actually say this was ours, this magical world so close to yet so completely removed from our troubled lives. Arriving was like crossing through a door to another dimension, one where my father would laugh heartily and he and my stepmother would sit with us late into the night, talking, reminiscing. Mornings, I alone would rise when my father did and follow him into the water, holding on to his shoulders while he dipped under and swam out toward the buoys. Days, I would sit on the beach and look toward the mainland and wonder at the impossibility of that life going on there while we were down here, inside this perfect snow globe, which was missing only the presence of my mother.

When my husband and I fell in love, we would stay up late in the cabin we rented in Montana and I would tell him dreamily about the island. How there was a water spring, and a lake so big and so full of secret pockets. How it was not perfect, the cabin was falling down, and when I was a teenager my brother's best friends had drowned there one night when they'd paddled out to see the moon in May, the canoe rotting and the water so cold. And still, how maybe one day Paul and I could winter the island together, just the two of us, watching through ice in and ice out.

When we moved east, we planned to go to Maine, and then maybe Vermont, and then to northern New Hampshire, but I wouldn't commit to any of it.

"You're orbiting," the wise man who performed our wedding ceremony said to us, and he was right: we were orbiting ever closer to the lake, and I didn't say yes to any place to live until we were right there at its shore. We were in Gilford, the town that would become our downfall. We felt from the start that we didn't fit in, but it didn't matter. What mattered was the lake. It had too many speedboats, the land was too bought up by wealthy out-of-staters, there was scarcely any public access. But it was the place I belonged. When I looked out at it, I felt something so vital, something so beyond words that it almost hurt to look, and I would wonder if some thread of my history that had been looking out at this view for hundreds of years accounted for such a feeling.

Now I can hardly bear to look at the lake. But I'm getting ahead of myself.

6

....

t was September, a few years before our child was born, when my
husband and I moved in with my grandmother in the center of Gilford Village, and on the very first day—before we had even gone to
buy bedding—I walked down the street beneath the turning maples,
past her church, to the town's library. It had been rebuilt that year, the
building now large and full of light, the collection extensive, with a
children's room on the ground floor and adult and teen spaces on the
main level. The woman working the circulation desk gave me a reg-
istration form, and when I handed her my proof of address she said,
"Isn't that where Elly lives?"

"She's my grandmother," I said. "My husband and I just moved in
with her."

She said she'd known my grandfather, who had died a year earlier,
and that I would probably see her son around, because he worked at
the town dump. She gave me a copy of that month's book discussion
pick and said it would be great to see someone my age show up. She
was a warm woman in her late seventies or early eighties, her white
hair in the same tight curl that my grandmother kept. "I'm going to
retire soon," she said as she winked at me, "in case you need a job."

I walked back on a trail through the woods—which could lead me to the mountains, if I wanted, or back to the road—and imagined how ideal my life would be if I worked in that beautiful space filled with books, just a few minutes down the road from my home. At the time, I was teaching college writing classes at a technical school some fifty minutes away, and I'd never felt the job suited me. I knew I was good at it, but I was also riddled with anxiety before each class and depleted after. The town library seemed like a dream.

I didn't end up reading that book for the monthly discussion, but a few days later I walked down to return the novel I'd read instead. A different woman sat at the circulation desk. She had a kind, serious look about her. As I returned the book, I told her I had loved it so much, and then I said I was interested in volunteering at the library. She handed me an application and asked if I was new in town. "Do you like hiking?" she asked, and she pulled out a large booklet of maps of the town's trails. She introduced herself, said that perhaps we could go on a hike together sometime, and that another librarian would soon get in touch with me about my volunteer application.

My volunteer job at the library was to sit in the back workroom and cover new books. Other volunteers were always there, too, and over time I got to know them. They were all women, all a generation or two older than me. "The Millers!" they would say when I told them who my grandparents were. "Of course I knew them." Some of the women had worked scooping ice cream at my grandparents' store; some had worked for my father after he'd taken over the family business. A few had been in plays with my grandparents back when the community theater still ran. "I used to go swim laps in their pool when they lived up on the hill," one woman said. "It was so generous of them to let me do that."

Slowly, I started to build a community. I went for hikes with one librarian, and I had tea and talked about books with another. By winter a position at the library opened, and I took it. I worked the evening shifts, and the woman I'd first met at the desk trained me. She showed me a folder where she kept newspaper clippings of ice-in and ice-out dates on the lake, and another with documents about an old island mansion. She'd grown up in the same Massachusetts town my grandmother had come from, and she'd worked in a library since she was a young teenager. I loved hearing her stories about the old days, like when she used to drive a van down to the lake to deliver books to all the young mothers without cars. It all felt oddly satisfying, like I was living out a short story about a small-town librarian.

"I always fluff the couch pillows at night," she told me. "And I do what the boss says."

But then another librarian told me something else in those first few days: "I don't buy any of this gay stuff." We were flipping through library trade journals of prepublication reviews, marking the books we thought the library ought to purchase. It was evening, dark, the library empty. "If it says LGB-whatever, you can skip it," she said. "People here don't read that."

An image of my little brother, Noah, flashed across my mind. We'd drifted apart over the years, but we had been so close when we were young. Now I wanted to challenge her, to tell her that my brother was a gay man, that I would read those books, that my husband and grandmother and my friends would. But I didn't say anything. I liked this woman, and I liked this job. I told myself that she didn't mean any harm, and I kept quiet.

For the better part of the next ten years, I stayed at that library. I worked the circulation desk, led book discussions, taught writing workshops. I listened to patrons' stories of their lives, of their connections with my grandparents, of the town and mountains and lake. I started a classics book discussion group, where a handful of diehard readers showed up every other month to sit in the small New Hampshire room surrounded by state archives and follow me down the long path of examining *Great Expectations* or *Jane Eyre* and its place in literature. I recommended books to patrons, and I read what they recommended to me. "I heard you don't read books by women," I once said to a voracious reader in his seventies whose book returns always had to be placed in a special box filled with coffee grounds to get the stench of cigar smoke out. He liked some of the same rough western novels I liked, and on this we'd felt a kinship. "You can't just say that!" I told him. "Try this, and this, and this." He read everything I suggested, loved some and hated some, and always gave me feedback.

A few years into my job, when I announced I was pregnant, my library community threw a small shower. When my baby was born, library people came to visit with cookies and casseroles, hand-sewn blankets and knitted hats.

The children's room of the library was an entity to itself, and in those early years before I had a baby I scarcely ventured into it, and there weren't many patrons my age who used the adult floor of the library, as most of them were already parents who stayed downstairs with their children. In fact, I remember only one couple—a woman named Katie and her husband, Dan. I met them in my first weeks of work. She was visibly pregnant, and watching them check out books about pregnancy and their new life ahead called to mind my own future, and the decisions my husband and I might make. I always chatted with them at the circulation desk. My friends—the ones I'd grown up with—lived a few towns over, and I wanted to make some friends my age right here. We talked about the materials they were checking out or returning, we talked about the weather, and eventually, when I realized that Katie skied, we talked about our shared love of the sport.

It never led to much, but years later, when my husband and I found ourselves at the center of a town debate that pitted Katie's family and mine against each other, I would be haunted by the clarity of those early memories. They had carved themselves so deeply into my mind. Why, of all the hundreds of patrons I mindlessly chatted with, could I recall the specific magazines this one couple had checked out, and the weather and light on specific days they'd visited? But I remember it. I remember the drizzly February evening when they came into the library in the quiet daze of early parenthood, their newborn in a carrier. She was covered entirely by a blanket, a makeshift canopy that stretched over the handle of her chair and protected her from the outside world. I whispered a hello to them, asked them her name. Katie lifted the edge of the blanket up so I could see in for a split second. I looked at this perfect infant who, in six years, would enter kindergarten with my yet unconceived one.

"Oh my goodness," I whispered to her parents. "Congratulations." I barely knew them, but I almost wanted to hug them. Instead, we smiled at each other, all of us entirely unaware that, one day, they would devote themselves to protecting this sleeping child from exposure to my own.

7

hen our daughter was two—and still known as a boy—and I was a handful of years into my position at the library, the children's room needed a new librarian and I needed more hours. It wasn't a position anyone would have envisioned for me—I wasn't animated and sociable, like all the previous children's librarians, and I didn't do crafts. But I cared deeply about literacy, and having a child meant I was learning a lot about children's books. I moved downstairs, to the children's room, where a woman named Lisa already worked. When she'd first moved to town from just outside New York City, she'd shocked me with her personality, which was so far from the reserved New England character I was accustomed to.

"We should go out sometime," she'd said the day we met. "What do you like to do? We could go for a drink? Or dinner? Give me your phone number."

Her nails were professionally manicured, her clothing bright. She was in high heels in the afternoon, and she had a large diamond on her finger. I was dumbfounded. "I really don't go out," I said pathetically.

"Okay," she said. "I'll work on you."

She'd started working in the children's room soon after that, teaching Spanish to elementary kids and leading a music and movement group for toddlers. We could hear her through the whole library while she taught, blasting music, singing children's songs, laughing. Sometimes she'd parade the children right upstairs through the quiet adult section, drums and bells in their hands. She and I were so different, and when I moved into her workspace, my academic approach collided with her joyful one and neither of us knew how we would make it through. We bickered about where the books should be shelved, how the story times should be run, what the volunteers should do. We bickered about everything, and sometimes we got so frustrated that we drove each other to tears.

But eventually, something emerged through all our differences: we loved books and we believed in their power. We were in an insular town, and when she and I chose books for the library, we chose the ones that would expose the kids to a larger world. If our director didn't purchase them, we filled out little paper slips to request them again and again. We made it our mission to diversify the collection. We believed it was the best thing we could do for the children of our community, and we learned to work together for it.

My grandmother had passed away by the time I worked in the children's room, and Paul and I had used every last dollar we had—including the forty thousand dollars in government bonds I'd inherited from a great-aunt in Chicago, and the cosignature of my mother—to purchase her house. For a few years after we bought the house, Paul stayed home with our daughter while I worked in the day, and at night he went to a local restaurant to bake. They weren't easy years. Something had happened to Paul's hip—we didn't yet know what—that made walking painful on most days, and nearly impossible on some. Also, he missed the west, and working a low-wage job in a rural restaurant was taking its toll on him. It became a growing seed of discontent between us—he dreamed of returning to Missoula and made passing comments about being stuck in New Hampshire because I wouldn't leave the lake; and I snapped that if he wanted to go back west, he needed only to take the initiative to make it happen.

In truth, we both knew we didn't have the energy. We were so tired. Our child had spent the first year of her life waking up every hour, and by toddlerhood she still had not progressed to anything even close to a full night's sleep. We understood that she was different; I'd read every parenting book I could get my hands on, and nothing added up. She hit us, threw objects at us, hit herself in the head. She had not spoken until the age of two, and she rarely responded to her name, but by four she was putting together robots and snap circuit kits made for someone twice her age. She would use only one particular spoon, one particular fork. My father had gifted her a garbage truck when she was three, and for two entire years she had played with that truck and nothing else. She meticulously cut paper to put in toy trash cans, and then she spread the cans around the house to drive the truck to pick up the trash and empty it into the toy dumpster. For her fourth birthday, she asked friends to bring garbage so she could send it down a chute and sort it. She loved Halloween not for the candy but for the wrappers. She mystified us.

In those early years, Paul would put her in the bike carrier and pedal her down to the children's room for story times and library programs nearly every day. She did okay there so long as she could have the same exact cushion every time. But if the space was too crowded, she would become overwhelmed, cover her ears, and dart around in a panic. Sometimes, as I read a story aloud or glued googly eyes onto construction paper, I would watch out of the corner of my eye, heart breaking, as my husband carried our screaming child out of the library because she had begun to melt down.

But the children's room was still a home to us, as it was to other regulars like us—families that came to all the library programs and checked out mountains of books each week. One was a girl our child's age and her dad, and he and Paul gravitated to each other. His name was Eric, and soon he became our first real friend in town, the kind who would come over for an afternoon and unexpectedly stay all the way through dinner. Eric's wife, Robin, traveled often for work, so it was some weeks before I met her. He'd told me a little about her, though—I knew she loved to play video games, and I knew she worked in finance; I knew we didn't have much in common. Eric was easy for me—he liked to read and draw, and to talk about the process of making art. But when Robin first came over, our conversation was stilted. We seemed to have nothing to talk about, not until we landed upon what it looked like to raise a girl.

"She's only three," she said about her daughter. "And there's already so much shit about body image everywhere." We were sitting on the old couch I'd bought for fifty dollars when the library was getting rid of it, in the small room whose layout I never could get right. Robin worked for Mercedes-Benz, which meant she drove one, and I'd felt shy about the state of our house and our clear lack of wealth. But she had a relaxed way about her. She'd brought a bottle of Coke for herself and laughed at the salad we'd made, filled with random nuts and seeds and dried fruits from the back of the cupboard. "Eric warned me you all ate like hippies," she said. Of her daughter she said: "There's so much shit about what she's supposed to like and not like."

Of course I knew what she meant, and it existed for my child, too, though in a different form because we still thought we had a boy. There was a dress-up bin at the library, and when my child put the princess dress and plastic high heels on—as she often did—people stared. When boys in the children's room tried to check out picture books with mermaids or princesses, their parents told them to put them down because they were for girls.

"It's so stupid," I'd said to Lisa once. "All this gendered stuff."

"I don't know," she said, without looking up at me. We were in the back workroom, the story time crowd just cleared out. I noticed a shift in her—and she, surely, in me. We had come to know each other well; we knew that we were both strong-willed, and we could recognize when our bodies tensed and our voices became a little more forced—

a warning that our deeply held opinions were about to bump up against one another. "I wish I had a girl," she said. "I would love to dress her up like a princess."

"But these parents who don't let their boys check out princess books. It makes me sick," I said. I knew I was speaking forcefully, knew I was attempting in my tone to leave no room for argument. And we both knew what we were really discussing—my child, known to the world as a boy, who put the princess dress on every time she visited.

Lisa kept her attention on the pile of cardstock in front of her. She was getting ready to cut out shapes for a craft. She lovingly made elaborate crafts with the kids, the kind she hoped they'd save for years. It wasn't my style to do that—I tended to just throw a pile of playdough or fingerpaints on the table for them. "Sure," she said as she sorted paper. "But also, I really appreciate gender roles."

I didn't press it. She was my friend. In many ways, she and I had seen the worst of each other, and we had come out the other side with a loyalty to each other despite our differences. But when I heard Robin question gender roles, I felt an immense relief. Compared to the liberal college city Paul and I had moved from, this town felt so conservative, its social norms so crushing. I needed someone who would help me swim against them.

8

My daughter was four, a few weeks short of five, when I first took her to a store to buy something new for her to wear. She was about to start kindergarten as my sweet, wild, angry, funny, high-needs little boy. Prior to this, she had always worn hand-me-downs from the boys she'd grown up with, the children of my childhood friends. She had never seemed to care what she wore anyway—or actually, the reverse is true: for the most part she refused to get dressed. It would sometimes take half the day, sometimes not occur at all. When it did, it usually involved screaming on her part. Not *These clothes are all wrong for me,* but "I don't want to get dressed, I'm not getting dressed, you're stupid, I hate you." Kindergarten would start at eight thirty every morning and last all day, my child still spent a third of the night on most nights awake, and I was terrified of what we were about to enter. I thought of holding her back, but then she had never been to preschool. To keep her home as an only child for another year seemed like the wrong decision.

"Where's the girls' section," she said when we walked into the shoe store. Not a question so much as a statement. I asked her why she wanted it and she said plainly, "I want pink sneakers."

. . .

We were in Laconia, the city where I'd been born, in the same shoe store my mother had taken me to every year to get my school sneakers and Sorels. It still had the same gleaming yellow metal slide in the children's section, the same balloon machine by the door. It's in the center of downtown, a ten-minute walk from the house my father lived in while I was in elementary school. Back then, in the constant absence of supervision, my stepsister Courtney and I spent hours out on those streets alone. We'd sneak into the movie theater, smoke cigarettes behind the garage, slash open all the bags of leaves in the neighborhood. We'd parade up the dark road in the rain drinking stolen nips of liquor. We'd shoplift our family's Christmas presents and then watch with shame as my father would unwrap his Old Spice and say, "Ooh la la," impressed that Courtney and I could afford such a gift.

"We raised you all with a fierce independence," my father and stepmother say now, when we ask basic questions like, "Where were you?" and "What were you thinking?"

Once, I had a friend from school come to sleep over at my father's house, which was not a typical occurrence. My friend and I were nine or ten, though I'm guessing she came from a household much different than mine and in that sense was much younger than I was. I still remember the large, empty feel of the spotless white kitchen in that house that my father had paid so much to have renovated. My friend must have been surprised at our apparent wealth, and also surprised to discover that we had no dinner. I don't know where my father and stepmother were that night—probably at the family store, though maybe they were on the lake. Now my father tells wild stories of nights on the lake, and despite what they meant for my own childhood, I thrill to hear them. Stories of when he and my stepmother would take the boat to private, exclusive restaurants on distant islands. Of cutting through storms, lightning at their heels. Of coming home so drunk that he would spend the night walking the neighborhood streets, then sleeping in the backyard under the glow of the stars. Imagining, I am sure, the lives of the heroes of the novels he loved and the men who had written them. Not imagining, then, the lives of his children.

That night, my friend and I went downtown with my stepsisters. We somehow had money. We bought candy and soda and watched a movie and I know there were boys involved, boys with my sisters, and I know that I felt so humiliated and afraid, to have my cold home exposed in such a way. After the movie we went outside and stood on the curb near the car—whose car?—and my friend stepped to get in and suddenly vomited, her candy and soda coming up from within and spreading across the sidewalk and over the curb, under the car. My stepsisters erupted in laughter and I thought, *Good, get out now. Have your parents pick you up and go home. There is no love here.*

We bought the pink sneakers on that late summer day before kindergarten started, and then my daughter put her token in the machine for her balloon, and we left the store. We walked past that movie theater—now closed—that was on the far side of the river from the mill my great-great-grandparents had owned and just steps away from the block that had been razed during urban renewal but before that had been stamped with my family's name. She carried her yellow balloon and I held her hand and told her that she was walking the same streets that her grandfather had walked, and her great-grandparents, and her great-great-grandparents, and on and on and on back until a time before the roads were built.

She didn't care. What she cared about was that she finally owned something pink, finally owned a tool to help her communicate to the world who she really was. She'd worn the sneakers out of the store. The cashier had made some stupid comment, something along the lines of *You're sure this is the color you want?* and I'd responded with something that felt rude at the time but would comparatively have been so tame; within a year I would get so much practice in the art of standing up for a child.

I took a picture of her on the sidewalk that day. In it, my daughter—

still known to the world as a boy—is full of joy and hope with her new pink sneakers and balloon. I think of that photo now, of my child standing where I stood so many times as a girl, and it reminds me of the one and only thing I was sure of when entering parenthood: she would never have a childhood like mine; I would never, ever let her. Instead, my child would be safe and secure, whole, and never lonely with her own family, never scared.

Two years after we bought those first pink sneakers for her, a stranger would stand up at a school board meeting and talk about my child, say he would love to scoop her up and bring her into a loving place.

A loving place? I thought when I heard that. *You poor fucker, our place is drowning in love.*

9

The night before kindergarten began, Paul and I took our daughter to the open house at the school. We saw the classroom, met the teacher, and walked slowly down the halls looking at the colorful artwork and reading the bulletin boards about kindness and a growth mindset. I told her it was the same school her grandfather had attended. Tears flooded our eyes as we told her how exciting it all would be. We sat together in the cafeteria and ate pizza, and Paul got a phone call—he'd been offered a new job as the bakery manager in the natural foods cooperative in Concord, a small city just under an hour away. It meant a pay increase, benefits, a better work environment, and a schedule that wouldn't leave us feeling like we were ships passing in the night. We'd had such a hard few years, and that night as we all held hands and walked home in the evening light, the mountains behind us, we felt like our family was about to turn a corner.

Yet in the very first week of school, I realized things would not be so simple. Our child came out of the building crestfallen, a red paper armband taped around her bicep, the words *parent contact* stamped on it.

"What is this?" I asked as we walked home, but she wouldn't

answer other than to say she hated school and was never going back. I had to look in her daily folder to understand. The armbands were a colored system: blues and greens for the children who had behaved well or really well; yellow if you had needed to *stop and think* but had not done so; and red, like this one she had, if you had been so bad there would be *parent contact* before the day was through.

"It's like a fucking dunce cap," I said to my husband when he got home, but then I decided to have a little faith. This teacher had been there for years; she must know what she was doing. So many people reported loving her.

"Why'd you get yellow again?" I'd ask our daughter in those first weeks, the moment she walked out of the building. "Oh no, why'd you get red? Maybe you can earn a blue tomorrow," I'd say. But she never could—day after day, she seemed to be the only child to walk out of class with a badge of shame wrapped around her arm.

I worried, and then in October of her kindergarten year I happened to read a novel with a character who struck me as true to our child. The boy in it was around twelve and my child only five, but their essence felt oddly kindred. Two-thirds of the way through the novel, it was revealed that the boy had Asperger's. I was in bed, headlamp on.

"No, he does not—" I remember that I began to say aloud. And then I woke my husband up. "We have to go to the doctor," I said. "Our child has autism."

It wasn't the first time I'd thought this. It was just the first time I let the thought come wholly to the center of my mind and take its space, the first time I didn't convince myself that it was all just a phase.

Because the medical care in our area was less than ideal, I pushed for a referral to the Children's Hospital at Dartmouth-Hitchcock, where our child could be seen by a neurologist who specialized in the field of autism. Weeks later, we finally had our appointment scheduled. It was five months away.

As we waited, I contacted the school for help. I spent hours contacting them—the teacher, the principal, the guidance counselor. I even tried calling the nurse. I stood in my living room and looked out the window toward the school, phone pressed hard to my ear, desperate for someone within that building to understand that my child did not mean to be rude, that when she melted down it was not because she was being stubborn or spoiled.

"I think my child has autism," I said to the nurse. "I've been trying to get her help at school."

It was another dead end. She—everyone I called—listened, but no action was ever taken. Months passed. The armbands continued, along with visits to the principal's office and notes from the teacher: our child was *unaware of social cues;* she *tends to lose her temper when things don't go as she wants;* she *doesn't ask for materials when sharing;* she *tends to leave out explanations;* she *needs some extra time and support to finish her work;* she was *often distracted during lessons;* she *often makes noises or appears to ignore the conversation;* she *may need more practice with social skills and conversation.*

I spent my free time researching autism and public education, and one afternoon it occurred to me that I knew someone through the library who worked in the special education department at the elementary school. I called her immediately and overshared every telling detail about our child, desperate to convince her of what I knew to be true.

"You have to put it in writing," she said when I was through. "And you have to say specific words. Write to the school and say, 'I want to refer my child to the special education department.' Say exactly that."

It was January. We had just returned from holiday break. I had spent the entire fall saying what certainly amounted to that to so many people. Now I was baffled. Why had they waited until I used this precise language?

I did as she said, and within weeks the school began their testing, which I'd learned they had to do regardless of whether or not our child received a medical diagnosis. Speech and language, adaptability, psychological. For every test, a parent survey was sent home, and we had to fill in the correct bubbles to describe our child's behavior. I sat at our table for hours with those forms, worrying over my answers and what they might mean for her future. I had no previous experience with autism, though it was no secret that neurodivergent minds seemed to run in my family. My mother is a dyslexic woman with a lifelong struggle to understand the meaning behind people's words; my oldest brother, Will, had told me he believed himself to be autistic; and my brothers and I had often spoken of the neurodivergence of our uncle and our physicist grandfather, who'd died before I was born. So many of these people—including our daughter—had an uncanny understanding of motors and machines and how moving parts worked, coupled with a lack of basic social and executive functioning skills that come so naturally to so many others, and this had made elements of their independent adult lives nearly impossible—maintaining work and family relationships, maintaining a house, communicating their needs in a way that would not isolate them from those they loved.

I thought of my daughter, of the life I wanted for her, of all I knew she was capable of. I thought of all the support and understanding my family members had not received, and of how much suffering could have been alleviated had someone taken the time to help them identify their struggles and build in coping tools. By that point, I'd read every book about autism I could get my hands on, and only one fact had emerged for me with crystal clarity: early intervention mattered. Our daughter—who we still thought was a son—was already five. I sat with those parent surveys spread before me while Paul paced up and down the hallway that my grandmother had once paced. Did our child dress herself *always, usually, sometimes, or never,* and what if I colored in the wrong bubble? What would it mean for her future?

"Sometimes," we said. "Yes, sometimes. Wait, no, never. She never dresses herself."

I'd color the bubble in, but then we'd look at each other. "Maybe sometimes?" we'd say, and erase it, then color it in again.

Her teacher had to fill out corresponding surveys, and then a specialist would meet with our daughter during the school day to run a final portion of each test. I wasn't informed of when it was happening, and after school I would always ask our daughter leading questions to try to find out. "Did you go to a special room today? Did you do anything different?" I never got an answer, but a month or so after the testing began, I got the call that all the forms were complete and ready for my viewing. It was a drizzly late winter day. I was at work in the children's room. Susan, the woman who had been assigned as our daughter's school case manager, said she was headed to the preschool in the church that shared a parking lot with the library, and she could meet me outside with the paperwork. She had recently found out that I was a writer, and she'd bought my first book. She'd spent over an hour on the phone with me, listening to my concerns even though she'd already gone home for the day. Finally, it felt like the help we needed was on the horizon.

I went to the back workroom and opened the thick envelope, poring over the results. Every single test they'd administered put my child within the autism range. In the psychological screening, the teacher's ratings placed her *at risk* in the areas of adaptability, social skills, anger control, developmental social disorder, emotional self-control, executive functioning, and negative emotional resiliency; and with *significant deficits* and *extremely elevated range* in executive skills and emotional control. It was an odd feeling, to look through these papers detailing my child's struggles and feel grateful for the documentation. Months before, I'd sat in her kindergarten classroom, in a tiny chair at a tiny table across from her teacher, and worried aloud that our child had autism.

"No," this veteran teacher had told me. "We had a leaf blower in here for a project, and your child loved it! People with autism would hate the sound of a leaf blower."

"Your child doesn't have autism," another teacher had said. "Your child wants friends, and people with autism don't want friends."

Now, in place of stereotypes, I had actual data. But then toward the end of the packet, I saw it was coupled with something else—the woman I knew, the one who had finally told me how to get this process started, had written that though my child fell within the range of autism, further inspection reveals this is *likely due to lack of opportunity or traditional behavior.* With that, the team determined that she did not have a disability, and that she would therefore not qualify for special education services to address her needs.

In the weeks that followed, I studied that packet of testing results like a textbook, taking my highlighter to it as though some passage in there could magically open the doors to the help my child so clearly needed but was being denied. *Lack of opportunity or traditional behavior,* I read over and over again. I thought of my friends, the ones I'd grown up with, the ones whose children my child had been with since birth—countless hours running around together, playing in the dirt and making mud pies, reading books, building LEGO creations, eating crackers and banging on random instruments. I thought of all the story times we'd been to, all the library programs, all the hours upon hours of play groups. Wasn't that opportunity? Wasn't that traditional behavior?

I didn't know much about the woman who'd written the report—only that she was an expert seamstress and a kind and loving mother. Sometimes her husband filled in a shift at the library, and I considered him a friend. Once, when my lawn mower was broken and my lawn was so overgrown that we could scarcely walk through it, he'd delivered his grandfather's old push mower to us and taught me to use it. He and I had laughed about it, but what had she thought? I used to stand outside school pickup and feel so small, so out of place and misunderstood in that pristine neighborhood. I knew that Paul and I didn't exactly fit in. We had dead or overgrown grass; we had peeling paint and blankets on the windows in winter; we had an old rainbow flag nailed to our garage in the center of a street lined with crisp American flags. I knew we stood out, but it had never once occurred to me that that would get in the way of a professional assessing our daughter's disability.

Lack of opportunity or traditional behavior.

Was it the overgrown lawn and the pathetic excuse for a garden where grass should have been? Was it the pride flag? Or was it the fact that we allowed our child, still known to the world as a boy, to show up in pink sneakers day after day?

Though I was proud of my child—proud of her courage, and proud to see that we had raised a little feminist human, a child who understood in her bones that *female* did not equal *less*—those pink sneakers were not easy for me. In fact, I am now ashamed by the amount of anxiety that entered my life because of them. I understand that they should not have been worrisome, and that to many parents they would not have been. But that street we lived on, that town. Once, when my daughter and I walked to the library together for a music program, we ran into a neighbor who happened to live in the house my step-siblings' father had grown up in. My daughter's hair had grown out slightly, though it was far from long. She wore a pink T-shirt, but she was still known as a boy.

"Do you have an addition to your household?" the neighbor asked me. She was pushing a stroller. I stared blankly at her for a beat or two. I thought she was asking if we had built onto our ranch house. I don't remember how we arrived at the actual question she was asking: *Who is this child, and where is yours?* Because somehow, in that town, it was more conceivable that I had brought a new child into my home than it was that a child known as a boy should wear pink.

In those early days of my child's school life, I would stay up late, hiding the glow of my phone beneath the covers to read strangers' thoughts— should I allow my boy to wear pink sneakers, even though he will be ridiculed? The opinions were strong and varied, and none of them felt right. Eventually I mentioned it to my stepmother, who suggested what should have been obvious to me: buy a second pair of not-pink sneakers, and let my child choose each day. Pink when you want to be yourself, blue when you don't want to be picked on. Because she was picked on, instantly and consistently. A few times a week, she rode the school bus down the road to the town library, where I would meet her on the curb just as I finished my shift. There, children I had read to in story time for years would hang out the window and point. "Why is he wearing pink?" they would yell. "Is he a boy or a girl?"

"They're asking because they don't know," my child would sometimes say. "Duh! Why would you ask a question that you already know the answer to!" She would cackle, and I would hold her close, grateful for her clear, literal mind.

Sometimes, though, she knew when people were picking on her. I'm not sure why. I'm not clear exactly what those kids said, or how they said it, that alerted her. But she would tell me, and I would ask her if she'd like to wear her other sneakers instead. "No," my child would always say. "No, those people should just disappear."

"We just have to make it to March," Paul and I said to each other. March, when her appointment at the children's hospital would finally arrive, and we would get some answers.

While we waited, I collected every note ever sent home from the school, and I wrote down the details of every phone call. I took it all to every meeting. "This isn't her choosing to misbehave," I said. "It's outside of her skill set. She needs special help."

Yet—as if my folder of data didn't exist—I would be told she was doing great. And as much as I wanted to believe that, I knew it just wasn't true. Each morning, our child screamed and yelled and hit when it was time to go to school. Often, she would be late. After school, she hit herself, called herself stupid. On nights when she slept, she yelled out in her dreams that she hated herself. Sometimes I had to write to the teacher: *Up all night again, will be a few hours late.*

Finally, March arrived. The biggest snowstorm of the year was predicted for the day of her appointment. The hospital was two hours away, so I called the day before and asked what we ought to do. They gave us a room in the house for families whose children were hospitalized. I remember being so heartened by that room, that home in honor of a child who'd lost his battle with cancer. It was large and warm and full of love. Volunteers arrived to deliver meals; snacks lined the cupboards. We played Mouse Trap and thought about how we were about to enter the rest of our lives. The snow had started and fell unendingly, silencing the world around us and closing us in. A little girl with cancer toddled around the house with her grandmother, who told me they lived more often in that house than their own home. I felt wrong being there as I heard their story, wrong taking space for my child when this one was fighting for her actual life.

In the morning the snow was up to our waists. We caught the hospital van to the children's wing, and we were led into our appointment. We were there some two hours, during which the neurologist spoke and moved like a robot and my child took tests and had a meltdown when offered a bin of LEGOs only to discover it was filled with Duplos. Eventually, the doctor left the room for a few minutes, and when she reentered her demeanor had shifted into something human. She said our child had all the signs and symptoms of autism. She told us, and wrote in her report to us, that our child required special education services to help her with social interaction, executive function, and self-regulation. She handed us a list of therapist contacts and pointed to one.

"You're near Concord, right? Do whatever you can to get in with this place. If you have to pay out of pocket, do it. Borrow money from family. Do anything you can."

I still wonder every single day what I would have done without that contact, and the ability to pay for it. What would have happened to my child, to me? The doctor was in the doorway, almost out the door, when I said, "What about all this rage?" My child woke up angry, went to bed angry. She had thrown a hammer at my head, a screwdriver. She had hit me thousands of times. She had broken a cupboard and a Kindle and countless toys.

"You have to imagine what it's been like for your child," she said. "Imagine that all this time she's been trying to communicate with you and you've been trying to communicate with her, but the two of you are speaking different languages."

I'm not sure I could understand that then. I know that my child's skills in language and eye contact belie the fact that she is often operating on a different plane than most of us. But there are moments of insight. Sometimes they're the kind that make my heart grow, ones that I try to draw into comic strips and collect. There's the one where I begin to brush her hair and say, "Oh my god, there's a giant rat's nest back here," and she responds by running into the yard screaming, panicking for me to get the nest out. There's the one where my husband says, "Please don't talk and chew at the same time," and, mouth still overflowing with food, she exclaims, "Obviously I stopped chewing to talk!" Or when I say, "I'm on the phone, go find something to do," and when she asks what she could do, I say snidely, "Dig for fossils in the backyard"—only to discover an hour later that my yard is pockmarked with holes as deep as her legs are long.

But there's also this: "Turn the iPad off and get in the car. Grandma just had surgery and now she's home. I have to go take care of her. Hello? Did you hear me? We have exactly two minutes to get in the car. Hello? Hello?" And finally my hands reaching for the iPad, closing its cover. She screams and hits. I go to the car and wait. My child arrives, climbs into the back seat. It is winter, cold and dark, almost Christmas. She begins kicking the seat in front of her. I tell her to buckle up, and when she does not, I turn around in my seat to buckle her myself. She lifts her foot and kicks me in the face as hard as possible.

I remember the drive after that. The silence of it. My mother's house, the house where I grew up, was fifteen minutes away, and ten minutes into the drive we had to stop at the pharmacy for her post-op prescriptions. I had been at the hospital with her the night before, and the surgery had gone well enough except she had been given too much anesthesia and watching her struggle to wake up had been terrifying. I was tired, and now I was angry. But we walked through the pharmacy quietly. I held my child's hand and every single fiber in my body screamed to her that I would not take any more shit. We got back into the car, and it was as we were pulling out of the parking lot that she said, "I'm sorry, Mom. But you made me lose my video game."

It was only then that I lost it. I yelled at her, which is not typical of me. I yelled that, just that day, she had told me of a classmate who had stomped on a computer, breaking it. "Do you understand that what you did is worse?" I yelled.

"Why would it be worse?" my child asked innocently.

"Because I'm your mother! I'm a person, not a stupid computer!"

A moment of silence. And then: "Actually, Mom, you're wrong. Computers are actually incredibly intelligent."

I've read a lot of books about my daughter's diagnosis. I've watched experts take this moment when my daughter kicks me in the face and pair it with her very true statement that computers are intelligent and deduce from it that she and others with autism lack empathy. I am shocked by this impulse to place a value and intention inside the minds of an entire group, shocked and deeply offended by the ease with which my daughter's full humanity can be cast aside.

My daughter is the clearest thinker I know. She sees people without judgment. Her mind is a filing cabinet of information. At night, when I tuck her in, she runs her hands over my cheek, then pats my head. "Good Mama," she says, and then, sidling her body in closer to mine, "You're my favorite person in the world." Afternoons, when she comes home from her new school in her new city, she picks up her chickens and walks proudly with them, telling them they are good. She lounges with our cat on her giant beanbag. She plays her video game and then she whistles for our dog, puts her bird identification book in her backpack, and goes with him to the woods. Sometimes she asks if she can walk up to our elderly neighbor Hope's house to see if she wants help with farm chores. My child is wise and kind and enormously, painfully empathetic, and sometimes she struggles to communicate it. Sometimes her emotional regulation is taxed to a degree that I have never experienced.

Our daughter's therapist saved our lives, taught us the methods through which our child could stay calm and use words and behave safely. It was not a miracle. It was three years and hundreds of dollars a month out of pocket to learn how to help her function in a society whose rules she does not intuitively understand or respect. It was charts and timers and praise and visual schedules and just so much effort, so much focus. But the alternative was too bleak.

Over the course of a year, our daughter learned to be safe, and she was immeasurably proud of herself for it. First, Paul and I went half a day without being hit. And then a whole day. Three days, a week. A month. Two months! Eventually, we could not remember the last time we had been hit.

Yet school continued to be a challenge. Diagnosis in hand, coupled with the written recommendation from the neurologist that our child receive school-based special education services, we set up another meeting, sure that we would finally move forward. My husband and I took the day off from work and we put our nice clothes on and walked down the street together, holding hands, too nervous to speak. We signed in at the office and then went across the hall and took our seats at the long table in the small, windowless room that had become so familiar to us. Susan, the case manager, passed out paperwork, and immediately we saw what we'd feared: another form, already signed and dated, denying our child special education services.

"But she has a disability and she clearly needs help," I begged.

"A medical diagnosis does not guarantee an individualized education plan," Susan said.

There were so many people sitting at the table—teacher, guidance counselor, case manager, speech therapist, occupational therapist, school psychologist. This was what they called her *team,* and we, her parents, were supposed to be equal members of it.

"Look at everything she needs," I said. "Why is she being denied?" I thought of my child hiding in the coat cubby when it was loud, being sent to the principal's office when she melted down.

"It's not our kid's fault if you all don't believe in autism," my husband snapped, and I kicked him under the table.

"Perhaps the problem is that she doesn't know how to tell you about the good parts of school," the specialist who had referenced our child's *lack of traditional behavior* said. "Families just get into routines. It sounds like your child has difficult behaviors at home, and you just need to work on that."

"I don't understand," I insisted, pages of data before me. "It seems so clear."

"She's performing at grade-level standards," Susan said. "By law we can't approve an IEP if a student is doing fine academically."

"That's not true," I said. I'd read the law in its entirety. I'd even printed it out and marked specific passages. I had it in a blue binder in front of me, and I knew just which section she was referring to. I flipped through the binder and pointed to a place I'd highlighted. "This is the portion of the law that refers to grade-level standards," I said. "It does not apply to autism."

"I'd have to call our director of student services at the administrative office if you want more details about the law," Susan said. She was so kind, so thorough. I didn't want to be rude to her. But I told her to please do that, and then my husband and I sat awkwardly in that white room and waited, our mouths dry, my husband sweating profusely while my body shook. Susan returned a few minutes later with a printed page of the law in hand, faxed over to her from the director.

"That's the page I just showed you," I said. "It refers to 'specific learning disabilities' like dyslexia. Autism is not in the category it's referring to. It says it right here."

"I'm sure our director knows the law," she said.

"Maybe," I said, terrified by my powerlessness. "But in this case she is clearly wrong."

It didn't matter. Nothing I could say would change the fact that they had already decided to deny our child the supports she needed. We sat in that room for hours, rehashing the data, pushing against their denial, but eventually we just said that we never wanted our daughter in another armband again and we went home. We gave our child as much love as possible, tried our hardest every single day to keep her from blaming herself for the struggles she faced at school. And every day, I searched the internet and made phone calls to try to figure out how to get her to a place where her strengths and her clear needs would be recognized and accommodated. I called schools in surrounding towns, asked them how they would support my child. I called my former high school English teacher and bombarded him with questions about school connections in the state. I talked to my cousin in Manhattan, listened to her tell me about the school her son attended, which was built for children who learned in all the ways my daughter did. My oldest friend, Ingrid, had moved to California by then, and I called her crying, telling her I'd heard a report on the radio about these private schools in cities like Portland, Oregon, and Boulder, Colorado, where they specialized in helping neurodivergent children like mine thrive. "So she only gets a shot in the world if we move and then pay like one hundred thousand dollars a year," I said hopelessly.

Finally, at the suggestion of a friend, I called the Disability Rights Center in our state. I spoke with a lawyer, and I learned that many aspects of my daughter's denial were likely in violation of the law.

"Report them to the Department of Education," my friend said. "That will get things moving."

"You get more flies with honey," suggested another woman I'd been put in touch with for advice. She was a friend of a friend who worked in special education. It was spring, the school year almost over. I was walking the pavement outside the mechanic shop, waiting for my tires to be changed over from winter to summer. The lake was across the street. Decades ago, my grandfather had advocated for the land there to be converted to a public park, but now it was just a strip of fast-food restaurants and box stores.

"I don't have any more fucking honey," I snapped at this kind woman I had never met as I looked at the drive-thru restaurant my stepsister Courtney had loved to go to for sub sandwiches. What had this year done to me?

"Why don't you just move to Concord?" my mother-in-law would ask. She wanted us out of that small town and closer to my husband's work.

Our daughter's therapist asked the same thing. She said she'd never seen anything like what we were experiencing in Gilford. "The schools here in Concord have been really good," she'd say gently.

"We're not doing that," I would always respond. It was so far outside of what we'd ever wanted; since we were twenty years old, Paul and I had always decided where to live based on our immediate access to the natural world, and Concord was just another mill city in the center of the state. There were no mountains in Concord, there was no lake.

There had to be a way, I told myself repeatedly, and when I could see no other option, I took my friend's advice and called the Department of Education and reported the school's suspected disability rights violations to the state. It seemed to work; finally, in June after her kindergarten year had ended, the director of student services approved an IEP to follow our child into first grade. Yet it seemed clear to us that it had only been approved because we had forced it, and the specific supports our child needed were still not put into place.

"How did we live through this year?" Paul and I said to each other every night as we sat on the couch utterly exhausted, mindlessly staring at the walls. Because at that point, we believed the work it had taken us to get there was all we had to give. But now, what a joke. What a cruel and absolute joke; there was just so much more coming our way.

10

....

When my daughter was four—and still known to the world as a boy—she wanted to be a witch in a dress for Halloween. But then she'd watched *Wall-E,* the animated movie about a robot who collects trash, and two of her favorite things collided, so we made her a costume of the robot out of a cardboard box. Then, in kindergarten, she wanted to be a witch in a dress again.

"You mean a wizard?" my mother-in-law asked one early fall afternoon as we stood on our porch overlooking the yard that had been my grandparents'. The leaves of the silver maples had started to fall, and I remember thinking that the neighbors had already raked and as usual we had not.

"A witch," I'd snapped back, though the truth was that I, too, was concerned. Not logically—logically I understood that our gender norms were problematic. But also, my child was in school now. In such a conservative town. Where even the pair of pink sneakers had become gossip.

I worried, but then my five-year-old discovered vampires, and somehow that took the place of the witch that year. But in first grade, the witch came back.

"How about a witch in pants?" I asked.

"A dress," she insisted.

"What about these pants that are billowy like a dress?" I asked, holding up a picture on my phone. "You'll be warmer."

"I want to be a witch in a dress," she said.

The conversation went on for days. I remember searching online for pictures, desperately trying to find some masculine-looking version of a witch. I remember that I even asked the exact same question that I'd snapped at my mother-in-law for asking: "What about a wizard?"

I also remember that the Halloween dress was not the only dress my child asked for. Six years old, she'd swim around the center of my bed while I stood at my closet, asking when I would buy her dresses.

"You can wear this one," I'd say, and hold up one of mine, an invitation for a game of dress-up.

"That's dumb," she would say. And then finally, the moment when the absolute wrongness of what I was doing to her sunk in and I regretted every moment I had not given her the clothes she'd asked for: "Mom," she said quietly, from the center of my bed. "Is it illegal for me to wear a dress?"

I went to the fabric store, bought a pattern and materials, and sewed her the best witch costume I could imagine. I called my mother to help me, and we spent an absurd amount of time on it, and money. When Halloween came around, my child beamed.

And then her first-grade teacher contacted me. She used the exact language my husband and I had: *beaming*. She wrote that our child was *beaming in the dress*.

But she also said she'd found her crying in the corner and asked why.

And the response, choked out through tears: "My mom only lets me wear dresses to school on Halloween."

11

································

My brother Noah used to be a dancer. Tap was his specialty, and he was something of a star in his dance company. Each year, beginning as a toddler, he had a solo routine, just my sweet little brother tapping away in the center of the big stage. Eventually, he began traveling to Boston and New York to dance, and then to London.

My daughter was nothing like Noah—Noah was a showman who loved to dress up, to put on plays, to sing and dance. My daughter preferred to take electronics apart and dig in the dirt. Yet her desire for dresses called him to mind, and when she was six years old I signed her up for a dance class. At the time, I had been trying to help her, trying to show her that she could be any kind of boy she wanted. I had done other things to encourage this. I'd bought a book of photographs of all kinds of boys—boys with long hair, boys who wore makeup, boys with jewelry.

"Look!" I would say as we read. "Just because you don't see these boys does not mean they don't exist!"

It was the first book I had ever seen my child angry about. She grunted and punched at it whenever I brought it out. She threw it on the ground, she told me she hated it. I told myself I did not know why and, shamefully, I continued to place it strategically within her sight.

"I hate myself for being a boy," she would whisper to me at night. "Can people change?" she would say. "Why do you make me be a boy?"

These questions came at calmer times, but at other times she hit her head against the wall. "Stupid, stupid, stupid," she would yell at herself. We spoke with our psychologist about this action, though we were oddly quiet about its precise cause. That is, we learned how to keep her safe, but we took so long to learn about her gender.

Noah quit dancing when he was a young teen. I don't know all the details that led up to his decision. It's likely that he just didn't want to do it anymore. But there's also the fact that in rural New Hampshire in the 1980s and '90s my little brother was fiercely bullied for being gay.

My father claims that he knew Noah was gay when he was just an infant. Classical music had been playing and my brother, in his infant chair, began to wave his hands with the rhythm, and something about the graceful motion indicated his eventual sexuality to my father. I know the story is problematic. But also I can hear where my father is coming from. Back then, at least in our corner of the world, when a boy was gender nonconforming, it signaled that he was gay. And my brother was gender nonconforming from the moment he could maneuver his body to access what he wanted to reach: girls' dance costumes and tap shoes, high heels, his mother's slips to refashion as wigs.

At some point in Noah's early childhood, my father and stepmother visited a psychologist to discuss their son's desire for female clothing. There, they were instructed to not let him see his sisters naked, to give no attention whatsoever to his love of femininity. To continue to allow him to dress how he wanted only if it was *play* and *fantasy,* but to never let it out of the household. They listened, and there we must have the birth of shame—a fact I was aware of as it related to my brother yet somehow managed to smother in the early days when my daughter asked for dresses. But what else could a child be expected to feel when it registers in their mind that they can be who they are at home yet not in public? It is such a clear lesson: your identity, the core of who you are, is not okay with the world.

My daughter—still known as a boy—actually wanted to join the dance class, which came as something of a surprise to me, because she typically put up a fight if she had to leave the house. I was careful about the studio I chose. I avoided the one Noah had gone to, which trained their dancers to become competitive. I also avoided the one in our town, where I worried she would be judged. Instead, I signed her up at the cheapest place around, in Laconia, just beyond a renovated freight depot that still carried the name of my mill-owning side of the family. I always pointed this out to my daughter as we crossed the tracks and drove past it, but she didn't care.

She was signed up for a tap and ballet class, and on the first day I bought her shoes from the teacher. The girls' ballet shoes were pink and the tap shoes were Mary Jane style, tied with a pink bow. But I bought the only shoes offered to me, the boy ones—both pairs shaped like sneakers, all black. My child fussed and kicked as I put them on her feet.

"Put these on and go join class and you can play *Minecraft* when you get home," I said. Then, after she grudgingly went onto the dance floor, I texted Noah. He lived in New York at that point. We hadn't seen each other in some five years, and we'd spoken only a handful of times. He'd met my child only once, back when she was a baby. Still, I knew Noah was the person in my family who would hear me.

My kid wants the girl dance shoes, I texted him. He asked me if I could get them. My child, on the way home, asked me the same question. I said I would find out. It was a lie.

The next week, when it was time to put the shoes back on, my child cried about them. She did the same the following week. Dance class started in October and ran through May, and I am deeply ashamed to say that I told my child I would ask every single week. Meanwhile, it got harder and harder to get her feet into the shoes. She screamed, cried, stomped her feet, and threw her belongings. "I'm supposed to have the girl shoes!" she yelled. Why wouldn't I listen?

Around the same time that our daughter began dance class, her first-grade teacher sent another note home. She said our child's hair was getting in her eyes, distracting and frustrating her while she tried to work—could we please put it back? We asked ourselves what we could do that wouldn't be too feminine for that cookie-cutter town. We tried to convince her of a haircut—even just bangs.

"I want my hair as long as a girl's," she said. "I want girl hair."

We didn't make her cut it, but we didn't exactly listen, either; we ordered sweatbands for her and tracked down pictures of cool boys wearing them. She refused. Now I think back at how easy it could have been. Buy her barrettes, buy her a headband, put her long bangs in a topknot, anything. Just overcome your fear. Be proud. Instead, her growing hair continued to get in her eyes for months.

And yet, we continued to read children's books to her that showed boys in dresses. *It's okay!* these books said. *It's great!* Only for us, in practice, it clearly wasn't; and anyway, that wasn't the issue—we did not in fact have a boy.

12

There were perhaps ten girls in the dance class, one boy, and my daughter. Frequently, the teacher would separate them—my child and the boy in one position, the girls in another. "Why can't I be with the girls!" she would yell, no question in her tone. Just absolute surety that the adults had gotten it all wrong.

I got to know a couple of the other moms while we sat there and watched. My daughter wasn't the only one whose behavior was less than stellar in that class, and this led to some good—rather than judgmental—conversations. One mom consistently noticed my child's distress about being given the boy clothes and put in the boy roles. She asked me if there might be a group of gender-nonconforming kids in the area. She wondered aloud why we made kids follow such ridiculous rules of gender. "Can't we just let kids be kids?" she asked. I appreciated her, though I also wondered how far her support would really go. If I let my child be a girl, with a girl name and a girl pronoun, would this mom still believe I was letting her be a kid? Or did letting kids be kids stop firmly at the clothing my child wanted to wear?

Anyway, who was I to wonder? There my child was, miserable in her boy clothes and boy shoes.

. . .

By winter, my child's hair was long enough for a ponytail. One day at dance, she noticed a little basket of hair elastics on the teacher's desk. She started to play with them, and she asked me why they were there.

"In case someone forgets their hair tie," I said.

She gave me a look she often gives—*I want to do this thing but I know you're going to say no so I'm going to just ask like this, silently, with my perfect little face.*

I stood up, got the elastic, and had her turn around so I could put her hair in a ponytail. At first, once her hair was up, I thought the difference in her face was simply because her hair was finally out of her eyes. But then I watched her go into the dance studio, where mirrors lined the front walls. She was looking at herself, turning her body, looking more. She was not just satisfied. She glowed. All through that class, she kept her eyes on herself, and now and then reached back to touch her ponytail, to see if it was still there.

13

....

wish I knew more about my brother Noah's life, but one of the heartbreaks of divorce and blended families is the vastly different realities that the children experience, and the distance it can create between them. Noah is the child of my father and stepmother, meaning that we saw each other only when I was on visitation to my father's; and as the years went on and I got more control of my schedule, I stayed with my father less and less. In part, this accounted for how far Noah and I had drifted apart, but once that dance class started, I could not stop thinking of him. One night after class, I went to the cold walk-out basement of our ranch house so my family couldn't hear me, and I called Noah to talk about my child.

"My kid wants to wear dresses," I said.

"I used to wear Dad's long T-shirts to preschool," Noah told me. I had vague memories of this. It had been because he wasn't allowed to leave the house in a dress, and the T-shirts had felt like the next best thing.

"Do you think Dad and your mom were right, though?" I asked him. "What if they'd just let you wear the dresses?" It was he, after all, who had asked me if my daughter could get the girls' shoes in dance.

But he surprised me in his response. "Oh, honey," he said. "If I could have worn what I wanted, it would have been absolute social suicide."

Better than actual suicide, I thought, but did not say. Because our family had worried about that outcome multiple times, and then he'd attempted it once, recklessly swallowing a handful of pills at the end of a days-long bender. By then my husband and I had moved back to New Hampshire, I was pregnant, and Noah was on the other side of the country, in Arizona, intubated in a hospital bed. My little sister flew from Hawaii and my father flew from New Hampshire to be with him. At some point my father asked me to come out to take his place because he had to return to work. I was livid.

"He doesn't want me," I said. Noah's life was on the line, and I knew my father was the one person he really needed. I knew I couldn't take his place. "Who cares about your job? I'm not coming, he needs you."

Now, whether or not I was right, I'm still so sorry that I didn't immediately get on a plane. How could I have failed to do that?

I was twenty-eight years old—four years away from parenthood— when I first watched *Milk,* the film about LGBTQ+ rights activist Harvey Milk. It was 2008; it would be another seven years before marriage equality even became law in the United States. Paul and I had been in our upstairs apartment in Missoula, lounging on the futon after a long day cross-country skiing on the other side of the mountain pass. We'd rented the movie on a whim, without thinking about how heavy it would be. We sat there stoned, eating heaping bowls of ice cream while I cried soundlessly, tears soaking my face as I thought of my brother. The movie had an afterword that flashed statistics—the extremely high percentage of gay men who struggled with addiction, the extremely high percentage who had attempted suicide. I paused the movie to back up and read them all again. The statistics astounded me. How could I have never put it together before, that Noah lived in a completely different world from the rest of our family, that the doors that had always been open to us had never been open to him? It wasn't something our family had ever discussed. Noah was gay, of course we loved and accepted him, and that was the end of the conversation. But I read those statistics and finally I realized that my little brother, whose laugh I still miss, had not been born with a troubled brain, that his struggles were actually society's struggles. Why hadn't I learned this earlier? Why hadn't we all? And what about him—had he learned this? Has he now? Or has he spent his entire life believing the problem is within him?

When my daughter changed her name and pronoun a few months after dance class ended, I was aware that many people from her life would be shocked. This was a child who'd lived for a garbage truck, whose favorite birthday gift ever had been a toy chainsaw. I had once driven her across the state just to find a real-life feller buncher for her to see. *Really?* I knew they'd say. *A girl?* And then: *Does she still like tools? Trucks?*

Her dance studio was the one place where I knew no one would be surprised. The recital was in May, and as the date approached, the teacher sat all the children on the floor while she handed out the dance costumes, one for tap and the other for ballet. The first piece to come out of the bag was a big, sparkly red hair clip. She passed one out to each girl. My child said she didn't get one. I'm not sure if she was told they were for girls or if it suddenly dawned on her. She stood up, picked up a costume from the floor, and threw it at the teacher.

"Why do girls get all the good stuff!" she yelled.

The teacher gently but firmly reprimanded her for her behavior, and then continued passing things out. My poor kid came out with just a sparkly red vest for ballet and a baseball shirt for tap. She was furious.

I spent the next few weeks trying to get her to like her costume.

"It's sequins!" I would say. "It's so shiny!" I got the costume out one spring day as we stood near the back door, looking out at the rhodo-dendron that was getting ready to bloom. The middle and high school was visible across the field beyond our backyard, and it was where her recital would be. I told her so.

"I'm not doing it," she said.

"But you've worked so hard!"

"It's too embarrassing," she told me. "I'm not wearing that dumb boy costume."

"Wait," I said. "It would be less embarrassing to wear the girls' one?"

And then, after she'd tried so hard, in so many ways, to tell me, she said the words that began to crack open the wall I'd built around my understanding: "Duh," she said. "That's the costume I'm SUPPOSED to have."

I hugged her tight. I apologized. And then I wrote to our psychologist, told her I needed her to refer us to someone with expertise in the field of gender.

14

························

I t turned out that our psychologist's colleague had some expertise in the field. We made an appointment with her, but it was some four weeks away, and it felt like an eternity. We pushed for something earlier. We felt we were on the crest of a wave that was about to crash.

By that point, our daughter still wore her pink sneakers, but she'd also found a pink sweatshirt at the bottom of a hand-me-down bag. I remember that she was nervous to wear it to school, aware that she would get picked on. But I also remember that the nerves didn't sway her decision—she was wearing this shirt, it was going to be hard. I emailed the teacher, asked her to please keep an extra eye on my child. By the end of the day, I had an email back, and there was that word again: *beaming*. My child was *beaming* in the pink sweatshirt, so much so that a teacher in a neighboring class had even noticed and commented, saying, "Today is a good day for you!"

That was in April of her first-grade year. At the end of the month, I flew to Missoula, Montana, because I had been invited as a guest writer for the writing program I'd attended. My husband and daughter would meet me there a few days later, and from there we would rent a car and drive to his brother's in Oregon.

The morning after I arrived in Missoula, I left my hotel to walk the river trail toward downtown. It was sunny and warm, the trees budding bright green and the light glistening off the Clark Fork River. People were out and happy in the way they always seem to be in that city—riding bikes, playing Frisbee, picnicking in the park. I texted my husband from the walk. *I think we need to move back here,* I wrote. I told my husband of the boys I saw in the city, my language revealing the fact that I still failed to see the child we had. *Boys in pink,* I wrote, *boys with long hair, boys in skirts.*

My husband agreed immediately, as I knew he would, and on that day it seemed so simple: we could just pack up and go. The prospect of raising our child in this small, liberal city we so loved suddenly eclipsed nearly all the worry about how hard the move would actually be.

They would arrive the night before Easter, so I wandered the downtown shops buying things for my daughter's basket. A pink octopus. A pink T-shirt. It wasn't a dress, but it was a start. I also found myself going down the same rabbit hole of the internet every night and ending at the same place: *If you're wondering about whether your child needs to socially transition,* the website said, *many families find relief in going away, even for a weekend, and allowing your child to live in their preferred gender. The experience can be illuminating.* Why hadn't we done that? Why weren't we doing it now? What were we so afraid of?

I saw old friends during the days that I waited for my family to arrive. At lunch with one friend, I talked about my gender-nonconforming kid who also had autism, about her anger, about her insistence that she was a girl.

"My friend's kid was the same," she said. "They let her change her name and pronoun and all those anger problems went away." She told me that the daughter was on puberty blockers now, probably eventually hormones. I was shocked. I had read about transgender children, but I wasn't aware of meeting any, and anyway, though deep down I knew just who my child was, the decision to allow it seemed so totally extreme.

. . .

When my husband and daughter arrived, we spent a few days in Missoula showing her all our favorite spots. We ate croissants by the river and milkshakes at the tea shop; we took her on the carousel, then rode the city bus to a restaurant we loved. She did it all in her new pink shirt. At night, I scrubbed whatever she had spilled on it out in the hotel sink and hung it to dry. After a few days, we left the city for the seven-hour drive that would take us over the continental divide and to the mountain range in eastern Oregon where her uncle, aunt, and cousins lived. She was ecstatic about the trip—to see the clear mountain rivers, the pines, the jagged and snowcapped peaks. Her hair was long, she had pink to wear, and she was safe with her parents. Along the way, she kept wanting us to pull over, to take pictures, to throw stones in the river, or to walk just a little way into the woods.

But once we arrived, and she saw her younger cousins she had been so excited to connect with, it all fell apart. She fought and melted down and tried again to interact and failed. My husband and I were desperate with the anxiety we always had in social situations with her.

"She's on the edge," we said to each other. "Quick. Do something so she doesn't tip over."

We took her for walks alone, and every afternoon we let her rest on the air mattress and watch TV for a few hours. We made sure she ate well; we played the game where we rolled her up tightly in a blanket, *like a burrito,* because the pressure seemed to calm her. Nothing worked for very long. Of course it didn't. She was growing her hair out and wearing pink and moving, as much as we would allow her, into her true self. But she was still being introduced as *he.* Her cousins were still being told she was a boy.

My brother-in-law, Neil, and his wife had a sign in their front yard that has become familiar but was at that point still somewhat rare: *In this house we believe . . . no human is illegal, love is love, science is real.* Before noticing the sign, I knew our daughter would be fully accepted by her uncle; he is a kind, gentle man who loves nature and poetry and who is always willing to open his mind. Still, that sign and its rainbow background made me feel a little more at ease. Yet one night after the children were all asleep, the four of us stayed up late talking and eventually our conversation veered to our child's gender expression. We'd sent a photo to my mother-in-law that afternoon—all her grandkids riding a giant purple dragon together at the park. Her response had been that my child sure liked to wear pink, that hopefully it was just a stage. We talked about how to respond, about how pink was just a color and certainly it was okay for any child to love it.

But then Neil, a devout scientist, said, "But these transgender people. I think that's going too far. Chromosomes are chromosomes, male is male, female is female."

At that point, I was still so scared to see my own daughter. But at least I knew that if millions of people around the world were in fact transgender, then obviously being transgender existed.

Even him, I thought. If he, with that sign in his front yard, could say this, then what hope was there in the world for our child? I said good night, went to the playroom and lay down on the air mattress next to our willful child for whom the world felt so difficult, and cried.

By May our child had long hair, pink sneakers, and now a pink sweatshirt and a pink T-shirt. We did laundry constantly so she could wear her two favorites multiple times in one week, and we waited anxiously for our appointment with the doctor who had some gender expertise. I met my daughter as she got off the school bus at the library, and I sent vicious looks to the children who hung their heads out the window to mock her.

"Why is your kid wearing pink?" a child once yelled out to me from the bus.

"Because it's a color, duh," I snapped at him.

But school was almost over. Summer would spread wide before us. I would have a rest from all the meetings. She would be home, free from the possibility of bullying, free from the shame. We walked down the sidewalk together.

"Kids on the playground ask me every day if I'm a girl or a boy," she said.

"What do you say?" I asked.

"Girl," she said.

I said I was sorry they asked that, but my sweet, literal child did not understand why I would be sorry. I said I thought that they were maybe teasing.

"Um, no, Mom," she said, just as she'd done a year before. "Why would anyone ask a question they know the answer to!" She cackled at me. We kept walking, hand in hand. I was gentle, quiet. It was not typical of her to share with me in this way, and I didn't want to push.

"Mom?" she said.

"Yeah?"

"Then they ask me my name, and when I tell them, they laugh because it's a boy name."

I squeezed her hand.

"Mom?" she said again.

"Yes?"

"I need a new name."

We had a birthday party to go to that weekend. It was the first one our child had been invited to all year. We didn't know the little girl or her parents, but I talked my husband into going with us to ease the horror of it. We stood near a bouncy house and spoke awkwardly with other parents I knew from the library. When Robin and Eric—our closest friends in that town—arrived, Paul and I glued ourselves to them. After an hour we were all ushered into a smaller room, where a woman dressed as the Disney princess Elsa entered. She had a microphone. She asked the children to sit on the carpet. My child and the other girls sat down, and the princess started to sing. The boys never sat down, and soon their bodies squirmed farther and farther away from the scene. Eventually, they were all in the other side of the room, running around the tables, pretending to shoot each other with machine guns.

No wonder, I thought. *If these are the options, of course my kid chooses girl.* Because she didn't have an interest in war or weapons. And, more important, because I still didn't get it—I still thought she was looking at two choices and choosing one.

After the song, the princess told all the girls to get in line for their makeup. My child got in line with them. My husband and I moved away from the other parents, closer to her. A wall of protection. But suddenly one boy—the roughest in the class—dropped his imaginary weapon and got in line, too. His grandfather, who had brought him to the party, came up next to us.

"Oh, here we go," he said loudly. "Oh, Jesus. I need to make him get out of that line."

"He's just having fun," I said. "You don't need to."

"What are you, a girl?" the grandfather taunted loudly. The little boy heard him, turned, and slowly backed out of the line. "Wimp!" his grandfather yelled. "Too scared to go through with it, are you?"

When my child got to the front of the line, she shyly asked Elsa for pink eye shadow. I can't remember what she was wearing that day, but it must have been something that communicated male. "How about blue?" Elsa asked.

"Pink," my child said, and closed her eyes, tipped her head up. When it was done, she ran to me, asked me to take her to the bathroom so she could look.

"I can't even see it!" she yelled as we stood in front of the mirror.

"It's just light," I said. "Lots of eye shadow is like that."

"I can see the other girls'!" she yelled. She started grunting and kicking, and I wished I could communicate telepathically to my husband to come help. He could always calm her down, could always make her look outside herself and laugh. But it was just me with her. Eventually, I got her to leave that bathroom with the promise of cake and ice cream. She sat alone at a table to eat it, no friends around her, miserable that her eye shadow did not show.

15

....

remember the moment it struck me that Noah had lost his laugh. We were in the small A-frame cabin in the woods near my mother's house that our brother Henry had built in the wake of his friends dying in the lake my senior year of high school. It was a place we went to have bonfires and party in the summer, and a place I went alone to have some sense of freedom and independence. We were sitting together on the old, dirty couch that must have been sickening to my little brother, whose sensibilities were so much more refined. We smoked cigarettes, listened to music from a battery-powered boom box, and talked about his future plans. He was fifteen years old, and he had just dropped out of high school. It was a private school where my father and stepmother must have thought he would be more protected. He wasn't. But he had finally found a hobby he loved there, photography. One night he got permission to use the darkroom with me. I picked him up from our father's in the little Volkswagen my mother had passed on to me, and we went to the school. We walked the campus grounds, smoked a joint by the tennis courts, sat together in the huge, empty ice rink because my brother loved the vacuous feel of it, and then we went to the darkroom, where he developed photos he'd taken on the farm where he lived with our dad. He marveled at every step in the process, and so did I.

Soon after, a camera was stolen from the school and Noah was blamed. My father confronted him. We all knew that Noah was a child who broke the rules, but he was also one who had no shame in doing so. In middle school, he'd stolen my father's credit card to order himself a king-size bed. When it was delivered, he'd proudly come clean, asking my father if he really wanted to pay to ship the bed back. Now it seemed that Noah would have admitted if he'd stolen the camera, and also that if he'd really wanted a new camera he could have found a way to buy one.

My father went to the headmaster, insisting the thief had not been Noah.

"This is because of his identity," my father said.

"No," the headmaster said. "We've had a gay here before without problem."

Before my brother dropped out, some boys smashed a whoopie pie in his face while at school lunch. He began to spend lunch hiding out behind the dumpsters, smoking cigarettes. This would have been a year or two after Matthew Shepard had been murdered. Did Noah think of that as he hid? *Fag* had been a constant in my brother's life, and it had crept into his psyche; I remember him saying in those years that though he was gay, he wasn't *one of those flag-flying fags.*

But what if he had flown flags? What if our family had flown them for him, for his survival? Now our home is filled with reflections of my daughter's life—flags, but also art, books, T-shirts, stickers, all of it to celebrate her, to prop her up against so much hardship. My brother's childhood home lacked that. True, my father and stepmother did their best; and in that era, just loving and accepting my brother as gay seemed a revolutionary act on their part. But what if he had been surrounded by absolute pride, the kind that trickled down into his bones? My brother's struggles were not chance. There were eight children in our family, and not one has struggled in the ways he has.

He had a job by the time he'd dropped out, in a Ralph Lauren at the outlet mall. He'd buy clothes with his paycheck, but also bedding and towels and curtains as he worked to curate a life so far from the one he lived in the New Hampshire woods of my father's house. Nights, he sat at the woodstove in his bedroom and blew the smoke from his cigarettes up the chimney. He flipped through catalogs and earmarked what he wanted. His plan was to move to Phoenix, where he could live with my stepbrother—his half brother—and get a job at the upscale Ralph Lauren there. No matter that they said they didn't hire people his age, or people whose sales experience consisted of an outlet in rural New Hampshire; as we sat together that day in the dirty A-frame our brother Henry had built, Noah told me it would all work out, that he would make them see how good he was and he would get the job.

I was afraid for him, and I was aware as we sat there that there was something vacant between us, some access to him that I no longer had. I told him so. He laughed and told me not to worry. But it was a guarded laugh, almost performed, and it struck me suddenly that when we were very young, his pure and full laugh had been the best sound in the entire world to me; it—he, his arrival in this world—had broken through the loneliness I'd felt at my father's house. Now that laugh was gone, never to return.

16

....

I n my daughter's final month of first grade, our appointment with a doctor who had some expertise in gender finally arrived. Our psychologist, whom we had worked with for over a year now, sat in the corner of her office while her colleague sat next to our child with a notebook on her lap. She drew a few pictures. She explained that sometimes kids are born with girl bodies and on the inside they're girls. Sometimes they're born with boy bodies and on the inside they're boys. And sometimes kids are born in girl bodies but are boys on the inside, and sometimes in boy bodies but are girls on the inside. Sometimes kids are neither, and sometimes kids are both.

"Can you circle which picture is you?" she asked. We couldn't see, but we knew which one our child chose.

"Great," the psychologist said. "The word for that is *transgender*!"

She talked some more with our child, her demeanor happy and calm. After a while, she looked up at us. She told us that the best possible thing we could do was to support her gender expression. She told us it was actually quite common for autistic people to also be transgender. "I expect she'll want to change her name and pronouns soon," she said.

I stared at her. It felt like she had just peacefully dropped a little bomb on us. But then I looked at our child. For at least a year, our psychologist had jokingly referred to her as a grumpy old man, and the assessment fit: she had functioned as alternately grumpy or irate for most of her life. But when our child heard that word, *transgender,* it was like the light in the room shifted. The sun shone on her for the first time. All of us noticed it, instantly. A weight she had carried her entire life suddenly fell off her shoulders, onto the ground. We practically heard it drop. She stood up. She straightened her back.

"Can I go get a toy?" she said.

I saw that our psychologist had tears in her eyes. "How did I miss this?" she asked. And then, when our child reentered the room and sat herself in the middle of the floor, "It's a totally different presentation. Entirely, completely different."

The colleague referred us to the Boston Children's Hospital's gender clinic. "You won't have to think about anything medical yet. Parents just feel more at ease, checking in with the leading experts."

When our session was over, our daughter chose a prize from the bin and we left. Because of work, my husband and I had come in separate cars, and now our daughter rode home with him. I got to drive alone. I was on the highway when I started crying. Not just tears but full-on heaving. I took a breath and looked at the car passing me. It was Paul, with our daughter in the back seat. As they passed, she smiled and waved, and the image is burned into my memory. I am not exaggerating when I say that I had never in my life seen her smile like that before. So light, so free.

I didn't drive straight home. Instead, I called my husband to say I was stopping at my mother's, where my brother Henry was visiting. In childhood, our visitation schedule had put Henry, Will, and me with our mother two-thirds of the time and our father one-third; but when I was five years old, my brother Will stopped coming home to my mother's in a 1980s divorce agreement that still eludes me. Will was eleven at the time, and he did not see my mother again for the next seven years. Our home with our mother became just the three of us, and her house—with her, Henry, and me in it—was my oldest sense of safety.

I let myself in that night and found them in the dark living room, on the couch in a scene so totally familiar. They were watching a police procedural, the volume loud, my mother's legs stretched out to almost reach my brother, who had squeezed himself against the arm of the couch to not be touched. I cried and caught my breath and cried more and eventually I told them my child was transgender. "You have to just accept it," I said. "I need you to accept it."

"Okay," they said. But then, "Some doctor tells you that, so you think it's true? Someone spends ten minutes with your kid, so you believe it?"

"No," I said. I started to defend our child, still using her former name and pronouns in the process. I started to list all the evidence. My head pounded, and suddenly I realized that my mother and brother, here before me but unable to see what I had seen, were not in fact the family I needed. I left.

At home, I was shocked to see that Paul had already put our child to bed.

"I asked her about pronouns," he said, and he told me that she'd said she wanted to change hers. "She's so happy," he said, using *she* for the first time. "I told her she was a great daughter and you should have seen her face," he said.

"No," I remember telling him. "Can we just slow down?" I hadn't done enough research, I didn't understand enough. I was angry with him for saying things I hadn't approved of first. I went into my child's room and held her tight. Then I went to bed.

17

ust after that appointment, I went into my daughter's first-grade classroom early one morning, before the bell rang. We loved this teacher—she was more creative than disciplinary, she took the children outside every moment she could, she gave our child love, and she even read books to the class about gender-nonconforming kids. "Can boys like pink?" she would ask in circle time. "Of course they can!"

I had requested the meeting. I wanted to know how accepting the classroom truly was. If I sent my child to school in a dress, would she be protected from bullying? We sat in children's chairs at a low table. The teacher had a stack of papers in front of us, but before she began flipping through, she pointed to the high section of the wall. It was covered in self-portraits students had colored after choosing one of two templates, boy or girl. I scanned the pictures for my child: there she was, blond ponytail and dress, big crayon smile. A little girl on her first day of first grade. I have a picture of that day—she's dressed in a decidedly male fashion, fire engine shirt and joggers. What if I had allowed her to wear the outfit she'd colored in this self-portrait instead?

The teacher began shuffling through the papers in front of her.

This wasn't schoolwork but more artwork, mostly more self-portraits. Girl after girl after girl, all year long. As I looked, I remembered that this had been the pattern in kindergarten, too, though we'd written it off as a phase, or as a signal of her disregard for social norms.

"We did a skit once," the teacher told me. "I wasn't thinking. I assigned your child to a male role." My child had refused to play the role. "I went to the principal's office this morning," she went on. "I told them they need to do something about a transgender policy." That word again, out loud, before I was prepared. "This classroom is safe," she said. "And there's a bathroom for all students right here. Your child can wear a dress."

I went home, stood on the back porch, and I called my mother, and then I called my brother Henry. The rhododendron in our yard was huge, the biggest I had ever seen, and in full bloom now. I stared at it with that same feeling I'd had when our child had been diagnosed with autism—an answer, a pathway forward, a relief. But also, a lifetime of struggle ahead. On the phone, I told my family that my child had been identifying as female for at least two years. I told them my child was saying "I'm a girl" to classmates on the playground. But no one would listen.

"A phase," they said. "Remember when you wanted to be a boy."

I did. I had been four or five, and I had wanted my name to be Leroy, after my favorite character on *Fame*. I wanted to wake up and have a penis—the only proof, so far as I understood it, of being male. But even back then, when I wanted to wear my brothers' clothes, I still felt fine wearing my own female ones. I just knew my brothers were cool, cooler than me. I knew they had more freedoms. I believe I knew what the world was teaching me about gender, about my worth.

Anyway, I got over my desire to be a boy before I turned six. It was nothing really. I had wanted it, it had been a fantasy, but it had not caused unhappiness. Yet as my six-year-old began, before I had okayed it, to tell classmates that she was a girl and needed a new name, I heard my family, their reminders of that period of my life, and I let that small piece of my history be louder than all other signs. And when someone did finally listen to me, to my initial pleas for people to hear what I was saying about my child, I dismissed it. It was my oldest friend, Ingrid, who lived in a California city where her children had rainbow flags in their public school classrooms. She alone sent me links to trans-related information and stories, and I responded over the phone by reminding her that my child had always liked trucks, had never been into "girl stuff."

"Huh," Ingrid said. I knew what she meant because I have known her virtually all my life; I heard her disappointment in me. And I saw myself in her lack of response, saw that I was defending the gender norms we had been challenging for years. That evening, when my husband returned from work, I told him we had to go to the department store, had to finally let our child choose some new clothes.

"Choose what you want," we said as we stood at the edge of the children's clothing.

"Where's the girls' section?" our child said plainly. We pointed, then followed her to a ring of summer dresses. She looked at them and looked at us and then she looked at the dresses more.

"Choose a few you like," I encouraged her. She reached her hands out, touched the cheap cotton, then looked back at me again, silent. I could see exactly what she meant to say: *How is this thing I have wanted for so long finally happening? How have you finally listened to me?*

She chose three dresses, and at my urging a pair of shorts, which were bright pink and very short. We bought the clothes, drove home. She went in the house and asked if she could put a dress on. I told her they had to be washed, and anyway it was time for bed. We tucked her in, said good night, and then my husband and I sat on the couch and repeated the same thing back and forth to each other: "Did you see how happy she is? This is real."

. . .

When it was time for school the next morning, our daughter woke up and immediately asked to wear a dress. I encouraged her to wear the shorts instead.

"Why?" she asked.

"People might make fun of you," I said, but the moment the words left my mouth I wanted to pull them back, to swallow them down. What kind of message did I mean to impart? "I want to talk to the teacher first," I corrected. "I'll get too nervous." Still not right. I should have listened better. I should have looked at my daughter and listened.

She wore the pink shorts. I was scared for her all day, scared of what she might tell me at the end of it. I went early to the school for pickup, stood alone waiting. She came out happily, ran right up to me. She said, "Can I wear a dress tomorrow?" And then on the walk home, "Cammie was mean. She said I wasn't wearing the right shirt with the shorts. They sell a matching shirt and you didn't buy it, dum-dum."

That evening our daughter, for the first time in her entire life, went into her room, found her own clothes, and got changed. She came out in a pink dress with pink hearts and asked if we could ride bikes to the playground. My husband and I were dumbfounded; where had our child gone? For years, leaving the house on any occasion had felt like an insurmountable task.

We walked behind our daughter as she rode her bike down the sidewalk on her first voyage into the world in a dress that was meant for regular life rather than Halloween. I would like to say that my pride, like hers, was larger than my fear, but it wasn't, not yet, not at all. I was scared, and so was my husband. When we passed our neighbor out in his lawn, we moved a wide distance from him, right off the sidewalk and into the street. None of us offered any hello. We were so relieved to find the playground empty.

The dress flowed behind her as she pedaled circles around us. My husband took a video. Of course he did. We had never, ever seen our child so happy.

One of my favorite photographs is of our daughter standing in the early morning light in front of the blooming rhododendron, wearing her rainbow dress and pink sneakers. It's May of first grade, her first day wearing a dress to school. Her stance is tilted, her hands held neatly in front of her body, so girlish and content. My husband took another picture of her and me together, my arm wrapped tightly around her body, her joy and my anxiety so evident behind our smiles. Then we walked down the sidewalk to the school, her dad on one side and I on the other, a barrier against the cruel world. We waited outside the building until long after she went in, expecting someone to run back out, to say, *What were you thinking?* and *How could you let your child do this?* Instead, I got messages throughout the day: our child was doing great, our child was glowing, children had stared a little but no one said anything.

I even got a YouTube video, sent from the guidance counselor, a woman whose support of our child had been unwavering. *I saw this and I thought of you all,* she wrote. It was a video of Nicole Maines, the transgender woman and actor whose family had fought for her rights in Maine. I wasn't ready for it, though. That word, *transgender,* being given to me so carelessly again—even on that day, it made me nervous. My fear, still, was so much larger than what was in front of me. But the fact in front of me was so astonishingly clear: my daughter, she heard that word, *transgender,* and the clouds parted for her. *Here,* that word so obviously said to her, *you are not strange, not wrong. You are so common there is a word for you! Here,* it said, *come through.*

I had learned not to press her, so after I picked her up from school I just waited for her to share. Finally, after dinner, when I could wait no longer, I leaned on her bedroom doorframe while she lay on her bed looking at a book and I said, "Did anyone make fun of you?"

"Yes," she said, without looking up.

"Do you want to wear your old clothes tomorrow?"

"I'm wearing girl clothes every day forever," she said plainly, and she turned the page of her book.

One morning after school drop-off, I ran into Eric in the parking lot. By this time, Paul worked daytime hours, and my irregular schedule of writing and part-time library work meant that Eric and I were often the parents available to attend school functions. We'd stood together in the woods to watch our children run by in an obstacle course; we'd squeezed in next to each other on metal chairs to watch an afternoon assembly. He'd helped me when I needed a truck to get rid of old furniture, or when I needed advice about yet another broken lawn mower. I'd begun to get to know his wife, Robin, more, and sometimes Paul and I watched their daughter for them, and we'd all had dinner together a few times by now. More than once they'd witnessed us standing outside the school building for pickup after a long, relentless meeting, my husband's fists clenched and my body shaking with nerves. They'd listened to us go on about our struggles with the school, and they always checked in to find out if things were improving.

Eric decided to leave his truck in the lot and walk with me to my house. I'd just gotten a box of finished copies of my second novel in the mail, and he wanted to come over so I could give one to him.

"Paul said you're going back to Montana?" he asked as we walked.

"I hope so," I said. I told him we didn't have specific plans yet, but that we were looking for jobs to apply for. "It just feels like Missoula would be so much more accepting of our kid," I said.

He understood. "It's so great," he said when we were inside. He was referring to the dresses our child had begun to wear to school. He said he remembered how she'd often put the princess costumes on at the library. I told him about the conversation I'd had with the first-grade teacher, about the psychologist's appointment, about that word, *transgender*, being used by both the teacher and the doctor. I told him that I'd made an appointment at the Boston Children's Hospital, where we would see a doctor who specialized in gender. I told him what our child had said before the dance recital: "Duh, that's the costume I'm supposed to have."

"I talked to Robin about the dresses," Eric said. He's a large man whose arms are covered in black tattoos, a hobby welder and metalworker who collects knives and loves violent video games. "I really never thought about gender much before," he said. "I honestly didn't know anything about being trans." He said Robin had shown him some videos, and she'd read books with their daughter to help her understand.

We didn't have a chair in our living room, only the one couch, and I felt awkward talking to him while sitting side by side like that. I turned to look toward the back porch so he wouldn't see tears in my eyes. Aside from the teachers, I hadn't spoken to anyone in town about what we were going through yet. I'd been so afraid of judgment.

Eric told me you read some books with your daughter about gender, I texted Robin the moment he left. *Thank you.*

I'll do anything I can to help, she texted back immediately, and she stayed true to her word.

Soon Susan, the special education coordinator who had worked with us since kindergarten, sent home a bag of books that she'd purchased for the resource room. *Might be helpful to read!* she'd written brightly on a sticky note. I sat alone at the kitchen table and took the books out one by one. *I Am Jazz. Who Are You?: The Kid's Guide to Gender Identity. Jacob's New Dress.* I had read every single one before. In the fall, I'd sat on the couch and read *Jacob's New Dress* with our child slowly, pointing to the pictures and remarking on how grateful I was that books about boys in dresses existed. But what had I meant? It would be months before I bought her a dress.

Our library hadn't owned *Who Are You?: The Kid's Guide to Gender Identity,* so I'd put an interlibrary loan request in for it. When it arrived, we'd sat together one early winter afternoon and read it. There's a wheel with cutout windows at the back of the book—you spin it to show which description fits. My child had not hesitated for one moment in her choice: *boy body, girl brain.*

"Okay," I'd said, and then I'd just closed the book and returned it to the library.

Every year, I'd help the library celebrate Banned Books Week. I'd walk the stacks and collect all the books that had been challenged or banned throughout the country, and I'd put them on display. I'd print posters about the harm of censorship, the human cost of blocking access to books with characters whose lives reflected actual ones. I'd make bookmarks to show that, year after year, nearly all the targeted books featured LGBTQ+ characters. I'd put my pin on my bag and I'd wear my special socks—I READ BANNED BOOKS. It was my favorite library week of the entire year.

Yet as I sat at my table that late spring morning with the books from Susan spread before me, I remembered not reading *I Am Jazz* aloud to my daughter. It's a simple picture book that explains Jazz Jennings's social transition when she was young. I'd had my husband read the book, and I'd even asked him if we should read it with our child. She still wasn't *her* to us yet, but I think she was to herself. Paul had shrugged, said it didn't matter either way, which I see now as half true—it could not possibly have hurt her to read it. But it could have helped so much.

What had stopped me? Had I actually believed that information about transgender children could create a transgender child? And so what if it did? Now I can say with every fiber of my being that I wish only for the world to have more of these resolute humans who look at the adults around them and risk everything they have to say over and over again until they are heard, "You are wrong. I know myself better than you do."

When Susan sent the books home, I finally read *I Am Jazz* with my daughter. She wore dresses now, but I kept trying to delay a new name and a new pronoun, kept wanting our appointment in Boston—some four months away—to come first.

She seemed to like the book. Nothing remarkable happened. She listened, then went to her room to play LEGOs.

· · ·

That would have been in early June. Some three weeks later, once school was out, she and I went to our family's cabin on the lake alone together, which we had never done before. It hadn't been our plan— Paul had backed out at the last minute, and I suppose his absence on that first summer trip to the island marked the beginning of what would become his absolute descent.

In part, Paul did not go with us because his hip pain had progressed to the point where he could not walk on uneven ground, and we had just learned that he needed a major surgery to correct what we now knew was a congenital hip displacement. It was a long, difficult procedure that we'd been told only a handful of surgeons specialized in, one of whom was in Boston. We'd scheduled the surgery for September, after which Paul would be out of work and in a wheelchair, then on crutches for three months.

But had his hip been okay, would he have gone?

At that point, I spent my time daydreaming about our move back to Missoula, but the complexity of it had only multiplied. Months after his surgery, Paul would need a follow-up procedure to remove the screws that would be placed in his hip. Could he even get that done in Missoula? And how would we afford it? My husband had spent his entire working life in kitchens, and he'd only recently found a job that paid well, that offered benefits and vacations and hours that fit with our family. It wasn't easy to find in his field, and there was so much competition in Missoula, where pay was low and benefits were scarce. We knew that if we moved, he would no longer be getting health insurance through his employer.

I don't know how to describe my husband's longing for the west in a way that does not sound insignificant. I can list the individual parts. He misses the wide-open landscape and the more open people. He misses the cold, fresh creeks flowing from the mountains, and the way he would lie down in them, hold on to a rock, and let the current wash over his body until he was nearly frozen. He misses the freedom of Missoula, where he would ride his 1969 Schwinn across town to

smoke a joint on the front porch of an old friend's house while looking out at the sweep of the valley. He misses gathering quarters to play
pinball and *Ms. Pac-Man* at the bar; and backpacking, hiking to hot
springs, driving over mountain passes to see what is on the other side.
He misses his family, who still lives there. But these parts do not equal
the whole. The whole for him in the Rocky Mountain west is akin to
something I feel when I look at the lake. It is deep and beyond words
and in those days—before our hearts were broken clear through—it
felt vital.

But Paul loved my family's spot on the lake, and before his limited mobility, he'd been adamant that we go there every chance we
got. We'd camp near the beach instead of sleep in the cabin, and we'd
swim and hike and just look out at the expanse of water. Paul would
keep a fire going all day, and he'd cook our meals on it. Our child was
calmer there, soothed by the water and woods. Her first trip there had
been when she was a month old, and it was a home to her now, as it
was to us. In those early years we were all so sleep deprived, but out
there it didn't matter so much; in the tent we'd wake to her cries and
just lie there with her under the glow of stars and the rustle of birch
leaves, and we'd get her to listen with us to the lapping of the waves or
the haunting calls of the loons or the sudden and uncanny predawn
silence. It didn't matter if we were tired. The next day we would swim
and rest and read and eat. It was the escape that kept us east.

But that summer my husband was worn out and in pain, and feeling trapped in New Hampshire, and I suppose he was also mourning
the loss of a son and staving off the fear of what it might mean to have
a transgender daughter. I wanted him to come to the island with us,
but I also didn't. His sadness was a weight I could not lift.

My daughter and I couldn't manage our canoe alone, so we hitched a
ride from a man I knew through the library who lived in Florida during the school year and spent the summer on the lake. He picked us
up at the town boat docks and drove us out slowly, circling the island

where his camp was to point it out on the way. It was hot, early July, with a storm predicted. At our camp, he ducked his head to come inside and look around. Now it's one of the worst on the lake—falling down, in desperate need of repair. But it's also one of the oldest and one of the few not owned by out-of-staters, and in that sense my family is proud, though the fact is that none of us has the money to take care of it.

My child was quiet, playing in the water and digging in the sand. The man and I talked about books, and after some time he left and the storm rolled in. We spent it inside, on the bed in the front room, the one nearest the lake. We played Battleship and watched the rain move across the lake in sheets of varying shades of blue to black. I took a picture, my sweet child with long hair and a purple dress leaned up against the knotty pine wall. The storm lifted, a rainbow appeared, and we went outside to sit in the sand at the edge of the water. There's a girls' summer camp less than a mile from our cabin, on the same island, and campers began to appear in the cove before us in their sailboats.

"Mom?" my child asked as we watched the boats. "Can transgender kids join the Girl Scouts?"

I understood right away that she had mistaken that camp and all others to be Girl Scouts, though I was slower to understand the weight of the question.

"I don't know," I said. "Why?"

We were sitting right next to each other, each of us tracing the lake with our eyes. I remember the feel of my fingers in the sand, the way the top layer was soaked but just below the surface the sand remained dry.

"Because I'm transgender and I want to join," she said. "Duh."

She had never said *transgender* aloud to me before, had never used the word to refer to herself. And finally, her saying it woke me up. My poor kid, for whom communication was already a struggle. She had tried so hard to get us to listen, but now here she was putting it in the simplest form possible. She should have won a gold medal.

I pulled her in close and we watched the sky. That night, as we cooked dinner over the fire, we brainstormed names. She would have a new one. One that told the world her gender.

21

....

When Noah was fourteen or fifteen, he made a date with each one of his immediate family members to come out to us individually. It was a long process; there were so many of us—his mom, our dad, eight children altogether. On the day when it was my turn to go out with him, I picked him up from work at the outlet mall and we went across the street to McDonald's. As we ate French fries and drank Coke he told me he was gay. I think I must have told him that I knew, that we all knew, that we'd always known. I wonder now what he was asking for in that moment.

"When I said I was transgender," my daughter said at dinner one night, some two years after she'd changed her name and pronouns, "it's not like you didn't already know."

She was right. I'd known it through and through, and my knowing wasn't the point. The point was that she was asking to be noticed, asking us to wake up and look head-on at the daughter we had and to rearrange our lives accordingly. What if that was what Noah had been looking for? What if, instead of telling him that the information he was giving me was obvious, I had congratulated him? I could have baked him a cake to celebrate, could have thrown him a party. I could have learned about gay history, gay pride; I could have promised him I would fight for gay rights, and then I could have done it. Why didn't I look for an LGBTQ+ youth group for him? There must have been one somewhere. I had a license. I could have driven him. I am pained to think of how much these simple acts could have relieved the suffering my little brother was about to endure for the next decade.

22

·····················

I t took a few days, maybe a week, to settle on the right name for our
daughter. I was working fewer hours at the library now, and writing
more, so summer meant that she and I were home together most days.
We'd walk around the house thinking of names, and I would call a
new one to her, practice it, see if it felt right. At the end of the day,
when my husband came home, I would tell him whatever new name
we'd settled on. He never had much to say about it.

By that point I'd done a lot of research, and I'd passed it all on
to him, which meant that we were both just learning to shoulder the
crushing weight of the statistic that parents of transgender youth have
etched into their bones: without appropriate support, one in three
trans youth will attempt suicide, and nearly half will seriously consider it.

We existed under that dark cloud, together but so far apart. I would
tirelessly read and plan, and Paul would just go blank. At night, we'd
curl up on opposite sides of the bed, my shoulders clenched and his
eyes sunk into his phone, each of us aware that that measurement—
nearly half, nearly half—danced back and forth across our minds. We
knew it wasn't some nebulous mystery, knew it was attached to a very

clear anchor: *without appropriate support.* Meaning that our child's chances of survival depended wholly on our ability to provide that.

"What do you think of the new name?" I'd ask Paul, and then in the silence I would just continue: "Do you think we're doing the right thing? Should we wait until our appointment in Boston to use the name? How should we tell other kids? When should we have a meeting with the teacher?"

Eventually, Paul would reach across the bed, put his hand on my leg. "It's fine," he would say. "It will all work out." Then he would roll back over through the pain of his hip and sink into his video of fly-fishing in the mountain creeks of the west.

"It will work out only if we make it work out," I would snap at him. Sometimes, the conversation would escalate: he said I worried too much and I said he disappeared too much. Other times, one of us would just give up and leave the room, I to the couch to read or he to the basement to sleep. We both knew that a gap was widening between us. But we also knew that, for our daughter, we could still reach over it, could still find each other's hands across the dark abyss. We did that on the day she opened a book and pointed to a name she liked. He and I looked at each other and knew in an instant that it was right. Greta. A name as sure and bold as her.

It took longer to get used to the new pronoun. On the first day that we began to settle into both together, our family was invited out on the lake by the same man who'd just recently given my daughter and me a ride to our cabin. Paul felt up for the outing. As we cut across the water I walked up to the helm and yelled over the noise that our child had a new name. But I didn't say the whole thing—the name was still so fresh, so unfamiliar, and I was still so unsure. I cut it off at the first syllable, saying "Grey," a diminutive form that had also been occasionally used for her old name. I continued to do this throughout the night as I introduced her to the man's wife and children, plus two other couples they had invited over.

"No," my child stepped forward and said each time I introduced her. "My name is Greta," she would announce proudly. My husband and I looked at each other in awe, each silently asking the same thing: *Where did our child go?* Truly, where was that angry child who would hide behind us, who would never, not ever, offer even a hello?

Paul and I stayed on the porch overlooking the lake for most of the evening. We avoided pronouns entirely, avoided all conversation about our child. Meanwhile, Greta swam with the other kids, she ate her dinner, she answered questions when asked. "Is this how other parents live?" we said to each other quietly. Typically, any social event meant one of us following our child around, intercepting, negotiating, trying to keep the meltdown that was moving ever closer to us from crashing down.

But not this time. This time we enjoyed ourselves like adults do, and our child remained carefree and happy. Why wouldn't she? It was, essentially, her first time out in the world.

Within twenty-four hours of a new name and pronoun, our child started reading independently, when previously she'd generally only looked at the pictures. She stayed up late at night to read, moving through a simple chapter book a day. At the end of the week, I packed four of her books, plus our clothes, in preparation for a trip with my mother to visit my brother Henry in Maine.

Once again, my husband would not be coming with us, and once again, because of his sadness, I felt ambivalent about his absence. As summer spread before us and our daughter went out into the world as herself with me at her side, I began to think of that early decision of Paul's, to pair his life so quickly and completely with mine. It had been my fault we'd come east. And though any imagined altered past would erase the existence of our child, I could not stop wondering if maybe he would have been better off to stay away from me, and thereby to remain in the west.

23

We would be gone to Maine for five days. When my mother pulled into the driveway to pick us up, Greta ran out to the car in her dress and handed a note over. *Dear Grandma, I have a new name. It's Greta. Please call me Greta. Love, Greta.*

My mother, who would soon become a stalwart support, was not ready, not yet. She was shocked, she was afraid, and the new name sounded like poison or a joke coming from her lips. My daughter sat in the back seat with her headphones on and watched a show on the iPad while my mother and I silently seethed at each other in the front. A few hours into the drive, she needed me to look at her phone— something about the music or directions. I unlocked it and saw its screen still open to a text chain with a friend. *Now I'm supposed to call "her" by a new name??!!* my mother had written.

For a few miles, I tried to pretend I hadn't seen the message. We were on an empty highway halfway to my brother's, pine trees in every direction. It was the area my husband had lived in as a teen, and where my mother had taken us every summer as children. I always thought of that as we drove this stretch, thought that years ago I might have passed by my husband long before I knew him. That I might have noticed him in the grocery store or driven by him as he and his girl-friend headed to the beach.

I turned around and said Greta's name, testing to make sure she couldn't hear me beneath her headphones. Then I turned back, looked out the window away from my mother, and said I had read what she'd written to her friend.

My mother became instantly angry, her hands gripping the wheel, her voice rising. It was a familiar space for us; we had spent so many years clashing. But I needed her now, and Greta needed her. Their minds were not far from each other's. "I don't think in words," my mother had once said to my brother Henry and me. We'd been in the kitchen, home from college for a visit. She was making the chocolate chip cookies she'd made every week of our entire childhoods.

"That's not true," we'd told her. We were both readers, both writ-ers, our minds so much more similar to our bookish father's, though it was our mother who had done the hard work of raising us. "That's impossible," we'd scoffed.

My mother got frustrated with us, with the way we were ganging up on her. Her profound dyslexia went undiagnosed until she was seventeen or eighteen years old, and that lack of understanding had a brutal cost—all those years with all those people, herself included, wondering what was wrong with her, wondering why she couldn't read if she just tried a little harder. All the myriad ways she must have been told she was stupid. I'd carried that story with me into every single special education meeting for my daughter. It was like a little stone tucked into a locket with all the others from my family—my brother Will, my uncle. I would not let the school make that my daughter's story, too.

Henry and I had kept pressing our mother until she finally slammed her old spatula into the bowl of dough. "I think in god-damned pictures," she'd snapped at us, and she crossed the kitchen to turn the oven on. My brother laughed a dismissive laugh I have only ever heard him use with our mother, and with that, the conversation was done. But years later, as I watched my own child come into herself, it haunted me. Of course it was possible to think in pictures; of course it was possible to think in any number of ways beyond my grasp. As I got to know my daughter, I found myself apologizing to my mother for my utter cruelty.

When we'd faced difficulty with our daughter's school disability rights, my mother was in her element; between divorce and having Will move out, she had struggled for years, yet working hard and pushing back had become the biggest lesson she meant to impart to Henry and me. In Greta's first few years of school, I'd called my mother every single morning after drop-off. I cried, I yelled, I just talked, and she listened. She came over multiple times a week and played with my daughter while I wrote or cooked or cleaned or took a walk. I had needed her in those days, and I needed her even more now, and as she drove us the six hours to my brother's in Maine, I was furious at her inability to show up.

My brother Henry lives in the most rural section of New England I have ever been to, on conservation land he bought cheap at auction. He truly lives off the land there, felling trees to strip and build into a house, dropping a bucket down into a well for water. He digs clams for work, and he gets his vegetables and meat and milk from friends who relocated to that area as back-to-earthers in the 1970s. He lives in a hand-built one-room cabin with no running water, and for this trip, rather than have us camp on his land, he had arranged for us to stay in the oceanfront dream house of a couple who'd had it built some twenty years earlier, when they'd retired and left city life. That afternoon, I called him as we neared his town, and he met us on the dirt road at the end of the spit to guide us to the house.

"Greta!" he yelled as he jumped out of his car to greet us. He held up a gift of a yellow tote bag decorated with a portrait of Greta Thunberg, her name scrolled across the bottom. It was the first time he'd seen our daughter since her name change, and his absolute support brought tears to my eyes.

We have only a few photos from the trip. In my favorite, she leans against the porch railing in that house in her new summer dress on a blue-sky day with the ocean shining brilliantly behind her, and she looks so peaceful and happy. It was the first day of a family vacation as herself, in a house on the water unlike any vacation home we had ever been to. She had run through the place when we arrived, examining every room, and she'd chosen one for us upstairs with two single beds and a moose wallpaper border. We unpacked and explored, and for dinner we grilled on the porch. That night Greta stayed awake until eleven p.m., lying in bed with a headlamp on, laughing while she read, totally entranced by this world of a book that she could suddenly enter on her own.

The next morning, while she slept in, I tiptoed downstairs to find my mother in her bedroom. We both knew we were still angry at each other. But I tried—I sat on the end of the bed while she rifled through her suitcase and I told her everything I knew. I told her the statistics, the importance of believing and affirming my daughter's gender. I told her to just look—couldn't she see how happy Greta was now, how much she'd changed? Nothing worked. She again reminded me of that stage of my own childhood when I'd wanted to be a boy. She asked if I would let Greta be a dog if she said that's what she was. I wanted to shake her, to scream in her face. But also, I wanted my husband. Since our daughter's autism diagnosis, we'd been each other's only true witnesses, bound together by the fact that only we knew what we had been through and what our daughter needed, only we understood. Now we were bound all over again, and without him at my side the crack of self-doubt in me was widening.

Still, Greta is my mother's only grandchild and the light of her life, and we managed to have a good time together. Clam prices that season were the highest on record, which meant my brother couldn't afford to skip the morning tide, so my mother, Greta, and I spent each morning alone together. We walked the desolate beaches, played in the waves, inspected crabs and rocks and seaweed, built drip sandcastles, and generally avoided Greta's name or pronouns. Afternoons, Henry would come in from the mudflats and call my daughter's name loudly, and his presence would relieve us all. We'd cook a big lunch together, and when the tide was high enough, he would take my daughter down to the dock and the two of them would jump fearlessly off into the cold water some ten feet below. "Gre-taaaa!" he would holler as she jumped each time.

But somehow it all began to crumble. I remember nights awake alone, unable to contact my husband because we had no phone service. What were we letting our child do? I wondered all over again.

Had Paul been there, he would have said, *Just look at her.* He, like our daughter, has an uncanny ability to cut through the noise and see the pure truth; it was why I had fallen in love with him and why I was still in love with him. He was afraid, of course he was afraid, but from the moment we'd sat in that psychologist's office and watched our daughter transform, his mind had never again deviated from the clear path in front of us.

Now, without his clarity wrapped around me, I lost my own. I would stand in the living room with my family and talk about my child, and feel so embarrassed to use that pronoun, *she.* I would say it meekly, my tone suggesting that even I didn't believe it. When Greta complained that she was bored, when she grumbled about a chore I asked her to do, I found myself reprimanding her in front of them—and using that nickname, *Grey,* the one I knew she didn't want.

But Greta didn't say a word about it. She just got up each morning, put a dress on, found her family, and tried.

The day before we left, we had a dinner party on the porch with old friends we see there every year. Greta adores these friends, and she dreams of a life like theirs: women who live off the land, who built their houses with their own hands, who hunt and fish and grow their food, who make clothing from fur and leather and wool.

We had a feast for the party—fresh-picked clams and lobsters caught that day, corn on the cob, greens from their garden. My brother had told them of Greta's transition ahead of time, and as we sat together in the late afternoon sun one friend leaned over to me and quietly asked how Greta was doing, how the change was going. She was a woman some twenty years older than me who'd never had children and, since Greta's birth, had always asked me heartfelt questions about parenthood. I loved talking with her, but now I didn't know how to respond. I couldn't stop worrying that we had gotten it all wrong.

"It's going okay," I said quickly. Why couldn't I just be as sure as my child? Instead, I took Greta's hand and brought her off the porch with me, away from all possibility of conversation. We went down to the field that overlooked the ocean. It was covered in beach roses. We breathed their scent in, chased each other, pointed out across the water to the horizon. I held her close. I told her I was so happy to be there with her.

By the time we got back to the porch, two more friends of my brother's had arrived. We had never met them before. I remember wondering what they thought of my child—this six-year-old in a dress who proudly introduced herself as Greta but whose name no one seemed to use; this child who—when she was out of earshot—was referred to as *she* by the women who lived up here, but *he* by members of her own family.

The next morning, we got in the car to drive the six hours home. From the back seat, Greta said she didn't like any of the food I'd packed. Her drink was disgusting. She didn't want to watch the movie I'd downloaded. She hated the music. A few hours in, she started kicking the seat and screaming. Eventually, my mother pulled over on the side of the road and whipped around and screamed at her to behave. Only she didn't say, *Be a good girl.* She said *boy. Boy, boy, boy.*

I still remember my daughter's crestfallen face in the back seat. She wouldn't speak the entire rest of the drive home, wouldn't even eat the donut I offered her. When my mother dropped us off at our house, Greta darted inside to the safety of her room. I found her on her bed. I lay down beside her.

"I hate myself," she said. She punched at her pillow and grunted. "I shouldn't have done that," she cried. She meant she shouldn't have kicked the seat, shouldn't have yelled, shouldn't have acted that way in Grandma's car.

"No," I said firmly, hugging her. "I shouldn't have. Grandma shouldn't have." I told her the adults were doing a really, really bad job. I insisted it wasn't her fault. "Grandma will learn," I said. "I will learn. Pinky swear," I said, and I found her little hand in the bed, wrapped my finger around hers. "Pinky swear one million times forever," I promised my daughter.

24

My promise wasn't enough. Directly after our trip to Maine, Greta was signed up for one week of summer day camp at her school. I went to the principal ahead of time to tell her about Greta's social transition, bringing with me some printed pages from a national organization about safe schools for transgender children.

"Great," she said as she looked the papers over. "Keep the information coming."

But who was I? I was no expert. Our appointment at Boston Children's Hospital wasn't for another few weeks, and I still felt so nervous about stepping out into the world and saying boldly, *This is my daughter, her name is Greta,* before really sitting down with the doctors and talking it through. So that summer morning I found myself suggesting to the principal that they try to avoid pronouns entirely at camp. I suggested they call her *Gret,* a nickname that she liked. Later, I sat Greta down and told her the same. I said that no one at the camp understood yet.

"We'll get the teacher's help in the fall," I said. "But for now, I think this will be easier on you."

She didn't even bother to disagree. She just marched into the school cafeteria for summer camp the next morning and announced proudly, "I have a new name!"

I stood outside and watched through the open door. That spirit of hers—so full of trust and hope—I wanted to gather it up, to cup it between my hands like a flame in the wind, to protect it. Her peers were around her. I couldn't tell what they were saying. I just watched from the pavement until an adult walked to her side, and only then did I leave.

The school had promised that the counselors would keep a special watch on Greta. In Greta's telling, the kids kept their distance from her. It went okay, for the most part. Except when she had to use the bathroom, a situation I had astoundingly failed to plan for. I later learned that, on the first day, she'd been told to use the nurse's bathroom.

"I'm not doing that," she'd said. "No one else does that."

Instead, she held it all day. The second day, a counselor ran to me when I walked into the parking lot for pickup.

"There's been an accident," she said. It took me a moment to figure out that she meant my daughter had peed her pants. She rushed me inside, to the boys' bathroom.

"You there?" I said gently, and immediately I heard Greta crying, a full-bodied heave. I got her to open the door and come out of the stall. I saw they had brought her a change of clothes.

"Why would they bring me boy clothes?" she yelled. She banged her head against the hard cement wall. I knew I couldn't make her stop, knew that all my efforts to contain her body would only make her push back harder. Instead, I put my hand between her head and the wall to cushion the blow until she relented and collapsed into my arms.

"It's okay," I told her. "It's okay, Greta." I looked around: boys' bathroom, boys' clothes in a pile on the floor. How could anyone have ever thought it would be okay to send her here, to give her these clothes in exchange for her pink leggings and dress? Why not just say it to her directly: *You can play your little game of being a girl, but we're not going to play it, too.*

Greta calmed down for a minute and peeled herself from my body. But when I said she'd better get out of her wet clothes, she started to bang her head against the wall again.

"Why would they do that?" she yelled.

"Greta," I kept saying. "Greta, I understand." I know I'd said as much before—over and over again, I'd told her I understood, and then I'd failed to live up to it. But now, as I stood in the boys' bathroom with my daughter, my hand between her head and the wall, I think I really did understand. I saw her walking into the cafeteria that morning, so sure that the world and its people would hold her up. And now this—banging her head against a cement wall, crying, heaving because she was so alone, so misunderstood. Because she kept telling people exactly who she was and people kept refusing to listen. Of course this would be the result.

What would happen when things got harder? How would we protect that shining light of hers?

I rubbed her back, smoothed her hair. "Let's go home," I said gently. "We can sneak out the back door, no one will even see us." I asked her if she wanted to go in her wet clothes or put the dry ones on. She shrugged and went into the stall. I could hear her sniffling while she changed, this six-year-old girl who was risking everything just to be herself.

The moment we got home, Greta went to her room and tore the clothes off. I told her to get in the bath, but she just put a dress on and came to find me. She cuddled her body into mine.

"It's okay," I kept telling her. I promised her that it was, that it would be. I had no idea what the town and school and state and country was about to do to us, no idea what privilege really meant and what it might mean for my child to lose another layer of it. All I knew was that I would never again call my daughter by the wrong name or pronoun. I would never again fail to prepare the world for her. I promised her that it would all be just fine, with no understanding that to make it so would empty me out, would break my heart in half and rewrite everything I thought I knew. It would destroy me, but I would do it. I would protect my daughter.

PART TWO

25

....

After Greta was diagnosed with autism, Paul drove us home from the hospital. We took the back way. It was a winding drive that ran along a clear creek and circled a mountain we loved to hike. Greta was in the back, five years old, and I had a hundred-page booklet on my lap that the hospital had given us. Snow as high as our car was piled up on the roadsides, and the tree limbs were heavy, tenting the roads. I flipped through the pages, stopping randomly on a passage that told me that drowning was a leading cause of death in children with autism. I closed the booklet and performed some Google search that must have been representative of my catastrophic thinking, and there on the screen I read that the marriages of over 90 percent of couples with a child on the spectrum end in divorce.

I know that statistic must be wrong. It seems so outlandish I haven't even wasted the time trying to track it back down. Still, false or not, it occupies me, the knowledge that the promise we made one morning on the island of my childhood would require extreme determination to keep. Not because of who our daughter comes to the world as, but because of the toll we pay with our full selves to prepare it for her. On that early March day that we drove home from the appointment where she was diagnosed, thank god my husband and I chose to understand that the struggle would bind us, would seal a lock on the promise we had made.

That summer when Greta was six and socially transitioned, Paul and I were riddled with anxiety of what lay ahead—his surgery and her upcoming school year. He continued to retreat to the corners of our house, distant and alone, and I woke in pain every night, my shoulders clenched to my ears. But then we were also buoyed together by the newfound calm of our daughter. She was protected, surrounded only by those who respected her gender. She was in the clothes she wanted and her hair was long; she had her name and pronouns. It meant that a layer of dysphoria we had never understood—and had attributed solely to autism—had fallen off like the heaviest of capes. At six years old she was peaceful and content for the first time in her life. She woke happy, and she spent her days reading and playing LEGOs and exploring the backyard, whistling and singing to herself as she went.

At the end of summer, Greta and I once again returned to Maine without Paul, because he was in too much pain to go. We went with my mother, and we again met my brother. The trip marked the first time we fell together instinctively into the rhythm of shielding Greta. We were in the town that Paul had lived in as a teen, at the campground we'd stayed at with our mother for two weeks every summer in childhood. That annual trip had been my mother's proudest parenting accomplishment, or at least the one she remembers most fondly. She'd meticulously pack all our supplies, and then escape her endless stream of schoolwork and yardwork and housework to spend days on the ocean with her children. The three of us—or four, in the years before my oldest brother moved out—would sleep together in one big tent, and in the morning my brother and I would wake to the sound of the door's zipper as our mother crawled out to sit under the tarp at the picnic table to drink coffee, smoke cigarettes, and make pancakes.

Once she was up, Henry and I would roll quickly toward her vacated spot in the middle, racing each other for a few hours of sleep on her air mattress instead of our hard camp mats.

For years, my brother and I had said we would like to go back to that campground with our mother, and that summer—when I couldn't readily get to the island because of my husband's failing hip, and when I avoided the town beach where I knew my daughter would be stared at in her new bathing suit—I finally made the camping trip happen. We would be staying for just three nights.

I'm not totally aware of what happened in the interim between our first trip to Maine and the second. My mother knew of the pain Greta had suffered because of our failures on the previous Maine trip. She knew about the toileting accident at school camp. She knew I had finally become steadfast in my support. But did my brother send her information about transgender kids? Did she research on her own? Or did she transform because she simply accepted the proof of her granddaughter in front of her?

The campground had changed since we had last been there, the sites closer together and the beaches and bathrooms and camp store more packed. Unlike when we were young, people in the neighboring sites could see and hear us, and my mother, brother, and I were all aware of what this meant: we would not out Greta, we could not. She was counting on us. We would not slip up on her pronoun, would not revert to her old name. It meant that, finally, it wasn't just my husband and I who moved through the world as she needed us to—it was my family. As we jumped from the rocks into the water, as we caught crabs, as we rode bikes and cooked s'mores and helped her to play with the kids at the neighboring site, we did so with a daughter, a granddaughter, a niece.

Henry had always been supportive. He might not have truly believed my daughter was a girl yet, but he would always follow my lead. For most of our lives, it had been he and I together—he and I moving between parents, he and I with the same strange and particular reality. But the fact that my mother learned, that something clicked in her mind and at seventy-three years old she closed in around my daughter and never looked back, this gave me some amount of hope.

"My granddaughter," she began to say proudly by the end of the summer.

None of us could have guessed that, by fall, she would find herself saying, "You stay the fuck away from my granddaughter," to absolute strangers in my town.

....

26

There's a ski area on the back side of the mountains behind my daughter's old elementary school, and on winter nights we could see the glow of its lights from our front yard. My father had grown up on the side of that mountain, and as a boy he would trek from his house through the woods, skis on his shoulder, and come out at the top of a ski trail. Once, famously, he snuck out at night to go to the ski area with his neighbor and their sled. This was years before night skiing, but the moon had been bright and the snow packed down. In my father's telling, their sled went so fast down the mountain that when they hit a jump and landed, he vomited from the impact.

Years later, while I skied that mountain, I would remember these stories and feel like it meant something to be skiing over my father's tracks, my grandfather's. My father taught me to ski there when I was two, and my grandparents, in my understanding, had something to do with the mountain's beginning. The local hero who'd won the Olympics and had a chairlift named after her had been my father's babysitter, and once, in a joke, had named her dog after my grandfather. Which is to say I felt I belonged there, felt I had some claim to the place.

For most of my childhood, my grandparents would buy us kids

ski passes to that mountain, and starting when I was six or seven my father would drop us all off there on weekends—I and my siblings who were old enough to ski, plus one of our cousins. My stepsister Courtney and I were put on the race team, which my brothers and cousin always mocked us for.

"With the Gilford snobs all day," they would taunt. "Too good for us."

I understood what they meant; the other Gilford kids seemed rich and well cared for. They had good long johns while Courtney and I wore tights; they had wool socks and we had cotton ones. On the chairlift they would remove their mittens—making sure to not let their hand warmers drop—and they'd take candy from their pockets. At lunch, they would take their ski boots off and put their lodge slippers on and unpack the lunches that had been lovingly packed for them. They'd stand in line for the microwave with their instant noodle soup or they'd take their sandwiches from their ziplock baggies and Courtney and I would look on, desperate with hunger and longing because we never even had food for the day; no one ever thought to make it for us, and even if we had the skills, what were we going to pack in a house filled with raw meat, tripe, and alcohol? Sometimes she and I would ski through lunch to avoid the shame and want of it all; and sometimes we'd make the long trek across the ski area grounds to the main lodge, weave through the line of people buying hamburgers and French fries, and we'd load our pockets with saltine crackers and ketchup packets. Once, she stole a Skor bar for us. But most of the time we would just sit at the tables, she with her group and I with mine, and watch everyone else eat. They usually had a parent with them, someone skiing for the day who would meet them in the clubhouse to open the cooler and spread the food out and talk about the morning. I remember sitting across from those parents—moms, usually—and watching them unpack the food. Did they notice I had none? I would never ask them to share; I knew better than to do that. My stepmother had taught me to not even call my grandparents to ask if I could come over. Better to stay quiet, to wait for people to offer. They never did.

So I was hungry, and I was cold, and often I was dirty, but out there on the ski trails I was also alive. I loved being there, loved nothing more than the carve of my skis against the hard snow and ice, the cold bite of wind against my face, the silence. I loved all forms of weather on the mountain—even rain, when everyone else would retreat to the lodge and I would be left alone to ski wide, fast turns across the empty trails.

Back then, the ski area closed at four p.m. Courtney and I would trudge across the snow to the parking lot, and there meet up with our brothers and cousin, who were generally not as hungry as us—they were more wild, brave, and ill-behaved; they begged for money, they stole food, and sometimes they ended up with a cheeseburger to split between the four of them. But we were all equally cold, and the end of the day was the hardest for us all. The buildings were locked and the sun going down, the temperature rapidly dropping, and my father's van would just not pull in. We would climb the snowbanks; sometimes my oldest stepbrother would bully us all into a violent game of King of the Mountain. We'd get pushed down on the dirty ice, scrape our faces, and get back up again. And still my father's van would not pull in.

When it did, it would be five or six at night. Once, when my father and stepmother pulled into the empty lot in the evening and we all loaded into the van, cold and hungry, we saw them toast with champagne glasses. They were laughing, an open bottle and a picnic spread out between their seats.

It's not lost on me that I spent my days doing one of the most privileged activities imaginable, one that someone—my grandparents, mostly—had paid exorbitant amounts of money for. It's also not lost on me why, when I taught my daughter to ski at that same ski area, I made absolute sure she had the warmest of socks, that her boots were never too tight, that her jacket was zipped all the way up and her mittens were fully dry. I bought a bag of hand warmers and kept them in the car. I also kept extra socks, extra mittens, extra scarves, extra food. All on the off chance that some child I knew would need something someday.

As an adult, I would see some of those skiers from childhood while at the mountain or around town. One—the best racer on the team, Maggie, who skied so fast and so smooth and won nearly every time—was now my neighbor and a school board member. I walked by her house on my way to the library. The mom of another came to the library to check out books. I'm still trying to work out if they actually looked at me and saw someone less, someone small and low inhabiting their world, or if that interpretation is just the remnants of that childhood feeling of hunger and cold, dirty clothes and no toothbrush in a sea of rich and coddled children.

My daughter would not have that feeling. I would not be late to pick her up. I would not send her out in winter without warm socks. I would not forget to pack her snack and lunch and water bottle. I would not ever let her feel so cold and alone as I had felt as a child. Not even once. This is what I knew from day one. What I didn't know was just how hard it would be to make it so.

....

n August, a few weeks before my daughter started second grade with her new name and pronoun, I had a meeting at her school to discuss her transition. Paul and I were still talking about a move to Montana, but our only immediate plan was to get through his surgery, which meant that Greta would be in school in Gilford for at least part of the year. She would be entering a large class with two primary teachers and one assistant, and though I was nervous about her peers' understanding, I was also hopeful about second grade.

"That's the best class," parents had said to me at the library over the summer. "You're going to love those teachers." Her first-grade teacher had said the same.

I went alone to the meeting, and on the walk there I remembered all those books that Susan had sent home, plus the words the principal had said: "Keep the information coming." I felt confident. Special education services had been complex, but supporting her gender in the classroom seemed relatively straightforward—all the research said essentially the same thing: use her name and pronoun, and make sure her classmates did, too. Define *transgender* so her peers understand she's not strange.

We sat in the same small, windowless white room where all our meetings were held. Only her teachers were there, and my job was simply to explain to them the miraculous shift in our daughter.

"She started reading independently when we finally let her be herself," I said, the pronoun still so unfamiliar in my mouth. "She used to be so angry. She's an entirely different person now. She's joyful," I told them. "I would have never used that word to describe her before."

"That's amazing," one teacher said, and they all nodded in agreement. One of them had tears in her eyes. "We have a lot to learn," that teacher said, "but we are so happy for her."

"Can she draw a new picture of herself with her new name?" the other teacher asked. It was an activity the children had done in their new classroom on step-up day at the end of first grade, and for a moment it felt like the most pressing piece we had ahead of us. But then the assistant teacher looked directly at me.

"There's no bathroom in the classroom," she said. "When I heard she'd be in our class, I even wondered if we should trade rooms with another teacher. But our class is so big. It wouldn't work elsewhere."

I told them what had happened at school summer camp. I said that in public, with her parents, she'd chosen the girls' room her entire life, and we'd let her.

"Well then, maybe she can just use the girls' bathroom," the assistant teacher said.

"Maybe," I said, though I—and, judging from the looks on their faces, the other teachers—felt unsure. Would the school even allow it?

A few days later, Greta and I took our dog out for a walk on the trails behind the school. As we crossed through the parking lot, I asked her what she would think if there was a special bathroom for transgender kids.

"You mean the nurse's office," she said. I could hear her anger.

"Yes," I admitted. "What would you say if you had to use that bathroom?"

"I'm not doing that," she said simply. "No way, no other girl has to do that."

She was right. What was wrong with me, that I had to bring this up again, after I'd stood there and held my hand between her head and a cement wall?

I said I was sorry, that I would figure it out. I said I would make sure she could use the bathroom. It was a promise, because there was no other option; I couldn't keep telling her to be confident in her girl-hood and then send her off each day to a place that told her she wasn't a real girl after all.

My husband and I had never heard of PFLAG—an organization of support and advocacy for LGBTQ+ people and their allies—but we joined when an acquaintance recommended it to us. The group was held at a church in Concord, in a wooded section of the city that I'd never seen before. A pride flag hung from the church sign, and it felt like an absolute beacon of light. Chairs were set up in a circle, and boxed cookies and cheap coffee and tea sat on a table at the back, next to heaps of booklets. *Our Trans Loved Ones. Straight for Equality: Guide to Being a Trans Ally. Cultivating Respect: Safe Schools for All.* Paul and I took every one of them, and then nervously sat down in metal fold-out chairs next to a mother roughly my age and her teenage daughter. We went around the room and introduced ourselves.

"Our daughter transitioned pretty much on her own," my husband said to the room of twenty or so strangers when it was his turn. "We wouldn't listen to her, so at the end of first grade she just started telling kids on the playground that she was a girl."

Someone let out a high, quick laugh. I looked up across the circle to see a woman clap her hands together. "Good for her!" she exclaimed. Soon I would get to know her, and come to admire her fierce advocacy so much. She was in her seventies, and she'd waited out her entire career to transition. "I couldn't start until marriage equality passed," she said when she introduced herself. "I knew I was a woman, but I also knew I didn't want to divorce my wife."

"We're here to learn to support our child," I said nervously to the group. "She's about to enter second grade, and the school has been good so far, but we're nervous."

"Do they have a transgender policy?" the facilitator asked.

"I don't think so," I said.

"It doesn't matter," the mother in the chair next to me said. "They might say it does, but don't listen to them. My daughter is trans and has autism," she said, and then she turned to her daughter. "Is it okay I said that? I mean obviously everyone knows, we've been coming here for years." Her daughter nodded and fidgeted with her bracelet. "Sometimes you have to print the law out and bring it to them. If they give you any shit, tell me, I can fill you in about the law."

"Wait," I said. She spoke so fast, so passionately. I'd already spent two years reading and highlighting law to advocate for my daughter, so I recognized myself in her. But I didn't totally follow. "What law?"

The woman across the room explained that just a few years before, in 2017, the U.S. Departments of Justice and Education had withdrawn the landmark guidance that gave transgender students protection under Title IX. But in New Hampshire we had state protections now; our governor had recently signed a bill that granted transgender people equal rights in public spaces, like bathrooms, along with a companion bill that applied to public schools.

"Is your daughter in public school?" the mother next to me asked. I nodded. "Then don't listen to them if they say she can't use the bathroom even if they don't have a policy. Sorry, but the governor signed the law and it goes into effect September 17."

We continued around the circle. There were people of all genders and sexualities, and many parents of LGBTQ+ youth. Everyone was so kind, so supportive. The meeting lasted two hours. When it wrapped up and we walked out into the evening light, I was suddenly hit with the first migraine I'd ever had. It sank down and built itself a heavy nest. I could not keep my eyes open. We'd left Greta with my mother, and when we stopped to pick her up I didn't even get out of the car. When we arrived home, I skipped dinner and instead went straight to our bedroom. I hung blankets on the windows to keep the light out and I lay there in darkness for hours.

"You okay?" Paul came to the doorway to ask periodically. I would just mumble a yes. I couldn't explain what I felt. Social interactions typically exhausted me, but not like this. This was so heavy and so bewildering. I'd left that group feeling relieved, grateful. I'd looked around and seen a future for my daughter, a path ahead and a community to guide me on it. I'd left feeling like I could see exactly where I stood: I was at the crest of a crystal-blue wave, about to dive down into an actual recognition of and belief in my child, my *daughter*. Yet years later, I can still conjure the heavy pain that coursed from my mind through my body like a toxin that evening. Now I sometimes think of it as some deep warning of what was to come.

28

As September approached, I had another meeting with the teachers. The plan was to talk about how to reintroduce Greta, how to make her peers understand her transition. According to the administration, the town had never had a transgender student in the elementary school before, so I'd agreed that the guidance counselor and principal ought to be at the meeting as well.

A new conference room had been built over the summer, which meant we didn't have to sit in that windowless white room that harbored some of my hardest memories. The principal led me to the new room, and I was surprised when I walked in to see that an administrator from the offices down the road already sat at the head of the table. She was the director of student services for the district, and when I'd questioned the law, my question had gone to her. When I'd reported the school to the state, I'd essentially reported her. Since Greta's kindergarten year, this woman had occupied so much of my mind—I'd imagined her sitting in her office with a pen in her hand, deciding whether to *approve* or *deny* my daughter's special education services. Did she think of the vast power her little signature held over my daughter's future?

I handed the teachers Greta's new drawing of herself, her new name written at the top. She had been practicing writing it for a few months now, nervous that she might mess up and misspell her own name. We chatted about summer, about how well Greta was doing, and then we talked about a packet the guidance counselor had brought: what to say when a child asks about our daughter's gender, how to explain why she changed her name and pronoun.

"Susan bought books for the resource room," I said. "There's a whole stack of them. *I Am Jazz* explains it perfectly. There are other ones, too. I think a picture book is all it would take."

"Great," one of the teachers said. "We'll go get the books and take a look at them." It seemed like the best plan possible.

But I also knew it wasn't the only reason we were there. I took a deep breath and looked straight to the administrator. I said, "My daughter wants to use the girls' bathroom. The last thing I want is to have my family at the center of a public debate. But on September 17, a new law will go into effect rendering the district's current policy of sending trans students to the nurse's office unlawful."

"It will be taken care of," she said abruptly.

"Thank you," I said, taken aback by how simple and swift the conversation was.

"We're here to support your family," she said, and with that she shut her folder. She stood up, said she had to get to another meeting, and then the other teachers and the guidance counselor got up, too. They all filed out, shutting the door behind them. But I didn't stand, and neither did the principal. She sat directly across from me. The packets of responses to kids' questions sat on the table between us. She picked them up, smoothed their pages. I remember looking past her, out the window to the summer day.

"We have to balance the opinions of all the parents," she said to me. She wasn't pleading, wasn't apologetic. She was simply informing me.

"Excuse me?" I asked her. This did not seem like the same person who had told me just weeks ago to keep the information coming. But then again, I had experienced this same odd feeling with her once before. It had been when I'd gone to her office to discuss my daughter's special education services and been told that there were lots of children in the school with lots of needs, some of whom even needed food. Was she shaming me? It was embarrassing to be told in this way to take up less space. But it was also wrong. I would push forward. *Suicide, nearly 50 percent, appropriate support*—these words were storm clouds constantly threatening the front of my mind.

"We have lots of parents out there," she said. "All of their opinions are important to us."

"But the research is really clear?" I said to her, aware I was placing a question mark where there should not have been one. Our appointment at Boston Children's still hadn't arrived yet—it would occur during my daughter's first week of school—and just then I wished desperately that it could have been a few weeks earlier. I wanted the doctors' reassurance as I sat there. I wanted that reassurance to occupy me, to back me up. But I had to do it on my own. I said, "Transgender children exist. My child exists. If a parent doesn't believe my daughter should be trans, I really don't see how that would have any impact on how the school supports her. We don't stop teaching science just because a parent doesn't believe in it, do we?"

She nodded. She told me she understood my concerns. It felt trite, felt like a phrase that could be used to soothe any parent in any situation. I kept pushing. "But you agree, right? You know that another parent's opinion should have no bearing on what my daughter needs?"

"The school will do our absolute best," she said.

"Well, I guess I just don't see why it matters if there are lots of parents out there," I repeated.

"We hear your concerns," she said.

I kept pressing, kept trying to get her to say something definitive about how the school would support my daughter. But she wouldn't. Eventually she stood and said she had to go.

Three days later, all parents and guardians in the district received an email, its subject *Superintendent communication.*

Dear Gilford and Gilmanton Parents and Guardians,

 On July 18, 2019, Governor Chris Sununu signed Senate Bill 263, relative to anti-discrimination protection for students in public schools, into law. In compliance with this new law, all men's & women's bathrooms & locker rooms at SAU 73 schools will be transgender & gender nonconforming-inclusive. Additionally, there are single-user restrooms in all of our schools that are available for use by all students, staff, and visitors.

The email went on to outline the location of each single-stall bathroom in the district. What a fool I was to believe that, in this way, it had been taken care of.

29

On the first day of second grade, I took a picture of Greta as she walked down the sidewalk, and then another as she stood on the steps beneath the old school bell, right where my father would have stood as a little boy. As she posed for her picture, I imagined my grandmother having my father do the same, and then telling him to be a good little boy and to listen well. Greta had her hair braided, and she wore her rainbow T-shirt and pink leggings, and her smile in that picture is so plain and calm, so trusting, and in such opposition to the frantic and forced smile of every other first-day picture. *Finally,* that smile says to me. *Finally I get to be myself.*

That first week, I annoyed her with my endless questions each day, but she never said much. I understood it as a shockingly good sign, and I sent a note to her teachers to thank them, saying things had gone *amazingly well.*

By that point, I'd told friends around town about Greta's transition; I'd written to one library coworker who was now retired, and I'd taken a hike with another. But even though we still worked side by side in the children's room, I'd managed to avoid telling Lisa. I knew her so well; I could read her face like a book. If she was uncomfortable or disapproving, I would know in an instant. It hadn't been easy to get to a place where we were at peace with each other, and I didn't have the energy to undo what we'd created.

But with school back in session, I knew I had no other choice, and one morning I finally got the courage to talk to Lisa. I told her everything I could think of to explain: Greta's early insistence that she was a girl; the visit to the psychologist; the remarkable change that had overcome her the moment we listened.

"Thank you for telling me," Lisa said when I was done. "And I love that you think this whole town isn't already talking about it."

I froze. If there was anyone in town who knew what people were talking about, it was Lisa. She seemed to connect with more people in a week than I had in my entire life.

"I went to dinner with two girlfriends last night and that's all they could talk about," she said. She wouldn't say names, she never did. But she did say one of the women was a doctor. "I was glad she was there to defend you to the other mother, let's just say that."

"What the hell," I said.

We were at the children's circulation desk, a massive heap of books to check in piled on the floor between us. She and I loved to read picture books, and we'd made a shared goal of reading every single one on the shelves. We kept a running list together—our top one hundred favorites. We didn't know any other adult who loved the form as much as we did.

"I don't get it," she said gently as she looked up from the books to me. "But, Abi, you know I love all children. You know I will always respect your child."

I nodded. I did know, but it wasn't enough. I wanted to say more, wanted to make her *get it,* but I didn't have the strength to do that without crying or getting angry. Instead, I just left her with the pile of books and retreated to the staff room upstairs. Soon, retreating like that would become the central part of my life at the library.

. . .

Greta had soccer practice in the evenings that season. She'd said she wanted to sign up weeks before, and I'd worried about it, thinking that when the time came she wouldn't actually want to go, and I'd been right. Each time, I bribed her with an ice cream sandwich to get her soccer socks and cleats on, though I probably should have just let her quit. She hated standing out there on the field, hated chasing a ball she had no interest in kicking, and I hated standing among what felt like the entire town, wondering about their judgments.

Lisa ended up being a volunteer coach for my daughter's team, which was half the reason I made Greta stick with it; she was a woman who believed in showing up when you said you would, and I wanted to show her that I was a person capable of that. Three evenings a week, I would take Greta to the field behind our house and hover alone near the sidelines, wondering who was looking at me, who was looking at my child, who was thinking what. Lisa would stand in the field and cheer her on, calling her name loudly, and I'd feel so thankful for this small piece of public support. But I wanted to just hide in the woods.

Once, a woman who helped run the soccer program came to me while I sat in the grass on the sidelines. I knew her vaguely through the library. "Can I sit with you?" she asked. "It's so great, how you're supporting her," she said, and she waved her hand toward Greta. "I know it's not easy. My older sister is trans," she said quietly. "She didn't transition until after high school. If people saw the way she suffered before, they wouldn't judge."

I thanked her for telling me, and then we just sat together watching the kids practice. After that, each night I had to be out in that field, I wished she would come stand with me and help me hold my ground again, but she never did.

Where was Paul? I know his hip was so bad by then, and his surgery only a few weeks away. I know his fear of the long path of recovery ahead—and the possibility that he would not recover—had overtaken him. I know that he spent day after day, hour after hour, dreaming of when we would be free to leave our town for Missoula. But none of that explains why he never came to the field with me. He could have. He got home from work around five, and practice was in the evenings, just behind our house. I try to remember him there with me and I just can't, not one single time. It occurs to me that this should have been a sign of how low he truly was.

One evening as I stood alone at a game, I saw Katie—the woman who loved to ski and who I'd wanted to befriend in my early days at the library—cheering from the far sideline. The weather had turned and she wore a thick Icelandic sweater. She waved across at me, so I slowly crossed the field to stand next to her.

"How's it going?" she asked gently, and she motioned toward Greta. She had a slight accent—she'd grown up in upstate New York, in the same area my mother was from, which I'd told her many times. Her oldest daughter—whom I'd met as a newborn that winter evening in the library—was on Greta's soccer team, and she was an excellent player, scoring goal after goal every game. She was also in the same class as my daughter this year.

"Okay," I began, so grateful that she'd had the courage to ask. "There's a lot of judgment," I added, "a lot of misunderstanding from people."

She let out a hum. "Mm-hmm." The tone felt off, maybe disbelieving. "We all have our struggles," she said, her voice suddenly high-pitched.

Do we really? I wanted to snap. Her words felt so pat. *Do you struggle with a near fifty percent suicide rate for your child?* I wanted to demand. *Does your daughter struggle with no one believing she's a girl?*

"Have a good night," I said instead, and then I walked slowly back to the other side of the field. I watched the game. At one point my daughter finally got close enough to the ball to touch it, but she fumbled and kicked it in the wrong direction.

"What the heck is wrong with you?" an athletic six-year-old yelled at her. I'd known him for years. He lived on one of the richest hills in town, right next to the house my father had grown up in. I stared at him until he caught my eye, and then I gave him the dirtiest look I could manage. What was happening to me?

The next morning, I dropped Greta at school, then walked home. As I walked, Katie drove by, just as she did every school day. But this time, she slowed her car to a near crawl, leaned over the passenger's seat, and waved boisterously. I felt like I was losing my mind. Had I misunderstood her tone the night before? I resolved to be positive. I waved back. Maybe I would make a new friend.

30

After months of waiting, our appointment at Boston Children's arrived. It was only a two-hour drive, but the appointment felt so momentous to us, felt like the first official step we would take in the life of our *daughter,* so Paul found a hotel for the night. It was newly built, not quite finished, and deeply discounted because of it. It astounded Greta—so many floors, so many windows. She kept asking how many thousands it cost to stay overnight. The three of us did all the things we could do there—we lay on the bed and scrolled through every television station; we filled the ice bucket at the machine in the hallway; we rode the elevator to every floor and taught Greta just the right moment to jump before it stopped. We spent hours swimming in the empty pool. In the evening we went to dinner, and we clinked our water glasses together to toast our daughter. Later, when we should have been asleep, we ordered room service ice cream and sat on the bed watching television, Greta totally entranced while Paul and I teetered on the edge of a precipice, unsure of what exactly we were going to fall into.

· · ·

"Look!" we said to Greta the next morning as we entered the building that housed the gender clinic. A rainbow flag, a trans flag. They were huge, held up by flagpoles that tilted toward the walkway, a safe little tunnel we had to pass through. I still hadn't called her pediatrician in our town, still didn't know how supportive she or her office would be. I wished so badly that there was even just one medical office in our entire county that hung these flags, that told me in this simple way that our daughter would be cared for.

The doctor was a young woman with large-framed glasses and a high bun, and her crisp appearance made me feel disheveled. But she was so kind. She sat us all down at a circular table and asked us to tell her about our child. Greta colored a picture of *Frozen*'s Elsa and built a LEGO house as Paul and I went on. We told Greta's whole story—her anguish at being forced to be a boy, her insistence on dresses, finally her decision to just go ahead and tell other children at school that she was a girl. The doctor nodded and jotted down notes, asked us some questions, and then she turned to Greta and asked her some, too.

"That's quite a LEGO house you built," she told Greta, then gave her a worksheet to fill out. Greta took her time. I looked at the sheet out of the corner of my eye. It asked what she wanted to be when she grew up. I'd always figured she'd say a scientist or a video game developer. But here she'd written her answer: *A woman.*

I'd been listening to one specific song lately, sung by a woman who hadn't transitioned until adulthood. *One day I'll grow up, I'll be a beautiful woman,* she sang in a high, shaky, yearning voice that called to mind my grandmother's when she'd sat at her piano to play a hymn. *But for today I am a child, for today I am a boy.*

Greta finished the worksheet and slid it across to the doctor, then returned to her LEGOs. I gave her a little squeeze on the shoulder. My heart didn't exactly pound but reach; it was like I could feel my infinite love grow futilely outward.

. . .

The doctor told us the two populations she saw most frequently in the gender clinic were those on the spectrum and one out of a set of twins. She said there were theories to the co-occurrence, but nothing definitive. Eventually, she looked over all the information she'd gathered, and she pointed out how long, how consistently, and how insistently Greta herself had been telling us she was transgender. She said we needed to listen. It wasn't new information, but it did feel like clarity.

"For the next five or six years," she said, "you'll come here once or twice a year to see me and just check in and see how she's doing." And then, she said, Greta would begin to see an endocrinologist and we'd all start discussing our options.

"What sorts of options?" I asked. I already knew—I'd done my reading—but I wanted to hear it.

"Puberty blockers," she said. "If she chooses that, it will buy her time. Then, eventually, hormones."

I tensed at the thought. Back then, I wanted desperately for my daughter to stay like this, six years old and far from puberty, forever. Medical care terrified me. My mother had raised me to think carefully before even taking a Tylenol. And even without that background, it was so much to wrap our heads around. Sometimes I would try to talk to my husband about it. "I can't go there," he'd say. "Just stop. I can't even think about it."

"In a perfect world," I asked the doctor, "would people do this?" I was aware now—as I had not been before—that she, anyone I talked to, could be transgender; I was aware that my question might not just be generally offensive, but personally so, too. Still, I pressed. I was all thought, all the time. Save for the pain in my shoulders, I could scarcely even feel my body. Nothing I'd known made sense to me anymore; I'd spent years reading and writing and thinking and talking about feminism, and I'd come to the firm belief that, sexual organs and chromosomes aside, whatever difference existed between men and women was entirely cultural, entirely created. But here was my daughter, the fact of her, telling me otherwise, telling me there was something deep and vital inside her which made her know she was female. "In a perfect world, would my child still need to make her body female if society would just catch up and accept her any way she looked?"

"Yes," the doctor said, so plainly. I had the feeling she'd had to answer this impossible and useless question before. But yes—if in a perfect world people are just as varied and diverse as they are in the real world, then there would still be transgender people, and some of them would go down one path and others would go down another. Of course they would.

"We've been doing this work for over a decade," she said. She said the data told them without question that when transgender youth are offered the care they need to eventually grow into the bodies that align with their genders, their rates of anxiety, depression, and suicide plummet. "And," she added, "what the data also tells us is that if they don't have the care they need, suicide spikes at puberty, when their bodies begin to betray them."

Did Paul and I look at each other when she said this? Did we hold hands, or find each other's feet under the table? Our daughter still worked on her LEGOs. The doctor spun around in her chair, faced her computer and scrolled for a moment, then spun back.

"One of our endocrinologists is hosting an information session for families in a few weeks." She wrote the date and time down on a slip of paper and slid it across the table to us. "That might be a good chance to get all your medical questions answered. But there's lots of time. She has years before puberty."

"Can she have a happy life?" I remember asking pathetically.

"Just keep doing what you're doing," she said. "Use her name and pronoun. Make sure her school and community do the same. When these kids are supported in their genders, their mental health outcomes are no different than their peers'. How's her school doing with the transition? Is she able to use the bathrooms?"

"She is," I said. "I think the school has been really supportive so far."

"That's great," she said. "That's so important." She looked at our daughter, then back to us. She had a way of adjusting her glasses that felt like a signal—like straightening a back or taking a deep breath—before an important sentence. "If all the other pieces are in place, I think the real question here is if she has the autism support she needs. That's what's going to help her interact, help her learn to read people."

I know Paul and I caught each other's eye then. I know that with those words—*learn to read people*—both of our minds darted together to the exact same terror. *Transgender* had really only entered our consciousness some six months earlier, but we had already become aware of a growing epidemic—so many trans people murdered by men. That afternoon, it was early September 2019. By the end of that year, at least twenty-seven transgender people would be murdered in the United States, most of them Black women. The following year, that number would be surpassed by August, reaching forty-four before year's end; and the year our daughter turned nine, the number would rise again, to fifty-seven. Was this risk—to be subjected to an actual hate crime—what the doctor was referring to when she said our daughter needed to learn to read people? "Let's just pray she's gay," Paul and I had said to each other. "Let's just pray she stays far away from men."

"With appropriate support," the doctor said, "the research tells us that your daughter will have an equal shot at a happy life."

When we left the office, we headed to the cafeteria for lunch, because my husband—who had attended culinary school for French cuisine—loved to eat hospital food. Greta was happy, skipping ahead. I was anxious and in a daze. How was Paul? In another two weeks, we would return to Boston for his surgery. That day, we went down a twisting staircase, almost spiral—why didn't we find the elevator instead?—and Paul had to grip the banister and step slowly, unevenly. At some point on our way to the cafeteria he spotted a painting of wildlife, and he called to Greta to come take a good look at it with him. But I just kept going. *Everything's okay,* I kept repeating to myself. *She has a bright future ahead.* But I didn't feel okay, not yet. I felt I just needed to get my food and sit down and take a breath, no task left ahead of me, and only then would my mind stop boiling.

Now I wish I had just stood with my husband and daughter to look at whatever it was they were looking at—bear or deer or something, painted in the woods, I think. My husband would have been making voices, saying something like, *Anybody seen the blueberry patch around?* in a slow bear drawl. I wish I had found it within myself to just be with them, aware in that moment, because that walk from the office to the hospital cafeteria would turn out to be the last cloudless one we would have for so, so long.

We got our trays and wandered through the meal court. I couldn't find anything I wanted to eat, and I was overcome with an unexplainable hopelessness, nearly crying in the lunch line. Somehow I ended up with the shrimp meal, even though at that point I ate a vegan diet.

"Why are you getting that?" Paul asked me.

"It's fine," I said. "Whatever. I'll just eat the vegetables and rice."

He asked me if I was sure and I told him to just go help Greta. I remember doctors and nurses around me, making their choices so efficiently. I remember feeling like I was blocking up the area, like I was in the way, like there was so much going on around me that I couldn't take anything in. Finally, we paid and found a table in the sun. I sat down and turned my phone on. Immediately it started dinging—a stream of text messages from Robin. Her first message: *The haters have come out.*

The rest of her messages were links to videos; the night before, while my family swam happily in the hotel pool and ate ice cream in the bed, people from our town had attended the monthly school board meeting to speak out against the new practice of allowing transgender students—and specifically our daughter—to access the bathrooms and locker rooms.

The videos had been recorded and posted to YouTube by a right-wing blogger in our town who documented all town meetings. I borrowed Greta's headphones and clicked on the first.

"I am here representing dozens of people that I've talked to," a man said as he stood at the podium facing the school board members and administrators.

I knew who he was. Keith. In June, he had brought his son—a classmate of Greta's—to Eric and Robin's daughter's birthday party, held at a local rec center. Paul had stood on the basketball court talking to the man for two hours.

"Keith seems really nice," my husband had told me on the way out of the party. "Maybe we could hang out."

Now I watched that same man motioning toward the windows in the video. "They couldn't be here—a lot of them are on that soccer field right now, they wish they could have been here." He referenced the email the superintendent had sent. He said that because of the timing—Labor Day weekend—many people hadn't even noticed it. "Their kids went to school today with this policy in place and they didn't even know, and they were floored." He went on: "We're talking about the most precious years of our children's psychological development. We teach our children to respect their bodies, their private bodies, and now they are going to be subjected to having to be in a bathroom and a locker room undressing with boys." He said he knew that wasn't politically correct to say. But, he said, "the biology."

I fast-forwarded the video, stopped. Keith was still talking. "Is my child going to be corrected by a teacher if they use the wrong pronoun?" He paused for a response but did not get one. "Because that is going to infringe upon their First Amendment right," Keith said.

I remember seeing that disgusting shrimp in its disgusting sauce and pushing my plate away. I remember my husband asking what was wrong.

"A little more background before we get into the next speaker," said the chair of the school board. "I touched on the fact that a student in the school who has regularly and consistently been identifying as the opposite birth sex—um, gender—that student's previous practice had been to use the single-occupancy bathroom." That student—my daughter—was happily munching away on a chocolate chip cookie and a bag of potato chips, methodically alternating between a bite of one and a bite of the other. Paul was making her laugh. The school board chair told the room that, "pursuant to the passage of the bathroom bill in the state of New Hampshire," the parents of this child in question had reached out to the school and the school had needed to respond. I scanned through the school board members, then focused on our neighbor, Maggie, who I'd been on the ski team with. I knew her to be kind and levelheaded. She'd once invited our family down to dinner at her house, but we hadn't been able to go because we were headed out on the lake for the weekend. I knew her sons. Every year, they came to the door to sell popcorn for their Boy Scout troop. At the playground, her younger son had always been exceedingly kind to my child. What did she think as she listened to the chair of the board say they just had no choice, that to comply with the law they had to allow transgender students to use the bathrooms? Did it occur to her that he should have framed it differently, and perhaps been positive about inclusive schools? Did it occur to her that he should have kept my family out of it?

Another man I recognized went to the podium. He owned a woodstove shop just down the hill from my mother's house, out on the main road. When I was young, the building had housed a movie rental store. My brother and I would walk there almost every day. That man asked the board what made this one family's opinion—my family's—more valuable than those of all the rest of the families in town. "I have three females," he said. "This is discrimination for them." He said the girls' bathroom was going to become a "dead zone" because none of the girls would set foot in there if a trans child—my child—was allowed to go in.

Fast-forward.

Another man I recognized. His wife was one of the children's room regulars. I was probably still eating the honey I'd bought from their children. He'd brought plans with him—bathroom redesign, all-gender bathrooms that would be private for all. I wanted to know his motivation. Was he saying that he wanted the district to spend untold amounts of tax dollars on single-stall bathrooms so we could finally put this argument to rest? Or was he saying he wanted these bathrooms because transgender girls posed a threat to his girls? I didn't have it in me to find out. I liked his family. I wanted to keep liking them. I closed the video.

"Those fuckers," I said quietly to Paul.

"What?"

I held my phone out for him to see what Robin had sent. He took it, started scrolling through. Clicked on a video. It occurred to me how dark a place he could go. I told him not to look. To give the phone back. Greta was still munching. She asked for a soda and we said no. Paul said he wanted to watch. I again told him no. I grabbed the phone. He asked me if I was going to eat and I said I was not. He and Greta began to eat my food. I sat there watching them, telling myself to not look at any more videos. Telling myself it didn't matter, wouldn't amount to anything. And then I clicked on another video.

At the podium, a man introduced himself as Keith's father. "I'm concerned about the psychological effects on the children," he said. "Is that something that the board is going to look into? You may be having counseling forever, with dozens and dozens of children, because of this." He said he wouldn't allow his grandchildren into a bathroom with men and women in it. "I don't think that's right, I don't think it's natural, and if you look at nature, the issue that is before us is very contra to nature, and please don't label me as a bigot," he said. "I don't know who this individual was . . . but I would love to scoop them up and bring them into a loving place." He said he wanted to teach this child—my child—about a man and a woman. He said my child was being brainwashed.

I fast-forwarded. I was going to turn it off. I remember thinking that: *I'm going to turn this off.*

And then a woman's voice. She was speaking as she approached the podium; I couldn't see her at first. "I have children to tuck in," she said. She entered the screen. Katie. At the podium, she read a concise statement: "Since Senate Bill 263 does not become effective until 9/17, I respectfully ask the board to motion to defer implementation of SB 263 to rethink interpretation as applicable to at least the elementary school. That's all I have to say. Please consider a motion."

She was the last speaker of the first public comment session. The school board chair told the crowd they would now move on to the next portion of the meeting, reminding them that there would be another chance to speak at the end.

The bigots know to wait, Robin had texted me, and then sent more clips. I knew from her texts that this second public comment session had taken place some two hours later. I could see in the video that most of the meeting had cleared out and that darkness had fallen outside. I opened the first video to see Keith speaking again. I fast-forwarded. Another man saying more of what he'd already said. Another. And then Katie, who must have decided not to go tuck her children in after all.

"I respectfully implore you to consider a motion right now before I walk away to defer implementation of the Senate bill and to rethink your interpretation as applicable to all the schools, but primarily the elementary school." She waited a beat. "So please consider a motion. Will you? Tonight?"

She stood at the podium. Silence, and then the chair of the board told her that he wasn't hearing a motion. He apologized. "Thank you for your comments. Thank you for staying."

"Mm-hmm," she said. That same noise again. "It's important to us."
That exact same tone she'd used with me on the soccer field just a few
evenings before.

"It's important to us, too," he said, rubbing his forehead. "Believe
me. We don't take it lightly."

I remember telling Paul I had to get out of there.

I remember saying I thought I would be sick.

I remember Greta, so happy in that cafeteria.

And then I remember pushing through the food court, searching for the exit, dimly aware that Paul was trailing behind me, angry,
wanting me to slow down, to help manage Greta and our things. And
I remember that I just could not.

We didn't go straight home. Instead, I insisted that we go to an outdoor sculpture museum that I'd always wanted to visit because somehow I had the determination to salvage the day. Paul pushed through
the pain of his hip. We walked the grounds, under and through giant
abstract sculptures that pulled my mind outward and saved me on
that day. I bought Greta a lemon ice cream frozen in a lemon peel and
bought myself a coconut sorbet frozen inside a coconut shell. We ate
them in the open courtyard. After, I took a picture of her beneath the
sprawling vine-like limbs of a tree that seemed to be but perhaps could
not have been a banyan. I sent the picture to Ingrid.

"She looks so different, so happy," Ingrid responded, because it was
true.

31

After Noah dropped out of high school and prepared to move west, he bought himself a plane ticket, plus a cell phone in the days when they were rare. According to the story my family tells, he took that phone out of his pocket the moment the plane landed and called the upscale store in Scottsdale where he was determined to be employed, and he announced that he had landed in Phoenix and would be arriving shortly for his interview. It worked. He is smart and determined and resourceful, he's funny, and he's excellent at telling people precisely what they want to hear. In this way he very quickly rose to the top of his company and made himself a name in the world of luxury clothing.

I was in college in Wisconsin, and then in Idaho with my brother Henry, and then briefly in Oregon, and then finally in Montana with my husband during the first handful of years that Noah was in Arizona. We talked some, but not often, and there were entire years when neither of us went home to New Hampshire to visit. Soon after he moved west, though, my little sister Margot—technically half sister to me, but full sibling to Noah—finished high school early and moved to Arizona to be with him. They were less than a year apart in age. She and I had always remained close, so her proximity to Noah meant that I—and the rest of the family—had more information about him.

After he left home, I don't remember a time when Noah wasn't an addict. I don't remember finding out, I don't remember any shock of information about it. It all just seemed to trickle in naturally, like a streambed that had dried in summer but would refill again once the rains hit. First he was home for a goodbye party, sixteen years old and not addicted to anything, so far as I know, other than cigarettes. He sat in the low couch, looking so confident and aloof during this odd ordeal held at a wealthy family friend's house in Gilford. The house had a pool in the backyard and a Jacuzzi inside, by the bar, beneath a photo of its owner posing with George H. W. Bush. It overlooked the lake and mountains, and in a handful of years my family would all gather there again the night before my grandfather's funeral. Noah would be there, his first trip home since he'd left. Clad in tight pleather pants, he would announce drunkenly that his underwear was also pleather. My brother Henry, also drunk, would insist to see, and Noah would run away from him, laughing, out into the cool October night. I would follow, and I'd discover my little brother beneath the trees, suddenly distant and panicking, and seemingly on more than alcohol. He had to get out of there, he said, out of that house, that town, that entire state. It would be more than ten years before I understood his sentiment.

Once he left, Noah entered a world so far from our family's sensibilities that every story I heard about him would be surrounded in a cloud of myth, until it didn't exactly feel that my brother—a living, breathing, pained human—sat at their center. Instead, this character—*look at what he does, it's so unbelievable.*

Unbelievable, for example, when we all traveled to Las Vegas to watch my sister Courtney get married. I was twenty-two years old, fresh out of college. It would be the first time all eight of us siblings were together in nearly a decade—and so far, it has been the last. Noah would fly in from Arizona with his half brother—my stepbrother—

and there would be some ordeal in the airport, something about Noah using a fake ID and getting drunk and missing his flight. We would all laugh. Later, he would sneak into the hotel bar multiple times, until finally the bouncer took his name down.

"Fine," my little brother would eventually say, and instead he would take himself to the oxygen shot bar, and then to the spa to get his eyebrows done, and he'd charge it all to our father's room, so the story of his constant drinking at seventeen became the story of him beautifying himself with our father's money and then flying back to Arizona before our father ever even knew.

More stories would arrive—Noah on pills, Noah among the top ten salespeople in the country, Noah getting a DUI. Every now and then a big story would stand out, and these have become stars in the constellation of my history. I know every house I lived in when the phone calls came in, I know where I stood while I talked, I remember the lighting. The first came less than a year after Courtney's wedding. I had moved from Oregon to Montana and met my husband, and now we lived in that cabin thirty minutes outside Missoula. It was on a hillside in a valley surrounded by mountains. A creek ran below, and in the evenings we'd watch deer and elk and moose and a few times even a bear walk down to get a drink of water. We had a woodstove and a loft, and we'd stay up late into the night listening to music, cooking crepes, dreaming of all the adventures we would take together. It was our perfect place to fall in love.

I was in the driveway, headed to the car, when my father called. My husband and I planned to go into Missoula to have dinner and see a movie, and then grocery shop. I was wearing the Carhartt overalls I lived in in those days. In my bag was a turquoise blue knife embossed with a butterfly from my older brother Will. A few years earlier, he'd given one to each of us siblings—even Noah—for Christmas, and told us to always carry them. I don't know why we listened. Maybe because it seemed so thoughtful and out of character for Will to celebrate in this way. He is a gentle, bighearted man whose good intentions often get buried beneath his difficulties to communicate; and he'd been going through a rough patch the year he gave us those knives, and he'd been trying to get back on his feet. I remember that the gift had seemed so important to him, so heartfelt.

"Noah's okay," my father began, "but he was kidnapped." He went on to explain that my little brother and his roommate had been kidnapped by a gang while walking home from a bar. They'd been thrown into an SUV, their bank cards had been taken, and then they'd been driven around the city to withdraw money at every ATM. After, they'd been taken out of the city into the desert, where they'd been tied to a fence. I would talk to Noah about it years later. He would tell me that after tying him up, one of the men held a gun to his head.

"I don't know why he didn't kill me," I can still hear Noah say. "I don't know why he didn't blow my fucking head off."

But Noah had that knife. Somehow, in the back of the SUV, he'd maneuvered it from his pocket to the inside of his shoe. Hours later, tied up in the barren darkness, he would reach that knife and cut himself and his roommate free and walk to the side of the highway and wait for someone to pick them up.

I don't know if that event was a hate crime, though it will always be impossible for me to think of it as anything else. And I suppose the truth is also that I don't know exactly what led to my brother's drinking, to the pills, to all of it. But once—one single time—I gave him a book for his birthday, a compilation of stories written by and about gay men. His face reddened and tears appeared in his eyes—something I had not seen since his young boyhood. By that point my father had moved from downtown Laconia to a farmhouse owned by his cousin that had been built in 1775, and the stairway had a latch door at the bottom and top. Noah took the book and went up the stairs, closing both doors behind him. Later, weeks later, and then again years later, he thanked me for that book.

. . .

On the September evening that we drove home from our daughter's first appointment at the gender clinic, the information the doctor had given us and the videos I'd just watched of the school board meeting spiraled around and hooked themselves into memories of my little brother. I thought of his path—bullied, dropped out, addicted, victimized. I thought of that one small gesture—only one—I had made to really support him, of how much it had meant to him, and I wondered if it stood alone. I thought of how my brother has survived, against all odds. I thought of the fact that my daughter would, too.

But I would change the odds for her. I had to.

32

....

Our house in Gilford Village was small and brown, with a pitiful front yard that I'd tried various times over the years to turn into a vegetable garden, but by the end was just alternately dead or overgrown grass. There were flowers at the house's edge, though—peonies and lilies that my grandmother, an expert gardener, had planted. I'd added the daffodils a friend from the library had given me, and one year I threw red poppy seeds into the yard and ended up with an extraordinary bloom. But otherwise everything I'd tried to grow had failed, and the yard had been a mess since the day after we'd signed the paperwork to purchase the house. That day, I'd walked home from work at the library to discover Paul sitting in the front yard, digging up the grass with his hands. He had been at it for hours, and now our lawn was a pit of dirt.

"What are you doing?" I'd asked, incredulous. He told me he wasn't sure—he wanted a garden there instead, or maybe some native grasses. His only clear aim at that point was to dig up the lawn. "All summer all I hear is lawn mowers," he said. It was true. "Ahh," he would say on summer weekends, "the sound of Gilford." I basically agreed with him; I understood the environmental cost of cut green grass, and I felt out of place surrounded by such pristine lawns. But there we were. Afternoons, I'd cross the road and hike up a trail, and I'd pass by a neighbor deep in the woods and feel as though I were living inside a bucolic scene of a nineteenth-century novel. On weekends, we'd go out in our canoe and pass by friends on the lake and time would meld; I would see my father, a teenager, sneaking out at night to steal his father's boat and go for a ride, and I would imagine my child years in the future doing the same—taking her grandfather's boat from the very same boathouse and going out on the lake to watch the stars. Around town—at the grocery store, the transfer station, the docks—I knew so many people, and they knew me, knew where I had come from. In the quiet of morning, as the mist lifted from the mountains, I would unlock the library and turn the lights on and once again feel myself living inside a book. At night, when I switched the lights off and locked the library up and stepped out into the burst of fresh air as the moon rose behind the mountains, my bags heavy with all the books I'd checked out, I would imagine myself performing the same task as an old woman.

Yet once I saw those school board videos, every time I stood in the driveway and looked at my house, I thought of that very first action my husband had taken when we'd bought our first home—not to improve it, not to beautify it, but to revolt against it. It occurred to me that we should have always known we were doomed there.

wrote to the principal and teachers after Greta's appointment in Boston. I said we didn't exactly have new information, just reassurance. I said the doctor had emphasized the importance of an inclusive school on the mental health of these kids. And then I told them what I'd seen in the videos: several parents, some of whom had children in Greta's class, vocally opposing the rights of transgender students. I said I worried that bullying would increase.

I was right. Within days of sending Greta back into school, phone calls from the principal began. The first time, she said she needed me to come into the school because there had been an "incident." My daughter had spilled her milk at lunch and screamed "bloody murder" about it, and when everyone looked at her, she stood up, threw her lunch tray at a teacher, and tried to flip the table over. When they got her into the hallway, she ripped artwork down on the walk to the principal's office. Now she was sitting with the guidance counselor. I sat in that windowless conference room with the principal and her teachers.

"I'm sad that happened," I said. It was true—I was so sad. But I was also not really surprised. All along, I'd known that Greta walked a tightrope at school; I'd known that at home she generally had the tools to calm herself, to communicate, to take a break; but at school, once her stress increased, she would have no choice but to fall completely apart. "This is exactly why I have been advocating for appropriate support since kindergarten," I told them plainly. I got her from the guidance counselor's office and we left. As we walked, she kept looking up at me, then down to the ground, grunting, kicking at rocks, and every now and then calling herself stupid. But I would not be disappointed in her. Also, I would not press her. I would wait for her to come to me.

"I'm not going to school," she said in the morning. "I'm never going again."

"Oh, Greta," I said. "Why?"

"They say I'm not allowed to be a girl."

"Who says this? When?"

"At recess," she said.

"Who?"

"Everyone," she said, and turned away from me. "I don't know who. Just everyone, okay?"

Within a few days, I got another call: a substitute teacher had used Greta's former name because it still appeared on the roll call despite what the school had promised. Classmates laughed. Greta flipped her table over.

Another call: a classmate had used the wrong pronoun. I'd heard about her—she repeatedly did this. Greta said it was on purpose and I believed her. Instead of ignoring it yet again, my daughter threw her lunch bag at the girl. She was sent to the principal's office. It was snack time, so maybe ten o'clock in the morning. Greta sat there the entire day. There was an all-school assembly that afternoon, and still my daughter was forced to sit in the principal's office.

At home, sometimes, Greta would open up. "A girl in gym called me my old name and said I'm not allowed to change my name," she'd say, crying. "People in the hallway point and say I'm a boy." I'd contact the teachers; most of the time, they already knew.

Mornings, I bribed her with M&M's to leave the house, to cross the road, to walk down the street. But once we were there, she would refuse to enter the building for ten minutes, twenty, sometimes even an hour. Once, I brought her in late and she rudely grabbed her late slip from the secretary and mumbled something under her breath.

"What did he just say to me?" the secretary asked.

I called the teachers. I went to the principal. To the guidance counselor. I sent email after email. *We promised her she wouldn't have to do this alone,* I said. *I promised her the teachers would help.*

It was only September. In one week, my brother Henry would come down from Maine to drive Paul and me to Boston for Paul's surgery, because I suddenly felt I could not handle it alone. I could not sit in the hospital for six hours while my husband, the one other human on the entire planet who understood how to care for our daughter, was utterly unreachable. My mother would come stay with Greta, would take her to and from school. "If she refuses to go," I remember telling my mother, "then forget it. Just have a good day with her."

We had a wheelchair in the living room, ready for Paul's return, which wouldn't occur until a week after the surgery. We had a new couch, one that he could sleep on, a huge new pillow, and a TV tray. We'd bought a Nintendo Switch so he'd have something to do in his recovery. We also had a ziplock bag of buttons: PROTECT TRANS KIDS written in a half circle across the top edge, and GILFORD across the bottom. My mother and her friend had made fifty of them in advance of the upcoming school board meeting. It would take place a few days after Paul was scheduled to return home from the hospital, on the first Monday of October, and this time the discussion of transgender students' rights would be on the agenda; the school board and administration had decided to draft an official policy to outline bathroom and locker room access, sports inclusion, name and pronoun usage, and student privacy.

At my mother's urging, I'd left a message for the trans justice advocate at the state's ACLU office to learn more about school policies and how to get them passed. She called me back one afternoon just before Paul's surgery. I took the phone to the cold basement, out of earshot of my family, and I looked out the window, straight into the immaculate yard of a couple who had been childhood ski coaches of mine. My entire body hummed with tension.

"I'm Kasha," she said, "my pronouns are she/her." She asked me to tell her about my daughter. "I'm amazed by her clarity," she said.

"So am I," I told her, so grateful to speak with someone who understood.

Kasha explained that a school policy was necessary to clarify the law by explicitly outlining student rights. Also, a policy would protect students immediately; without it, a school was held to the law only by the threat of legal battle, which was long and expensive and would not help a child on the day they needed help. She said she'd worked on many policies throughout the state, and that she was there to assist in mobilizing people.

"Get as many people as you can to come out to the meeting," she said. "Get people talking about it, educating themselves."

I told her that I would, that I already was. That I'd sent a long email asking for support to everyone I knew; that a friend had helped me start a campaign to send postcards to the school board members; that we'd made and distributed some fifty buttons, though only Robin wore hers proudly, everywhere.

"Do you plan to speak at the meeting?" Kasha asked.

"I'm not sure," I said, though I knew it wasn't true. I would speak; I had to. But also, I was so scared. I didn't know how far these people against Greta's rights would go. "We live in such a public spot," I said. "Right in the center of town." Would they throw rocks at our windows? Would they spray-paint slurs on our house? "I need to think about our safety," I said, as if people didn't already know exactly who we were, who my child was.

Late that night, sleepless, I got lost in my phone, sick with anxiety about the upcoming meeting. I wanted to know what people were saying, if anything. I typed *Gilford* and *transgender policy* into the search bar. Immediately I found an old newspaper article from before my daughter had even entered kindergarten. In it, I discovered that a few years earlier the district had drafted and passed a transgender and gender-nonconforming student policy almost identical to the one that was now being introduced, but they'd reversed their decision almost immediately because of the town's backlash.

Some of the same parents I'd just watched in the videos were quoted in the old article, including one quote from the man who'd come with plans for single-stall bathrooms—the one whose speech I'd skipped because I'd wanted so badly to keep liking his family, the one whose children kept bees, whose honey I still had in my cupboard. "You absolutely cannot jeopardize the safety of our students," the article quoted him as saying. "How can you do this to my children? I will take on a third job to give them an opportunity to be safe."

At work the next day, I told Lisa about what I'd read. "He's going to these meetings acting like he wants single-stall bathrooms because everyone prefers them," I said, "but he's conveniently leaving out the part where he thinks his daughters are in danger if trans girls are around."

"You have to understand that this is hard for people," Lisa told me. We were in the children's room. The story time crowd had just cleared out, and the room had fallen into its lunchtime lull before the afterschool crowd arrived.

"Yeah," I said dismissively. I remember turning away from her, looking at my computer screen. "Because they're fucking idiots and they're horrible people."

"No," she said calmly. "Abi, it's hard for me. I'm sorry, I just can't wrap my head around it."

I said nothing back. I just got up and went into the workroom behind our desks and shut the door. It was overflowing with crafting supplies in there, and over the years Lisa and I had bickered about the mess, but we were past that by now. I faced the wall, my body sick with tension, tears finally pouring out. I wanted to hit something, to break something. When I heard Lisa cautiously open the door and say my name, I whipped around and snapped at her.

"Why don't you just try," I said. "You know how to read. Read one fucking book, Lisa, one fucking article, and you'll see that my daughter's life depends on people putting even an ounce of effort into understanding."

"Abi," she said, trying to calm me down.

"I'm not fucking kidding you, Lisa. Do you know the suicide statistics for my kid? Nearly fifty percent if people don't do the basic minimum and let her be a girl." My nose was running, my face was wet. My body was shaking. "It's not that hard," I told her. "Can you imagine what it's like for my kid? To know so deeply she's a girl and to go into school and get bullied day after day in this fucking town and still just keep showing up? What do you think it's going to feel like when the adults decide she can't use the goddamned bathroom after all? When they cast their votes to say she's not a real girl?"

"I didn't know," she said quietly. "Abi," she said. "I can learn." It was such a simple response, given so quickly, but I believed her. She was a person who was always willing to open her mind, to learn. Yet when she went on to say that others could learn, too, I just shrugged, wiped my tears, and shook my head no.

"People can learn," she repeated. "They just have no reference point." I'd heard her say this before. She was a brown woman in a white town, and it was what she'd said to me about the patrons who made casual comments about her skin. "We could have a program," she said. "Host a discussion or something." She was always full of big ideas, and always so full of faith in people.

"You go right ahead," I told her miserably. "But I've got a kid who's being bullied, autism services to fight for, a school board meeting to prepare for, and in a few weeks my husband will become immobile for three months, during which time he also won't get a paycheck because somehow he forgot to sign up for paid family medical leave. But if you want to take on educating this town, be my guest."

She asked if she could give me a hug. She told me to go to lunch, to go take the afternoon off if I wanted. "Except," she said, smiling, "it sounds like you might need the paycheck."

34

Paul and I used to put our tent and sleeping bags and camp stove in the back of the car and go all over the Rocky Mountain west, sometimes backpacking and sometimes just pulling over on public land and camping there. He loved studying maps and choosing spots for us—never the highest peak, never the strongest river; instead some sparsely traveled spot he knew would be beautiful and overlooked. In our first month together, he took me on a five-day backpacking trip in a wilderness area in southwestern Montana that straddled the Great Divide. We camped in high meadows, and he fed us rich chocolate and cheeses I had never heard of. We floated naked in cold creeks, brewed cowboy coffee as the sun came up, watched moose drink from the mountain lake. After that trip we kept going—we hiked to backcountry hot springs, and at night we huddled together in our tent in the snow. Once, he took us to an old forest fire burn because that's where the morels were. I hated the hike, hated that the trees were gone and we were walking in the hot, dry, miserable sun, every direction apocalyptic. I trailed far behind him and I cursed him as I walked— for walking so far ahead of me, for gathering his wild mushrooms without even noticing my suffering, for bringing us here and being so damn clueless and happy about it. At the end of the day, I was dehydrated and seething with fury. We got back into our car and began the long logging road drive out, and suddenly wildlife just started appearing. First elk, lumbering down off the hillside and across the road. We slowed down and watched, then drove onward. Moose. We stopped and let them pass. Deer. Soon a black bear.

It was our first season together, my first season in Montana. Just before that, I'd lived with my brother Henry in Idaho, but then I'd met a man from the mountains of eastern Oregon and fallen in love with him in a dangerous way, my heart just wide open. In Idaho, I worked at a Barnes & Noble for $6.25 an hour; it was no reason to stay. I went to try love instead, and writing in that man's small mountain town. I lasted half a year, my heart stomped on every month like clockwork. In March a college friend came to drag me out of there and take me with her to Montana, where I could get a job on a trail crew. As I drove the high winding passes out of Oregon, her car in front of mine, I wondered what it would be like to just not turn the corner, to just drive off the cliff instead. I had never been so broken.

Exactly one year to the month earlier, in March of my final year of college, I'd spent a night drinking whiskey. Before that, I'd only ever drunk one time, when I was fourteen. I'd vomited everywhere, and I'd never really had interest again. But that night in college I won a writing award, and I felt good, and I drank whiskey and I smoked pot, and then I went to the dorm room of a completely sober friend. We kissed, and after that my memory is distorted—in parts it's blackout, but in the other parts I've flown up to the ceiling to watch from above while he has sex with my body.

It would take me nearly two decades to understand that night, to understand the word *rape* and all the ways it would lay waste to the years ahead.

But my husband, he got me back out into the world, into the wilderness. We walked and walked and walked, and something clicked in me. This was why I was alive. This miraculous natural world and its inexplicable waves, like the one that had kept my husband and me circling each other for years before we met. It rebuilt me, and it held me up.

In our first year together, the car I'd arrived west with broke down and the replacement we could afford was a 1980 Subaru that had some ignition trouble—there was a key by the steering wheel, but then there was also a key by the gearshift, and to start the car both keys had to be turned into position and we needed either to be parked on an incline or have someone push. A few months after we'd bought the car, a truck with a cattle guard rear-ended us on our drive into Missoula and the hatch door was destroyed. After that, we just duct-taped plastic wrap to the back of the car and kept driving.

"How the hell do you two get by in the world?" our brothers would ask as they watched our life. But they understood. Something about our upbringing had made us both painfully aware of the one small, precious life we had. We weren't going to give it over to convention.

Henry came down from Maine to drive us to Boston for the surgery. There had been years when it was the three of us in Missoula, sometimes the three of us in the same small apartment. At times, Paul and I had felt that Henry parented us in the way we would have wanted to be parented; when we worried—about the future, about a decision we'd made in the past, about the shapes of our lives—he always gave us his absolute faith. He'd done the same when I'd called him to say I was pregnant. "It will be great," he'd said right away while I cried. "You two will do great."

We piled everything, including the wheelchair, into the tiny two-door car that we'd bought in our final year in Montana. The three of us had crossed all over the west together in that car. Now, as I sat in the back seat next to all our bags, I was thankful to be with them like this, even if it was surgery and not a hot spring we were headed to. I yelled over the music that I was really going to find a good job in Missoula, that we could all go back there.

"That ain't gonna happen," my brother said.

"Don't be mean," I told him.

"Do you know how many people are trying to get the jobs you want there?"

"Paul believes in me," I said.

"Keep telling yourself that, sweetie," Paul said, and reached his hand around to pat my leg. The two of them laughed. I wasn't offended. After Greta's birth, Henry had moved effortlessly into his role of uncle, but I'd always felt I'd left him behind; Paul and I didn't give him the time or care we used to, and I missed it, missed us. Riding together in that small red car that we'd driven all over the west in felt good, familiar. It felt like a space I wanted to get back to.

"Ready?" Henry asked lightly as he pulled into a spot in the parking garage. Both Paul and I were too anxious to know what to do, so Henry led us into the hospital. It all happened quickly. We checked in at the desk, and then we sat in a waiting room with a buzzer. It lit up, Paul disappeared, and the next time we saw him he was drugged, lying in a hospital gown.

While Paul was in surgery, Henry and I walked the city streets. We drank Starbucks coffee in the sun, we ate pastries, a few hours later we ate Vietnamese sandwiches. I was wearing my TRANS EQUALITY NOW T-shirt. It had come with my first donation to trans advocacy work, and I remember that I felt loud in it. It contradicted my deeply practiced mode of telling people what I knew they wanted to hear. But I knew it mattered. Every day, every moment, every step—even while my husband's bone was being sawed apart—I was rehearsing in my mind what I would say in front of the school board and how I would say it so they would finally understand.

When Henry and I had tired of walking the streets, we went into the empty waiting room and occupied separate corners on the plastic-cushioned seats and alternately dozed or disappeared into our phones. Finally, six hours after we'd left Paul, his doctor came to say the surgery was done and a nurse would soon take us to see him.

"The surgery went well," I told Paul's father, who called a moment later.

He started crying. "I don't know how you two are going to do it all," he managed to say through tears.

"We're fine, no big deal," I said mindlessly, and then I hung up because the nurse had arrived.

Paul was behind a curtain, waking up as we entered. He saw me, grabbed my hand, and then started yelling for me to help. "Abi," he yelled, "it hurts so bad." He began to cry out unintelligibly, every muscle in his body visibly tensed. My brother ducked out from within the curtain and returned with a nurse. She upped Paul's medication and ushered us out. When we saw him again, he was awake in his hospital room and, somehow, he had that pin my mother had made on his tray: PROTECT TRANS KIDS – GILFORD.

My brother stayed a few hours with us, then took my car and returned to New Hampshire. Paul drifted in and out of sleep and pain all night while I sat in a chair and read an easy, transporting novel and imagined what our life would look like as soon as we returned west. It wouldn't be long; three months and he would be healed, six months until the follow-up procedure. There was a youth group for trans kids in Missoula. There were sensory-friendly hours at the museums and theater. The after-school girls' program I wanted to put Greta in noted on their web page that they welcomed all girls, including transgender ones. Hour after hour, I dreamed of giving our daughter a fresh start in that city that would welcome and protect her. We didn't need much. Enough money for rent and food, health insurance, and a good school for her, one where her autism and her gender would be understood and supported. One where she could be proud of her differences, not scared. During those hours in the hospital, it didn't seem like too much to hope for.

Paul's immediate recovery took longer than expected—his pain was higher, his mobility lower. I stayed at his side for two days, and then my father and stepmother came to pick me up with the plan that I would return to Boston in a few more days to get him. I went home. I was crossing the large parking lot of the middle and high school with Greta—where, in less than a week, a school board meeting would be held—when my husband called in tears. It was Saturday morning, an oddly warm late September day, and we were headed to a trail we liked. Paul said he couldn't do it alone; he needed me to come back. Greta had our dog on the leash, and she wore sunglasses and a dress. After years of awkwardness and anger, she looked so confident, so calm.

I stood in that parking lot gripped in fear. What if we'd made it this far, our daughter now our *daughter,* her true self, only to find out that Paul would never walk pain-free again? I called my mother, told her I needed her to come back and watch Greta. Then, because I was too anxious to drive myself into the city, I called my father. He was at my house within hours to take me to the hospital. I found my husband alone in his hospital room, falling apart.

I don't know what I did to help him, other than occupy space. But at a certain point, a haze fell over the room that we stayed in for another three or four days. I kept reading my transporting novel. I walked across the street for Vietnamese sandwiches and hibiscus iced tea. I called a number when he was hungry, and I pressed a button when he needed the nurse's help. When it was time for him to learn his exercises, I stood at the bed with the physical therapist and maneuvered his leg as she instructed. When she came back to teach him how to move from the bed to his wheelchair, I supported his weight as she told me to. I pushed the wheelchair down the hall, balancing the crutches across his lap, to the stairwell where she needed him to learn to go up and down two stairs, which was the number to get into our house. He had lost some fifty pounds ahead of the surgery to ease the weight on his hip, and he was so skinny now, his face nearly skeletal, and still he cried out in pain as he went up each stair. Sometimes, in the night, he woke in pain and yelled from the hospital bed until I woke up and pressed the button for the nurse, who would rush in to give him more meds. He'd quiet and fall back asleep. In the moments when he was awake, I assured him that everything would be fine. His body, yes, but also our town, our daughter. I told him it would all work out, would all smooth over in another week or two, and at that point it didn't feel like a complete lie.

35

When my husband was finally discharged after eight days in the hospital, a nurse wheeled him to the sliding doors and then left us there, my hands on the wheelchair, his crutches across his lap. I watched her get back in the elevator, shocked that someone would leave me alone to care for him. We stood on the curb waiting for my stepmother to pull in. Somehow, she and I got him into the car. He kept his eyes closed for the two-hour drive, and every now and then he made a noise to communicate that he felt carsick. When we finally pulled into our driveway, he threw the car door open and barked at us to help him out. We got him from the car to the couch, and he more or less spent the next three months there.

In that house we could never quite get situated, never figure out what furniture belonged where and which space I worked in, and in those days my desk and computer were in our bedroom. During that time, I kept a careful watch on his painkillers—convinced that if there was ever a time he could get addicted it would be now—and my alarm would go off at odd hours, alerting me that it was time for his medication. Also, he would call to me from the couch in the middle of the night—he needed water, he needed food, he needed me to empty his urine from the container the hospital sent him home with. In between all of this, I would sometimes lie down and bury my head beneath the blankets. More often, I would give up on sleep and instead sit at my computer to reach out to anyone and everyone I could think of for support at the upcoming school board meeting.

The bedroom had light blue walls and two windows, and it had been my grandparents' room. I'd visited my grandfather in there once when he was sick; I'd sat on one of their twin beds while he lay on the other, and I'd reached across and held his hand and told him about my life in Montana with Paul. After he was gone and we lived there with my grandmother, she would sometimes call me into her room and ask me to look through her books and take what I wanted. They were all either poetry or spiritual.

"I was born into a Christian family," she would say. "But I could have just as easily been born somewhere else and loved some other god."

Only her faith in the greatness of mystery was absolute. She'd had two experiences in her life in which she felt some godlike presence had stepped in to guide her, and these were central to her being. I thought of this—of her, her books, her spirit in that blue room—while I sat up through the night in those days. Once while I sat there, an email from her pastor came through. He still ran the church in the village, and he'd been one of the people I'd sent my plea for support to.

Of course I will do whatever I can to support you, he'd written back to me.

I didn't take it at face value, not yet. It seemed like the sort of thing people just said. Still, I remembered how much my grandmother admired this pastor, Christopher, who read and studied spirituality in the deep, open-minded, and varied way she did. In his early days at that church, my grandparents had asked me one Sunday morning when I was home from the west to attend church with them, to listen to this new pastor they so adored. I'd agreed because I loved my grandparents, not because I was interested in any way in their church. But the sermon, I was surprised to discover, was about welcoming LGBTQ+ people. I remember sitting on the pew next to my grandparents, thinking of Noah, feeling sure that they were doing the same. I think it must have been a few years later that I heard this pastor had lost his son.

I sat in the glow of my computer in that blue room and reread Christopher's concise email repeatedly—*I will do whatever I can.* His church was in the center of the village, next to the library, and it occupied a central place in our town. I thought of his connection to my grandparents and decided to believe him. One September morning I walked down the road to his office, and I was so deeply heartened to find him at his desk with a stack of books by and about transgender people and their rights. He asked me if I knew about his son, the one who had lost his life. I told him I had heard of him but did not really know.

"He was gay," Christopher said. "And bullied here. He took his own life."

I understood as he spoke that he knew Noah and at least some of the difficulties he had lived through. He knew my little brother had gone to that church to learn piano, knew his natural musical abilities had matched my grandmother's. Did he know my brother had also attempted suicide? He must have.

"I'll do whatever I can," he repeated.

I looked across his desk at him. I felt I could see into our minds—Noah in mine, his son in his, and now my daughter—this young human we could protect—hovering over both. I felt this pastor and I understood each other in the worst of ways; painfully we—and he infinitely more than I—understood exactly what the statistics meant.

36

The week before the school board meeting, I sat at my desk in the children's room at the library, wondering if Paul could get to the bathroom if he needed, if he had food, if he would just call me instead of risk trying to move when he shouldn't. I looked up when a woman said my name. It was the woman whose husband I'd just read about in the old newspaper article—the one who wanted single-stall bathrooms to protect his daughters from transgender girls. I couldn't face her. I said hello and then excused myself to run upstairs to the main desk.

"Lisa," I said. "You have to go down and cover me." This wasn't the first time I'd called on her for this. I'd done it when anyone who'd spoken at the meeting came in. Everyone I worked with was now accustomed to me hiding upstairs or in the back room, shaking in anger, waiting for a patron I used to talk with to just leave.

Lisa went downstairs as I sat at the main circulation desk and scanned the room. Regulars on the computers, a knitting group over in the corner. A volunteer behind me, in the circulation office. I'd spoken with her weekly for years. She was in her eighties, and she'd sometimes bring me cuttings of plants and handwritten recipes on index cards. What was her opinion of me now? What was anyone's opinion? Surely they'd all heard about my daughter—from what my friends and coworkers said, everyone had. I opened a magazine of book reviews and did my best to look busy so that no one would talk to me.

Lisa called my name through the intercom on the telephone. I picked up the receiver.

"I'm sorry," she said. "She's headed upstairs. She really wanted to talk to you."

"Jesus," I said, and I hung up just as she walked through the doors. She'd left her children downstairs. She asked me how I was and I looked at her blankly. I didn't have it in me to be fake.

"I'm sorry for everything your family's going through," she said. I'd always liked her, always found her so kind. But what was she doing, saying this to me?

"Isn't your husband one of the people who is fighting against my child's rights?" I asked plainly.

"He's for her," she said. "We all are. You're welcome at our house anytime."

"I read the article from a few years ago," I said.

"That article made him sound like such a bigot," she said. "I told him that when it was published."

I said nothing. I didn't know what to think. I'd enjoyed her visits to the library so much. I'd liked seeing her around town. I'd liked that she sat on the town beach relaxing in the sun while reading Madeleine Albright's *Fascism*. I'd liked her love of history. I wanted to keep liking her. And the truth was that I hadn't watched the entire clip of her husband speaking at the recent meeting; it was possible that he'd changed since the first time around, possible that now he just wanted single-stall bathrooms to give privacy to everyone and put the whole discussion to rest.

"Anyway," she said to me, "I came to tell you something. There's a man going around town. He's saying he'd love to find Greta," she said.

I looked at the clock on the wall. Nearly two thirty. School would let out at three. Greta was supposed to catch the bus to the library. Did the woman who came to talk to me just turn around and leave then? Was that the end of our conversation?

I went to the back room, frantically packed my things.

I looked up the number for the school, dialed. My hands wouldn't work right, I kept pressing the wrong buttons, shaking.

I finally got through. I asked to speak to the principal. The secretary put me on hold. A moment later she said the principal was not available. It was what she always said to me.

"Do not send Greta on the bus," I told her. "I will come get her right now."

I remember standing in the doorway of my boss's office, telling her I had to leave, that a patron had just told me someone was looking for my child.

"Who?" she asked.

I told her the patron's name.

"No, who is looking for her?"

When did I know? I have gone over and over it in my mind. The woman comes in, tells me a man is going around looking for Greta, and the walls close in around me. She must have told me who it was right then; she must have said it was Keith's father, the man who had spoken at the meeting about wanting to scoop my daughter up. But I don't remember her telling me at that moment. She said those words, *a man going around,* and everything in me shut down, and I only remembered the part where she said who it was later, once Greta was safe in my arms.

I ran down the sidewalk to the school. I called my mother as I ran. I told her I needed her to come over.

I saw the principal outside the building. Why was she outside? Had pickup begun?

"Someone said they wanted to find Greta and take her," I said to her. I felt stupid as I said it. Who would do that? Who would ever take my child? Why did I have to be so dramatic?

Greta came out. I held her hand. I asked her how her day was. We walked. We got home. I couldn't leave her with Paul. He still slept most of the day. I shut all the curtains. We waited for my mother. She arrived. She sat with Greta and read to her. I told her to lock the doors after I left.

I drove down the road to the police station. Got out, read the sign on the door, felt too afraid to enter, went back to my car. Got out again, went in. I told the woman behind the glass that I needed to speak to an officer about my daughter. I sat on a hard plastic chair and waited.

It clicked in my mind then, I remember that it did. I had misunderstood what the woman had said. This man wasn't driving around, wanting to take my daughter. It was just that he'd said it at the school board meeting, that he'd love to scoop her up. He'd said it rhetorically. He wasn't going around saying it again, he couldn't be. He wasn't driving up and down the road slowly, looking for my child. He said it that once, and now this woman was repeating it to me. Only the quote was off. A sick game of town telephone. It had to be. What was I doing, sitting at the police station?

An officer came out to the foyer and introduced himself as the chief. I was relieved. He'd recently moved to the area from the coast, and in the newspaper article that introduced him, his husband had been referenced. I assumed that meant he would not judge our daughter or us, that he'd understand.

He led me into the next room, dark and windowless, metal and cement. I sat across from him and told him what I'd heard. I said my daughter was transgender, and that the town was in the midst of heated discussion about a school policy.

"I've heard," he said. "The school has already asked officers to be at the next school board meeting."

"Are officers usually at school board meetings?" I asked.

He told me they were not, but sometimes, when there was a hot-button issue, they sent an officer along.

I told him what I'd been told by the library patron. "But I think I misunderstood," I said. "The man was at the last school board meeting, and he announced that he would love to find my daughter and scoop her up. But I don't think he's actually going around town. I don't think he's saying it again. I think I just panicked."

He took the woman's name. He said he would call her.

"I don't want him around my daughter," I said. "I don't even want him within sight of her."

"There's nothing that can be done," he told me. He listed the types of protective and restraining orders, and why none of them would be possible in this case. I understood. Nothing had really happened. But it still didn't seem right to me.

"So people are really just allowed to go around and say they want to find my child?" I asked hopelessly. I understood that it hadn't exactly happened that way; there was no man driving around, searching. But then again, it had happened—this man had stood at a school board meeting and said as much on camera. He had said he worried about the psychological effects that the mere existence of my daughter had on all other students. How was my town, my home, my neighbors, this police chief—how was everyone allowing this to happen to my family?

The police chief told me to keep in touch, to come back if there was any problem. He said we all wanted the best for my child.

And then he put his pen down. I remember that he sat back and looked at me kindly. "Is your daughter in therapy?" he asked.

"Yes," I answered. I explained that we had been in family therapy for years, ever since my daughter had been diagnosed with autism, though now her needs had changed. But as the words came out of my mouth, I was aware that I didn't want to share Greta's story with him.

I was only doing so to avoid judgment. I got up to leave. I suddenly felt so dirty. I felt like I'd failed my daughter, failed to stand up for her, failed to say what should have been said: *She doesn't need therapy because she's transgender, you know. If she needs therapy now, it's because of all the shit this fucking town is putting her through.*

37

Beginning when I was in middle school, with the help of my great-aunt in Chicago, my mother sent me to a YMCA sleepover camp every summer. I always begged to stay for as long as possible, and when I was thirteen or fourteen she finally let me sign up for every session they offered, some seven weeks in total. There was only one other camper my age who was there for so long. Her name was Sam. I had known her for a few years by that point. People called her a tomboy. She was kind and athletic and bookish, and because she came from a complete, wholesome family, she was much more innocent than I was.

At that point, I carried a secret that only my stepsister Courtney knew: the year I was nine, a teenage neighbor had begun to take me to the woods to touch my body and have me touch his. The experience had been like the strike of an ax across my memory; nearly everything that had come before was gone, vanished, and I'd been left with hours upon hours of looking at my nine-year-old self in the mirror, reaching out and touching my reflection, repeating, *That's my body, why am I not in it?*

I was so sure that when people looked at me, they could see those afternoons in the woods; they had become a cloak draped over me, impossible to remove. But not with Sam. I think Sam was my first true friend, or at least the first to give me the sense that I was being seen—and, in turn, to allow me to see myself: just a kid, not dirty, just a kid who liked reading and swimming across the pond, campfires, deep woods.

I hadn't thought of Sam in years, but as the school board meeting approached, she suddenly occupied my mind. What had become of her? Was she doing well? And how deeply had I harmed her?

Sam and I got into a fight at the end of summer. We were alone in our cabin that was surrounded by pines, just steps from the edge of the water, sweeping the sand from the beach out. I have no recollection of what caused our fight, but I know it felt vital in that way that teen friendships do.

"Are you even a girl, Sam?" I asked viciously. The words still echo in my mind. I can still see the way my friend stopped her sweeping and held her broom and just stared at me. Of course I'd meant what I said to be cruel. Bullying was familiar to me and I had been on its receiving end in my own family and at school innumerable times. But this moment when I turned the tables, when I took what I had learned from my bad childhood and shot it across the cabin straight toward this most basic part of my friend's being—it is crystallized in my mind.

I'd had trauma. But I'd never had someone debating my body, what it was and where it did or did not belong. I'd never had someone debating my actual self.

I am so sorry.

And what an entrenched, ubiquitous pathway to destroy a person.

38

On October 8, 2019, I dropped Greta off at Robin's. Her husband, Eric, would babysit, and Robin would meet us at the school for the first school board meeting any of us had ever attended. I gave Greta a big hug, told her not to play too many video games or eat too much pizza, and then I came home and positioned the crutches in front of Paul, who sat upright on the couch. As I helped him stand, it occurred to me that he occupied the same exact space of earth that my grandmother had occupied the morning of my grandfather's funeral, when she'd sat down to replace a button on her wool blazer.

I helped Paul out of the house, and then I left him standing there hunched over his crutches as I went back in to get the wheelchair. My mother pulled into the driveway just as I came out, and I didn't even bicker with her about how to get the chair into the back of her car. I just let her take over. I helped Paul into the back seat. I had my speech printed and folded up in my pocket. My mother drove us the sixty seconds to the school parking lot. She had worked at this high school when I was a teenager; my oldest stepsister had been sent here briefly when she'd had some trouble in Laconia; and Noah and Courtney had performed in their dance recitals here every year. It was the only school in the area rich enough to have a real auditorium, and it was the stage my daughter had stood on the previous spring, miserable and wrong in her boy costume.

We couldn't find an open door, had no idea how we were supposed to enter the school. My mother drove in circles around the parking lot, stopping every few seconds to let me out to test a door. "Shit, Abigail, shit," she kept repeating. Now and then she'd brake to let go of the steering wheel and rub her callused hands hard against her eyes. I kept snapping at her that she was going in the wrong direction, but the truth was I had no idea where to go either. We just kept frantically circling the lot while my husband sat in the back, drugged and miles away.

"Thank god," he says now. Thank god he was drugged and unable to walk, to run. Because when he imagines himself in that situation without drugs and a wheelchair, he has visions of the violence he might have inflicted on people, and he is terrified.

There was no signage. I kept jumping out of the car to retest doors. Everything was locked until suddenly it wasn't. My mother and I maneuvered Paul back into his wheelchair. We were so new to this, so unskilled. We pushed him into the building, but then we had to get upstairs and we couldn't find the elevator. When we did, it too was locked. My mother ran the halls calling for help. It felt like such an extreme emergency. Like in order to keep Greta alive, we had to just get to that room and tell these people what they were doing.

"Why did they have all the lights off?" I would ask my husband weeks later. He would look at me in bafflement. The lights had not been off. It had been bright. It was only my mind that was in darkness.

The room was packed, so many people, all of them white. Every chair filled, people standing, people pressed in tightly to every inch of space. I saw my father across the room. My big, burly brother Will, suddenly there next to me. Another familiar face at the back, the face of the man who'd said he wanted to take my child. When the meeting was called to order and a silence fell, I turned to Will and I pointed to that man and I said, "He's the one who threatened to take her. He's the one who said he would find her and scoop her up." I said it loudly enough for everyone around me to hear. The next time I looked back, he was gone.

The chair of the school board opened the floor up for public comment. My husband wheeled himself up to the podium ahead of everyone. I'd worn a sweater with a long, high neck, and I pulled it up over my nose and just breathed that smell of home and safety in. The administrators and school board members were lined up in a U shape behind tables. Paul sat before them, next to the podium, and began to read letters from schoolchildren. They had been sent to us by my college friend in Maine who had started the postcard campaign. Her neighbor had brought the topic up with her third-grade class, and they'd used it for an opinion-writing piece. She'd had my friend mail me some of the essays, which were really just letters to my daughter. I'd read them to Greta. *We're not afraid of our peers,* these kids had written. *You be you! We love all genders. We all deserve rights. If you feel that you are a girl, you are a girl!*

"Look," we'd said to Greta. "You're not alone. These kids might not be at your school, but they're out there."

Tears streamed down Paul's face as he read, but his voice remained so steady, so calm. He finished and wheeled himself back, his jaw locked in a tight grip. My heart broke for him. Did he suddenly understand that nothing we said would matter? Did I?

The school board chair called for the next speaker, and my grandparents' pastor darted up and weaved through the crowd. Someone tapped me on the shoulder; it was a woman from Paul's work. She had a cardboard box for me—a gift that I didn't open but just stuffed under my chair. I couldn't speak, could scarcely understand what was happening. Christopher didn't even cross the room to the podium, but just spoke from the corner on the opposite side.

"I speak as a parent who had a son many people would have labeled as different," he said. He said his son had attended Gilford High School for three years and "had some tough, trying moments." He quickly told a story—his son had been eating lunch in the cafeteria when some boys came up behind him and cut off his hair. "At twenty-six he took his life," he said, "something that happens far too frequently among kids and youth like him." He said he supported anything we could do to make our schools safer and more affirming. I watched him return to his seat. It was right next to Katie and her husband, Dan.

Next the man who recorded all the meetings and posted them to his YouTube channel came out from behind his camera to speak. Sometimes I saw him in the parking lot of the library, when he was picking up his grandchild from the preschool at the church.

"I'm not going to speak about emotions," he said. "I'm not going to speak about what is fair and unfair, but I want to speak about the law." He said that the law the governor had signed protected people from discrimination based on many factors, including religion, and that the proposed policy was "in complete conflict with a lot of deeply held positions of faith." He brought up pronouns, saying he'd already written to the school board multiple times about the issue. His concern was a specific clause in the proposed policy: "a student has the right to be called by their preferred pronouns." He said the board couldn't declare that. "I've searched high and low," he said. "At no point have I been able to find that the power from a school board presented here in front of us has the power to declare a new right." To him, the idea that a policy should include this supposed right was coerced speech, and worse. "If you have the right to tell a staff member, another student, or a visitor you must call this person by these names," he said, "you also have not just presented coerced speech but coerced thought and that, my friend, or friends, is the hallmark of totalitarianism." He asked people to think about what he had just said, and the slippery slope we were embarking on. People clapped. He returned to his camera.

Next a woman who owned a local fitness studio that focused on weight loss went to the podium. I was pretty sure she'd danced with Courtney and dated my stepbrother years before. Her studio was popular, her toned body and blond hair the gold standard in that town. Her son was in my daughter's class, and he came to the library often, usually with his grandmother, and always went straight for the nonfiction books about animals. I'd liked his visits well enough, though this year he'd been one of the students to tell my daughter she wasn't allowed to be a girl, so now I preferred to not see him.

His mother stood at the podium and said, "I am here tonight speaking as a concerned mother of a ten-year-old daughter and eight-year-old son, and also as a devoted Gilford resident since birth and alum of the Gilford schools from the village nursery to kindergarten and beyond." She was speaking slowly, looking around the room as she spoke. "Let me open by saying my family does not discriminate against any race, religion, or sexuality." She said she wanted "equality" for all children. "We want all children to have their rights protected, their privacy respected, and safety and comfort ensured." She said her heart ached for the parents, teachers, administrators, and citizens agonizing over this issue. "But we are all here for one reason," she said, "the same reason, and that is because we love and deeply care for the Gilford schoolchildren. Let's let that bring us together as we come up with a fair solution that will in fact equally address the needs, rights, privacy, comfort level, and safety of all the children of Gilford." Every time she said that word, *all,* she said it slowly, with extra emphasis and an extra pause. She asked that people be sensitive and support one another. "We are all entitled to our own opinion," she said, "but the power of a strong community comes in finding a unified agreement that regards all the views and protects all the children. What a valuable lesson that we can teach our children right now," she said, "and such a gift. Gilford, we must come up with an agreement that fosters a safe and comfortable learning environment for all of the children at Gilford." Finally, she came to the point she'd been circling around: "Unfortunately, the current policy does not do so." Once more, she reiterated that *all* voices needed to be heard and accounted for, and then she took her seat.

Keith went to the podium next. I reached out, put my hand on my husband's lap. This man occupied the darkest corners of my husband's mind in the same way that Katie had come to occupy mine; they were people we'd talked to, laughed briefly with, people we had at one point imagined as future friends. As the previous speaker had done, Keith also began by stating that he was a lifelong Gilford resident who had attended the school system from kindergarten through high school graduation. Then: "No one is saying that a child should not be able to express themselves in any way, shape, or form. What we are saying is that if that expression usurps the rights of other children, that is unacceptable." There was a little hum from the crowd after he said that. He said he was the father of three, including two daughters, and that he wanted to bring up some statistics. "One out of every nine school-age girls has been sexually assaulted or raped by a male. Do you think it's okay to force the girls who may have been sexually assaulted or raped to share locker rooms with biological boys and males, and do you think it's fair or reasonable to expect them to have to go use the single-stall bathrooms?" He brought up preferred pronouns: "It's compelled speech, ladies and gentlemen. That is a violation of the First Amendment." He went on: "Again, we want every child to express themselves the way they want to, but not at the expense of all other children's privacy and their comfort and their feelings . . . Again, I want to accommodate as many people as we can. We teach our children to respect with love and kindness. If I ever found my kid was bullying any kid, they would have a problem with me. But you cannot mandate speech." He wanted to know if the school would suspend a student who was "convicted, consciously, in their hearts, that you can go through this transition but biologically you're still an XX or an XY." He said that forcing a child to comply with this policy would be forcing them to lie to their hearts. Then, before leaving the stand, he reiterated the point he'd begun with: "No one is telling anybody you shouldn't be able to express yourself in any manner and we should all respect that, but when we start infringing upon others' rights, I have a problem with that."

I remember making my way through the crowd to the podium next, my head down, my chin tucked into the neck of my sweater. I remember how dark it was—it seemed—how I could scarcely see to get there. I had my speech in my hands, unfolded. I had timed myself. I took a deep breath and began talking. I was practiced at this. I had given many readings over the years. All I had to do was leave my body and enter the words on the page, fully. In that way I would cease to stumble, cease to be afraid, because I would cease to be in my body. I read. Suicide statistics. Bullying statistics. The difference between sexuality and gender. The list of all the major medical organizations—all of them—recommending these rights. On bathrooms, I said, "There has never, ever been a single recorded instance of a transgender person causing a problem in a bathroom, and nor has there been a recorded instance of a predator pretending to be transgender in order to access a bathroom." I told the story of my daughter wetting her pants one day and holding it on another. The chair of the board started to interrupt me, telling me my five minutes was up. I kept pressing, louder, faster. "I know we might not all agree," I said. "And I also know that no matter how far apart our beliefs are, I would stand up for your children. If they were being bullied, harassed, marginalized, or denied rights because of their identity, I would stand up for them," I told the board. "If we cave in in any way to the group of adults who are actively bullying some of our most marginalized students, we have to stop and wonder what message that sends to these children. If you are afraid to stand strongly with them, how must they feel? Can you imagine what it might feel like to know that because adults are so afraid to put their job or reputation on the line, that they instead put your safety on the line?"

I finished and folded my papers back up. People clapped. Some even stood up to clap.

Some fucking high school play, I remember thinking as I walked the dark tunnel back to my chair. Did I say it out loud? And why did anyone's opinion matter—why was this even the format?

An older man I didn't know went to the podium after me. He complimented my "courage and passion" and went on to say that he disagreed, and that there were "two genders." He said the issue was political, not scientific, and that bathrooms and locker rooms should not be "open," and that an "open bathroom" would not help the "marginalized student" anyway.

Another man. This one I recognized; I'd seen him in the videos of the last meeting. The one who owned the stove shop that used to be my movie rental store. I drove by it every time I went to see my mother, and I felt an odd ownership over it, that space where I'd spent so many hours of childhood choosing movies with my brother. The man said he was concerned about a teacher's agenda coming in. He told a story: "My daughter, six months ago, is walking through the store with my wife, and said, at nine years old, 'Why don't we have the same rights as men?'" People laughed, and then he went on. "She's being taught to be a victim before she's being taught the actual constitution and the history of everything else." He said he was seeing this in many cases, "right down to school projects . . . of having them do civil rights activists and this and that, they haven't been taught those rights, they haven't been taught the history that goes behind it, they're being taught one side of the equation and they're being trained to only see the negative and see that this is like this because of hate and that's really unfair." He came around to the policy. He said his daughter is religious, and she's taught that if there is a male in the bathroom, she does not go in it. Now, he said, his daughter "will not go to the bathroom at school anymore because she is afraid." He said it was biology, and then he turned to the suicide statistics that my husband and I had both cited. "We're looking at suicide from transgender youths," he said, "but it's actually suicide rates upon all youths and why is that happening? Because we're over-inundating them with all of this stuff, all of this hate, all of this fear, the suicide rates are through the roof for all children, not just transgender children."

I cut in then. From the back of the room I said, "The general population has a four percent suicide rate." The chair of the school board told me I could not speak out of turn. The man at the podium went on, said that if I wanted to talk about statistics we could do that, that "ninety percent" of children who have "gender confusion, it's gone once they hit puberty."

"Bullshit," I muttered. I knew the study he was referring to. The doctor who'd led it had been fired and his practice had been shut down.

At the podium, the man said he worried about "Pandora's box" opening. "You have no way to identify if someone is or isn't [transgender], it's based on what they're saying, so they're getting access into those bathrooms." He closed by stating that we all needed to come together, and finally—wrongly—that this bill people were talking about did not even apply to schools.

A doctor introduced herself next. I took a deep breath, relieved that someone with some actual information was finally speaking. "I have many patients—a few, not many—who are transgender, and I've spoken with them at length about how they felt as children." She said she understood that it was a real thing. But then she turned from the podium and found me in the crowd. Suddenly I had the feeling she was not going to be the support I'd expected her to be. I looked away from her, at the floor, while she spoke directly to me. "I agree with no bullying, no harassing, of course . . . and I don't think anybody here is arguing for ostracizing the transgender youth," she said across the crowd to me. The school board chair asked her to turn back around, to address the board. "Sorry," she said. Then: "I have no moral, ethical, or religious objection to transgender patients, people, I admire people who make a change in their life for the better as long as it does not hurt or infringe on anybody else's rights, and that's where this comes down to here." She gave a little history of Title IX, talked about the new state law, and then said that even her friend who was a teacher in "liberal Massachusetts" sent transgender students to the single-stall bathrooms, "of which there are many in all of the Gilford schools." She said it wasn't hateful for parents and girls to be uncomfortable with a "biologic boy" in the locker rooms. "My children are in their twenties. They've been through Gilford schools. When I told my older daughter about this, she laughed and said, 'Ma, I can tell you the name of five boys right now who say *Today I feel like transgender* and they go into the locker room to watch the girls undress.'" She closed by stating, "I'm in full support of transgender kids' rights." She said she would use the correct names and pronouns, and she didn't care much about bathrooms, but she had a problem with making the vast majority of the population uncomfortable for such a small minority. "Can't we just come up with a solution that works," she said, "like, Hey, can't you just use the single bathroom, and change in there?"

Robin nudged me and then went to the podium to introduce herself. "My daughter attends the elementary school," she said. "At seven, she is learning what it means to be transgender; she has a transgender friend. At seven, she is able to show compassion and empathy for those that are transgender, which is something we can all learn from." I looked across the room. There were other parents here, parents I'd emailed for support. Would they speak, too? "I want to distinguish that if you feel your child will be uncomfortable by the presence of a trans student in the same bathroom or locker room, that is not the same thing as feeling unsafe. Trans kids are more likely to be bullied, assaulted, and to feel unsafe in school; as a result, they miss more school, and the suicide rates, as we've already heard, for transgender people are alarming." She said that teaching students to use the correct names and pronouns is common decency, and failure to do so would be bullying. She said that people kept stating that they were worried about male students entering female bathrooms and locker rooms, but obviously that behavior was already addressed in the school handbook under the sexual harassment policy. She concluded by urging the board to offer more education on the topic for the community, and she took her seat.

One more woman spoke, advocating for single-stall bathrooms for all, which once again felt to me like a diplomatic way of saying what they'd all said: it wasn't safe to have transgender people in shared bathrooms.

The board announced that it would conclude its first public comment session and move forward through the agenda, and then hold a second public comment session. The room emptied. A woman stopped on her way by and asked if she could interview me, and I just looked the other way, said nothing. She handed me her card and I let it drop to the floor. Suddenly there were only fifteen or twenty people left: there were members of the high school student council; there was my mother, Paul, Robin, and me; there was Katie, her husband, and Keith; there was the man recording in his red hat; there was the man who owned the stove shop. There were my daughter's teachers, who sat a few rows behind me.

The meeting was called to order. The student council gave a report. Somebody mentioned that the school was a part of the Choose Love program. The superintendent gave a budget presentation. The principals gave their own reports. A teacher I regularly saw in the library asked for funding for a student trip to France.

Eventually, the board moved into their discussion of the transgender policy. Maggie, my neighbor and former ski teammate, asked her fellow board members if there was a way to ever really know how many transgender students there were in the school. Others talked about dividers in locker rooms. One member stated that all bathrooms should be converted to single stall to avoid town controversy. They agreed to send the policy back to committee for review, and then they opened the floor for public comment once more. Katie's husband, Dan, went to the podium. Robin tapped me, pointed to the back of the room, to a man in a suit who got up to record Dan with his phone.

"Lawyer," Robin whispered.

"At this point, there is not a policy being put in place as regards to the bathroom, correct?" he asked.

"There is not a policy," the chair said. "We do have a practice that was emailed out to the school."

"Is this the same practice that was in the 2017–2018 school year?"

The board talked quietly among themselves; nobody gave an answer. Dan continued. He referred to the email, citing its date and time. He said the email suggested there was a change in the policy. The board corrected him, saying it was a new practice, not policy.

"To me that comes off as a policy change," Dan said. "There was no vote on it, there were no minutes. I am asking the board to vote to either reaffirm the current position or to retract it until a formal policy can be made that's fair and just for everyone."

"Do we have a motion?" the school board chair asked.

"A motion to retract the current practice?" a member of the board said. "Yeah, I'll make that motion to retract the current practice until we've established a policy."

One of my daughter's teachers let out an audible gasp. If the motion passed, what would happen to my daughter tomorrow? I would not send her to school. I could not.

My mother stood up in the crowd. A stickler for the rules, she had done her reading. "That's not what public comment is about!" she yelled.

The board members spoke to one another about what it would mean to retract the current practice, and after a few minutes the man who'd made the motion announced that he'd changed his mind and didn't want to make the motion after all. Dan left the podium, and the man—the lawyer?—at the back of the room stopped recording and took his seat again.

The door opened. Lisa. She came up behind me, squeezed my shoulder, whispered that she was so sorry to be hours late. She walked through the room, to the podium, took a long breath, and introduced herself. She remarked that she knew nothing about transgender people, but that it didn't matter. "I may think differently in my house. But I think that what I personally feel, and a lot of people feel . . . is based out of fear." She looked around the room, then back to the board. "What I would like to put out there for the board to do," she said, "is perhaps to get parents education on this topic." She tried to suggest where to look for speakers, stumbled on LGBTQ+ terminology, then apologized. "I don't know," she said. "The point is to get educated. Not to make anyone feel something that they don't, but at least get information so that you're not making a decision based out of fear. At the end of the day," she said, "it is about the children. We live in a really small town. Do we really want our children walking and feeling like they're hated or feel the hate from parents?" She looked at the board and pleaded. "Educate us," she said. "Educate our school district. Have a forum, have a speaker, so parents can ask any question, good or bad, and be informed."

When she was through, the man with the YouTube channel came out from behind his camera and returned to the podium to reiterate his points, and then Keith went back up. He said he'd failed to talk about athletics earlier. He said that this country "has strived for women's rights for fifty-plus years, this would marginalize those girls," and then he spoke directly to Maggie. "You were a few years ahead of me, you were a phenomenal athlete." He referenced a lawsuit in Connecticut about "two transgender boys"—they were in fact transgender girls—"who had competed and won championships. No one is trying to discriminate against anybody, but what is fair, what is right, what is just." He talked more about the law and said we needed to "fight for the girls." He said, "Where are the feminists?" and raised his hands in question.

When Keith finished, Maggie stood up from behind the school board table, walked around to the podium, and introduced herself. "I just wanted to clarify . . . I was a Division One college athlete. I do not object to transgender children being able to play sports on the team with which they identify."

The board members wrapped up and the meeting ended. My memory is again a dark tunnel with my hands on my husband's wheelchair and my mother at my back, trying to push us out of that room, away from the crowd of people who were smiling and shaking hands, congratulating each other on their job well done. I felt we were drowning in them.

I saw Kasha, the ACLU trans justice advocate, on the far side of the hall. She was wearing a fake fur coat. Had I even known she was there? I went to her, pushing Paul ahead of me. I said hello. I reached out and ran my hand down the softness of her sleeve. It felt like some odd safety. I wanted to hug her. To apologize to her for having to also endure such hell.

Katie. Just behind us, talking to a newspaper reporter.

"Get me the fuck out of here," my husband said through clenched teeth.

"The elevator," I said suddenly. I pushed him down the hall. "Breathe," I said to him, to myself. I saw how tightly his mouth was pressed. "Mom," I said. "Do something, Mom." I was pounding the elevator button. The door wouldn't open.

"The key," my mother said.

"Mom," I said. "Fucking do something." But she didn't know what to do, either. I looked down the hall. People were still gathered outside the doors. They were just chatting. It looked like a party. I saw the husband of a coworker in the crowd. I had met him only a few times, but now I yelled his name. "We need the key!" I yelled. He heard me, found the janitor, found the key. When he brought it to us, I hugged him like he was my father. Where was my father, my brother? Why had they left me?

Outside, my husband's coworkers who lived all the way in Concord were at my mother's car, helping him in, loading his wheelchair. I hadn't even known they'd been there. Tremors ran constantly through my body. They had to open the car door for me. I couldn't buckle, couldn't stop shaking enough to click the belt in. My mother drove. Her car beeped.

"Turn the fucking beeping off," my husband said from the back seat.

My mother started frantically pushing buttons on the dashboard, the radio.

"It's my buckle," I said. "Jesus, Mom, just fucking drive."

Within one minute we were in my driveway. She helped me get the wheelchair out, then get Paul out and onto his crutches.

"Let me help you get into the house," she said.

"We're fine," I said. "Just go get Greta." I needed to see her, to hold her, to know that she was safe.

My mother pulled out of the drive. Paul took one step and his crutch slipped out on a wet maple leaf. He collapsed backward. My arms shot up and tucked beneath his, catching him in some horrible version of a trust fall. Neither of us knew how to get back out of it, so we just hung there together in the dim glow from the streetlight, silent and broken in the center of a town that would not protect us.

39

·······················

We didn't sleep that night. Every noise became a threat. When the wind blew a shutter, we thought someone had thrown a rock at our window. A dog's bark was a gunshot. My husband couldn't walk, could hardly move, so how would he protect us? All night, he scanned our doors in his mind: one garage door that locked, but the other with the broken motor; you could just grab the handle and pull that one up. The odd sliding doors at the back of the garage, where a porch used to be. The sliding doors in our living room. Our front door. The basement door. How would he block them all when they came for our daughter?

Still, I got up in the morning. I got Greta ready for school. I walked her there, and then I walked to work. I silently cursed every single person who passed by me on my way. Where had they been last night? They had become threats to us, to our daughter. Every single one of them had.

At the library, I stood in the staff room and listened to Lisa tell our coworkers about the meeting, about what she'd said and what she'd heard. It was interesting to them, to her. I left the room, went to the circulation desk.

"Was that you who spoke last night?" asked an older woman I'd been checking books out to for some eight years. She owned a Christmas tree farm. Once, she'd given us a sapling to plant in our yard. In those days, Greta had loved to take the shears out and clip the brambles. It was her favorite chore. One day, she'd been so engrossed in her task that she'd clipped the sapling right down.

"My husband said you did a great job," the woman told me. She had just put her returns in the book drop. She was here to pick up her next stack of reserves. How was I supposed to respond to her? It hadn't been a performance. Or had it? "This is our life," my husband had said. "This is our daughter's actual life you're discussing." I got the woman's books from the reserve shelf, checked them out to her, told her to have a nice day.

"I really didn't get it until last night," I said to Lisa when she came to sit by me. I was so tired, but a rage had entered my body and kept me moving, humming as though with too much caffeine. "All my life, I really thought this area lacked diversity by chance. How could I have been so stupid? Of course it's fucking on purpose. What else were those people doing last night than trying to run us out of this goddamned place?"

"I don't know that it's that clear-cut," she said.

"Are you fucking kidding me, Lisa?" I asked, and I walked away, down to the children's room, the heavy basket of returns in my arms. I sat at my desk and began organizing the books.

A few weeks earlier, we'd gotten two new, highly reviewed picture books that had transgender characters in them. Lisa and I had put them on display with all the other new ones. They were simple and colorful, and they gave me a little hope. Maybe people would learn, I'd thought, maybe some would. But day after day, they had just sat there. Until that day. I looked up and saw that one of them was gone. Suspicion flooded me. I checked the catalog. The book had not been checked out. I searched around. Finally, I went upstairs and asked a colleague who managed the library's technology to pull up the camera footage from the night before. It didn't take long to find a pregnant mother with six children in tow walk in, pick the book up, and drop it between the shelf and the wall. I knew her. I liked her. Her children read voraciously, loved the classics, and called newer, lighter books their *candy*.

I found the missing book on the floor behind the shelf and returned it to its place. Two days later, she would return and drop both books behind the shelf.

"The books are just right there where the children can see them," she'd say in defense of herself, when the director called her in for a meeting.

Why don't you just shove my daughter back there instead? I wanted to scream in her face.

Katie came in that afternoon. I was working the main circulation desk. There was no one in the room behind me to take over, no one picking up the phone when I called downstairs. She set her books down, and I pulled up her account, checked them each out.

"How are you?" she asked.

I did not answer. I could not even look at her. She picked up her books and left.

40

....

A few years after we met, Paul and I moved from Missoula, Montana, to Marquette, Michigan, so I could attend a graduate program in English literature. I'd chosen the school because of the location. Three years earlier, just after I'd finished college, my brother Henry and I had packed the little car my mother helped me purchase and we'd driven from New Hampshire to Boise, Idaho, where we would find an apartment together and he would attend graduate school. I didn't have much; my trunk was full of books, clothes, journals, and some art supplies. We took the northern route, going out of our way to drive the Upper Peninsula of Michigan, to the small town where we knew Jim Harrison lived. We went to the bar he frequented, and we just waited. When he didn't come in, we slept on the beach, and the next afternoon we returned to hold our post. He arrived around dinnertime. I sat down next to him at the bar and I told him I loved his books, and the rest of the night is a drunken blur that ended on the shores of that impossibly huge lake—because I drank now; after that night in college just three months earlier, I had started to wait all day until the moment when it seemed acceptable to begin numbing myself. The next morning, I emerged from a stupor with only the knowledge that to be a writer was possible, that a living, breathing human had written the words I'd so loved.

Our first year in Marquette, Paul and I lived in a four-hundred-dollar-a-month, two-bedroom apartment above teenage sisters with a baby, and sometimes their boyfriends. They had loud parties and vacuumed in the middle of the night. The house had a strange, chemical smell that made us suspect there was meth below. We slept on a bed we'd fashioned from wooden pallets covered with a foam topper, because we had just enough money for rent and food and nothing to spare. Paul worked at a bakery overnight, and he missed the west, and he began to wonder aloud if he should leave and return there. I—determined to be a writer—just kept on, with a strict schedule. I read, I wrote, I slept. Once I entered graduate school, I never drank again, never partied. I went to bed on time, I joined a group to practice meditation, and I exercised. I kept a tight grip on my life because I understood it as the price I had to pay to write books.

By our second year, we moved to a second-story apartment a few blocks from Lake Superior, on a noticeably wealthier street. The apartment kitchen was covered in built-in glass cabinets, and that year I would wake at four thirty every morning to sit at the kitchen table my mother's cousin had passed on to me, and which I still use, to work on my first book.

I was in that kitchen when I got another phone call about Noah. He was in Seattle, or just outside it. He had joined some kind of cult, or at least what my family thought of as one—when that call came in, had I already known this? Did I even know he lived in Washington now? Just a few months before, at Christmas, my father and stepmother had sent me a package, but it had been sent to the address I'd lived at the previous year. I went to the house, knocked, and asked the new tenant if she had received my package. She said she had not. But it was the only package my father had ever sent me and I wasn't about to walk away from it. When I told the young woman that it was a federal crime to take mail that did not belong to her, she disappeared down the long hallway and returned with the box, already opened. Towels from the store Noah worked at, and a Swedish cookbook. I remember being disappointed to find its contents, and so deeply disturbed that my father didn't know my address. What if I needed help? What if he had to come find me? More than fifteen years later I still have those towels, which now have gaping holes, and I use that cookbook every year at Christmas.

My father told me that Noah had to leave Seattle now and return to Phoenix. But at the moment, my father was afraid that Noah, alone in his apartment, might be suicidal. Didn't I have a friend from New Hampshire in Seattle? Could she go be with him?

"Ab," I remember that friend saying when I called her. "I can't do that. If your brother is suicidal, I am not the person you call."

"Right," I said, "of course." Was she right? Who was I supposed to call? I had no compass. Would a healthy family understand who to call?

I stood in that kitchen looking at the glow from the streetlamps that hit the glass cabinets and reflected back. I loved those cabinets, that kitchen. That year Paul and I slept on a narrow futon built for one that a friend had given us, pressed in so close to each other that neither of us could move. We had no other furniture save our table and its two wooden chairs. But that kitchen, with the built-in shelves, made me feel like a real person with a real life.

Noah didn't attempt suicide that night, at least not so far as I know. I suppose he might have. When I lived in that apartment, I had gone one day to the public library and come home with a pile of discarded magazines. One was a journal of art and creative writing. In it, I found a letter submitted by a woman I had grown up with. She had been like a sister to me, our families inseparable. She told her story of being in college, living in an attic room on the seacoast, and deciding one day to swallow her entire bottle of sleeping pills. She woke up days later, went downstairs, had a meal with her roommates. No one had ever known.

.   .   .

At the end of that school year, Paul and I flew to Arizona. We would visit Noah and Margot, and then go see Paul's grandmother. I came down with a stomach bug before we left, and by the time we saw my siblings I had lost more than ten pounds from the illness.

"Oh my god, honey," Noah said when I saw him. This would have been some two years after the kidnapping, less than six months after the phone call from my father about trouble in Seattle, and three or four years before the suicide attempt that would land him in the hospital, intubated for days. "You look great," he said. He held my hands and backed up to take my full form in. We hadn't seen each other since Courtney's wedding in Las Vegas five years earlier. "What have you been doing with yourself?" he asked.

"Vomiting for three days," I told him.

"You should really do that more often," he said with an earnest smile.

Paul and I stayed with Margot, and went to Noah's apartment only once. It was sparse and clean, with nothing but bottled water and Gatorade in the fridge. He was finally twenty-one, and he drove a Mercedes now, which in a few months—or years?—would have a Breathalyzer attached to it so the car would not start unless he passed the breath test.

Noah let us borrow that car to drive a few hours out of the city to Paul's grandmother's. When we stopped for gas, Paul stood at the pump looking proud as he said, "Do rich people feel this good about themselves all the time?"

We took his grandmother for a spin. She put her diamond and her opal rings on for the occasion, and she clapped her hands ceremoniously every now and then as we drove. "Wow," she kept saying. "Wow, would you look at us."

"My therapist just said I'm the loneliest person she's ever met," Noah announced in a comic and hollow voice when we returned to the city. We were in the car with Margot, on the way to an outdoor restaurant where he and I would argue about our father and my stepmother—his mother—and the various decisions we believed they should or should not have made. We'd argue again when I insisted he was too drunk to drive. I remember being vaguely aware that there were lots of pills in his life. I wanted to break him open, to knock down the wall that had never been between us in childhood. Instead, Paul and I spent most of our time with Margot, visiting the botanical gardens, eating Mexican food, going to a spa her friend gifted us passes to.

On the morning before our flight back, we went to find Noah at work to say goodbye. We stood under the awning at the upscale mall that misted us from above. My husband took a picture of Noah and me together. It's the only one I have. We're standing in the sun, arms around each other, smiling wide. I was so grateful to see him, to have him beside me, and so aware of how far away he was.

41

....

M om," Greta said softly from the back seat as we drove from school to her therapist. The outlet mall was to our right. It had been built one year while I was away at summer camp. I'd been gone for seven weeks, and when I'd returned the sandpit that I'd driven past my entire life had transformed into a mass of factory stores and stoplights.

Just before Paul's surgery, he and I had taken Greta to that mall to let her choose some school clothes. We'd walked into Old Navy and told her to look around to see what she liked, and she'd been so giddy with the freedom of access to dresses that she couldn't focus, wouldn't stand still, wouldn't try anything on. We'd left with a handful of dresses and a glitter cat ear headband that she wore now, as I glanced in the rearview mirror. I turned the music down so I could hear her.

"Nobody in this town understands what transgender is," she said. "So I don't want to be transgender anymore. But I can't be a boy, so I don't want to exist."

She had just celebrated her seventh birthday. What had this town done to her?

We were at the first in a line of stoplights, surrounded by the traffic and sprawl of that area that my husband so detested. If I turned right, I would be in the parking lot of the chain restaurant my mother had developed an uncanny love for in my first year away at college. It was just past five o'clock, the sun low and blinding before us. My breath caught and I clenched my teeth. How could my seven-year-old be telling me she was out of options?

I assured her that it would be okay. I had no idea of what else to do. As we crawled through the stoplights, I told her that the teachers would help, that we would make sure people got educated.

"But, Mom," she said, "the teachers can't help because they don't know what transgender is. They've never heard the word before."

"What do you mean?" I asked her. "Of course they know."

"No, they don't," she insisted.

"What? Yes, they do."

"Well, they won't say it," she said.

"What are you talking about?"

"They won't say *transgender*," she told me.

"What do they say?" I glanced at her again. Still so small she had to sit in a booster seat.

My daughter described what the teachers said to help her class-mates understand her transition. That "we all have feelings." That "we need to be kind to all our friends." That "in her heart," my daughter "feels like a girl."

"But they won't just teach them that you're transgender?" I asked.

She insisted they would not, and then a new thought must have occurred to her. It wasn't that the teachers didn't know the word. "They just won't say it because most people in the world hate trans-gender people like me," she said plainly.

42

....

October moved forward. The leaves turned their brilliant reds, but for us the month just spread horrendously outward in every direction, too slow because I dreamed only of getting to the point when my husband was healed and we'd be free to leave, and too fast because it angled ever closer to the hell of the next school board meeting, which would occur on the first Monday in November; and then the next, in December; and then the next, in January, at which point the school board would finally vote on the policy. Until then, the public would keep coming out to discuss it—to discuss us—every single month.

After that first school board meeting that I'd watched while we sat in the hospital cafeteria, we'd become determined to get out of our town and return to Montana. At the suggestion of Greta's therapist, we'd made a calendar: a countdown to our move. We marked off the weeks. "We'll be here for fall," I told her, "and then Christmas. Before we know it, it will be February!" I said that month, or maybe the next, we would put the house on the market. In March, Paul would return to Boston to get the screws in his hip removed, and then we would be gone. "You're going to love the mountains," we told Greta. "And the hot springs!"

"Where will we live?" she'd ask. She wanted to imagine the house we were going to.

We'd shrug. The housing market in Missoula felt impossible; there was no way we could afford to buy a house there.

"We'll find an apartment," I told her. "It will be fun."

"Like a hotel?" she asked.

"Maybe," I said. "I'm not sure."

"Will it have a pool?"

"Some of them do," I told her. "Some of them have pools and exercise rooms."

We started to draw pictures of the move: our house, a *For Sale* sign in the yard; our car, packed up with the three of us, our dog, and our cat. Our family on the way across the country and over the mountains to a safe little city we loved.

"Montana?" my father would say when we talked about our plans. "I would think that would be worse. I would think that would be a bunch of redneck cowboys."

"Missoula's not like that," I'd tell him.

"But what about when you go outside of Missoula?" he'd ask.

We'd list all the good things: old friends, a liberal college town, a place we felt understood. LGBTQ+ youth groups. Bike paths, rivers, mountains, hot springs. Paul's family, just a drive away.

By that point, an article had been published in our local paper about the school board meeting. It named me, it named Paul, it noted the school and grade our daughter was in. We kept our curtains closed against the world. Paul left the house twice a week for physical therapy. Otherwise, he lay on the couch, headphones blaring. When he wasn't playing *Breath of the Wild,* he was holding the iPad above his head, researching Missoula. He wrote to the school we wanted Greta to attend. He wrote to the organization that ran LGBTQ+ support groups. He also called the doctor who had performed his surgery, left a message for him: "What's the earliest possible date I could get my follow-up procedure?"

"March," he was told once again. Still March.

Sometimes we brainstormed ways that we could go now, then fly him back east for the procedure. But what about insurance? Having the screws removed out there wasn't an option; we'd agreed to that. Even if it was possible, we weren't going to risk a new surgeon completing a job that another surgeon had begun. So we'd say we just had to wait. Five more months; it was nothing. But then we'd circle back again. "Fuck it," we'd say. "Who cares if we go into debt. We can't live like this."

The bullying continued—daily, peers called Greta a boy, they pointed and used her old name, they told her she wasn't allowed to change her name, they told her she wasn't allowed to be a girl.

"Why won't the teachers just read a book so kids understand?" Greta would ask me constantly. Sometimes she'd cry, and sometimes she'd get angry.

I'd write to the principal, the teachers. I'd thank them for all the support, and then I would ask for more. I'd say that I'd been told age-appropriate language was being used to help the students understand Greta's transition; what exactly was the language? *If my understanding is correct*, I wrote, *and I would love it if it is not—the word "transgender" is not being used at school. Is that true?*

No response.

I'd try again: *What is the developmentally appropriate language that is being used? What stories, examples, and books are being used? I am told that the specific word "transgender" is not being used—is that true?*

Again, nothing.

I called, asked for the principal. She was never available.

. . .

One day, I got a message from a parent I hardly knew; her child had said that Greta was being bullied all the time. The next morning, I walked into Greta's room to wake her up for school, but when I saw her sleeping peacefully, I just walked back out and shut the door. I wrote to the director of student services to tell her that we would be keeping Greta home until there was appropriate support for her at school. I pressed send, then paced the house, nervous energy coursing through me. Paul was on the couch. I sat down to talk to him, but got right back up again, got dressed, and walked down the sidewalk to the school district's administrative offices.

"What am I supposed to do?" I asked the director of student services pathetically. Her desk was between us. I wanted to fall onto it, to put my head down and pass out. My skin was pale and blotchy, my lips dry. Deep purple bags had formed beneath my eyes. Surely, I thought, this woman went into this profession to help people. Where had we gone wrong? "How is Greta expected to function in that environment?" I asked. I told her I wondered about just pulling my daughter out of school entirely, teaching her at home.

She asked me some questions. She took notes. She told me she cared, that she was there to support us. And then: "It's very easy to homeschool in the state of New Hampshire. All you have to do is write a letter to tell us you're withdrawing her."

Was it a suggestion?

We sent Greta back after a few days. What else could we do? My email had been an idle threat. It wasn't even legal for me to keep her out of school in that way, and we weren't equipped to homeschool; we needed to work and, I believed, Greta needed to be around peers.

We will be hoping for the best, I wrote to the teachers, and once again I asked them to watch out for bullying. It was destroying me, so what must it be doing to her? All around, I could see nothing but attack. *Are you trying to ruin us?* I wondered with every single person I saw in town. *Are you? Are you?* At night, when I walked my dog down the sidewalk, my body clenched with each passing car. I would quickly scan my surroundings, trying to decide which direction to jump when I was shot at. When I drove, I would disappear from my body and then wake up pulled over on the side of the road, screaming at phantoms. I didn't know what was happening to me.

"Breathe," I would say aloud. "You can do this." I would call my husband. "It happened again," I would tell him. "I disappeared. I don't know where I went. It's like I blacked out, then woke up to my own screaming."

He would talk me down, tell me to wait a few minutes and then get myself home safely. He would tell me he needed me to stay saner than he was.

43

Christopher—true to his word—hosted an "Ask a Trans Person Anything" panel at his church one evening. While Eric watched Greta, we sat with my mother and Robin at a circular table in the basement where, five years earlier, Paul and I had sat with our refreshments in the haze that followed my grandmother's funeral.

The room was full. Three women were on the panel, including Kasha—the ACLU trans justice advocate—and a friend from our PFLAG group. They began by introducing themselves and telling quick stories of their lives, and then they opened the floor to questions. Christopher darted around the room with a microphone. I noticed the principal behind me. I wanted her to be there, to learn, but I also wanted her to leave. Her presence gave the wrong impression. It did not tell the room the truth: that she wasn't responding to my emails, that she wasn't responding to my phone calls. That three years into my daughter's life at that school, she still did not have appropriate support. That she was being bullied, yet no one within the school would answer my very basic question: *I'm told the word "transgender" isn't being used. Is that true?*

A friend of my mother's stood at the back of the room to ask a question. Christopher walked to her with the microphone. She told a story about her older sibling who had transitioned, or maybe wanted to and hadn't—I didn't follow. I couldn't follow anyone. All I could do was feel all eyes on me, and a dark, thorny vine squeezing my heart. It had grown up from my feet, from my husband's. It kept growing. My breath was short. I couldn't swallow. Where had these people been? They'd known my grandparents. They'd listened to my grandmother play the organ; they'd eaten the soup my grandfather had made each week. Why hadn't they stood up at the meeting, why hadn't they spoken? Sometimes we got cards in our mailbox: *I'm so sorry for what this town is doing to you. I imagine your family is having a rough time.* Once, we got an anonymous gift for my daughter, a necklace with a note to say she was strong. I threw it all away. I didn't need anyone's hidden support. I needed their voices.

The panel ended. People had cookies on napkins, they had juice, coffee.

"Do you really plan to move to Montana?" a woman asked me. I adored her. She worked hard for disability rights, and she'd helped me fight for Greta's support at school.

"I need to get the fuck out of here," I said to her. A circle of women was around us. I wasn't quite sure what I meant. Out of the room, the town, the state.

She hugged me. "Your mother doesn't want you to go so far," she said.

I pulled away to find my husband. He had already wheeled himself to the elevator. Soon he would regain some mobility and move from the couch to our bedroom, and we would become like magnets, clinging to the safety of each other in the middle of our bed, terrified to be left.

44

When Greta once again came home crying, I went to the school unannounced to track the principal down. We sat at the table in her office.

"Greta says the word *transgender* is not being used," I said. "Is that true?"

"Parents don't want their children exposed to this," she said. "We're trying to keep the hate out of the building."

I didn't bother arguing the point. I just pushed for the truth. "Is the word *transgender* being used?" I asked again.

Finally, after weeks, she answered. I wrote it down, word for word: "The superintendent has made a rule that the word *transgender* cannot be used in the classroom setting."

There was nothing left for me to say. I walked out.

Paul's brother called me because Paul wasn't answering his phone. I told him that our real estate agent had just come over.

"He says our house will probably sell in a day because of its location," I said.

"So you're really coming back?" Neil asked. We had talked to him about Greta as she'd started to wear dresses, and again when she changed her name and pronouns. He had learned, recognized his own blind spots, and accepted her without question. If you really knew our daughter, it wasn't hard to do. It took only one look to see that a light had been turned on inside of her.

"Yes," I told him. "Absolutely. We have to get the fuck out of here. You wouldn't believe what they're doing to Greta."

"Are you all doing okay, though?" he asked. "Do you need help?"

"We need so much help, Neil. We need any kind of help anyone can give."

He bought his ticket that night, and in a few weeks I picked him up at the bus station in Concord. If he had any lingering doubts about Greta's transition, they ceased to matter the moment he saw her, transformed. That night we all stayed up late together, Paul and I so thankful for Neil's light presence in our dark house. He cooked and he played with Greta, he talked with Paul for hours. He helped with the physical therapy exercises, and he made his brother go outside, into the fresh air and sunlight.

I had to leave them the next day to attend a literary festival in Vermont; it was the reason Neil had chosen that weekend to visit. As I drove across the state, I kept hearing the principal in my mind: *The superintendent has made a rule that the word "transgender" cannot be used in the classroom setting,* over and over again. I blasted music to make it stop, but then I woke up on the side of the road once more, screaming at people who were not there. *Breathe,* I told myself. I called Paul. He talked me down into my body. I drove the rest of the way safely.

I spent two nights in Vermont, distantly aware that beauty surrounded me. I went to panel discussions, and I gave a reading. But I wasn't really there, and I was not proud of what I had written. I was only broken. I packed up and left the moment my commitments were through, and I drove straight to Concord, to the monthly PFLAG meeting. I'd been counting down the days for it to arrive, desperate to see that group of people who understood, to tell them what the principal had told me.

I arrived some thirty minutes late and burst into the room like a storm, my rage bending the air around me. "My daughter is flipping tables at school," I yelled into the circle. "I don't blame her. I can hardly keep myself from going into that school and flipping every damn table there."

There were questions, comments. There was so much support. And finally, a quiet, steady voice: "They can't do that, you know. Reach out to the ACLU. Refusing to say the word *transgender* is discrimination and it's against your daughter's rights."

I promised I would, and then I went home to my family and the nest of my bed, and the next day I got up early to drive Neil back to the bus station in Concord. We stood in the parking lot by the entrance and I gave him a long hug.

"See you in Montana," he said.

"I cannot fucking wait," I told him.

45

Finally, the end of October arrived. We were thankful and terrified. Greta put her *Legends of Zelda* costume on and Paul draped
a white sheet over his body and we pushed him down the road to the
town's annual Halloween party, because I couldn't bear to go without
him and I also couldn't bear to tell Greta we wouldn't go. I took a
picture of them on the way there. It's one of only a handful from the
entire year. With him in a chair, they were the same height. One of
Paul's eyes was just barely visible through the eyeholes he had cut in
the sheet, and then only the frame of his chair and the bright green
point of one sneaker poking out at its base.

"I used to just lie there on the couch imagining all the ways I could
kill those people," my husband told me recently.

In the photo, Greta has her knees bent, a low, steady stance. She is
on guard, her shield up and her look intent. I look at the picture now
and I want to draw her in, to squeeze her with so much love. Her body
was so small, her will so inexhaustible.

46

························

But one more memory stretches out before the final leaves fall and stark November sets in. In it, my father parks at my house and steps out of his car, well dressed as always. My stepmother comes in to watch Greta while my father, Paul, and I head down the sidewalk to attend a sermon Christopher had told us we'd be interested in.

"I haven't set foot in the church since my mother's funeral," my father remarks. The sun is bright, a golden fall light. I'm uncomfortably warm. I keep my hands on Paul's chair. We have to turn a corner, and there the sidewalk ends and Paul is on rough ground, and my father and I have to work together to ease him over the road.

The church is packed. We sit at the back, where there's room in the aisle for Paul. Christopher and his wife welcome us. Light pours in through the stained-glass windows just as I remember it, and the sound of the organ that my grandmother's hands knew so well fills the space. I notice Katie's husband, Dan, and their daughters a few pews ahead of us. The service begins and the children file out. Christopher stands at the altar for his sermon. He tells the congregation that the son he lost to suicide was gay, that he came out just two months before their family moved from their city in Massachusetts to Gilford for this new job. In that old city, his son was "safe," he said, and the school was "unbelievably supportive."

"Had we known two months earlier," Christopher told his congregation, "we would not have come here. New Hampshire is not the most open-minded state."

I looked at the back of all the heads in front of me. Was Dan hearing this as I did? Was anyone? Christopher continued, again telling that brutal story of the bullying his son had faced in the lunchroom. He talked about meeting fear and ignorance with knowledge and love. But I just kept hearing that one phrase: *We would not have come here.* Did anyone else hear it as an indictment?

When the service was through, I walked to the front of the sanctuary, to the stained-glass window with my grandmother's name on it. I ran my hand over it, said a silent prayer to her. Despite everything, I felt seen, safe. Hopeful. I wasn't Christian, but I thought that maybe I could start coming here anyway. Maybe I could bring Greta. Maybe Paul would come. We were all so desperate for connection. Maybe if we unfurled ourselves from the ball of fear and rage we lived in and came out in this way, it would help.

My father and I led Paul out. Christopher gripped our hands as we passed him. His wife encompassed each of us in a warm and familiar hug. We stepped outside, into the blinding sun, and there ahead of us stood Katie and her children. I suddenly understood that she helped to lead the children's program. My heart fell. How exactly could I send my daughter to a Sunday morning children's group led by her? What would she do when Greta needed to use the bathroom?

A few days later, I received an email:

From: Gilford Community Church
To: Abi Maxwell
Subject: Re: Fwd.: Superintendent communication

Abi—I've been emailing Katie for a week or so. We've probably exchanged a dozen emails. She asked me to forward this to you. Christopher.

Katie's message began by saying she'd been disappointed with the email the superintendent had sent to alert parents that transgender students would be allowed to access the bathrooms and locker rooms; she told Christopher that it had created more "divisiveness, misunderstandings, and fear." And then:

> *Today I woke up emotionally exhausted. It takes a lot to make me cry sad tears and I have let my emotions wash over me. Dan and I asked our daughter if people are bullying Greta in her classroom and she indicated that some are. We believe that our church family reiterates our teaching that that is NEVER acceptable.*
>
> *Would you please consider giving Abby my contact information? I would like to sit with her and learn how I can develop the language I need to help our daughters be influencers to students who are misguided/bullying.*

My husband was asleep on the couch when I received the email. Greta was asleep in her room. I tossed and turned in the sea of my bed, and then I finally left the house to go for a walk. I called my little sister.

"This is good," Margot said. "Have coffee with her. It sounds like she's a person who can change."

"You don't get it, Margot," I snapped. "She's gaslighting me. She's trying to look good for her pastor while she also tries to kill my child." I was on the bike path that headed down toward the middle and high school. The streetlights were on. The field was empty. Once, Greta and I had lain in that field to watch a lunar eclipse.

"That's maybe a little dramatic, Abigail," Margot said.

I hung up on her, and I called Robin instead.

"This is a woman who appears to have hired a lawyer to fight against your daughter's rights," Robin said firmly while I cried. "Get the policy passed, and then talk to her if you still want to. But get the policy passed first."

I told her she was right. I hung up, walked around the school. On my way back, I found my cat in the field. I picked her up, carried her home while she purred. I got back into bed. Then back up again. I went to the computer.

Katie,

I am truly unclear about what you want from me. I cannot be the person to teach you that what you are doing is actively bullying children, but until you see that, you will not be able to teach your children how to be allies.

I am not sorry that you cried today. You should cry. You should also know that my husband and I have spent every day since the first school board meeting at which you spoke out in a state of inability to function because we are either crying or so angry that we cannot see straight. You should know that you and your husband are a part of the reason we are figuring out how to leave this town and get our daughter to a place that is safe for her. You need to know that you speaking out is a part of the reason that the school will not teach our children the word transgender, *will not even allow it in the class-room, which leaves my child in constant fear, leaves her coming home and telling me that she understands that most of the world hates transgender people like her. You and your husband are a part of the reason that I am afraid all day while my child is at school. And I am one hundred percent sure that my child is the only one in that whole entire school who is afraid to use the bathroom. You need to understand that what you and your husband are doing is essentially saying to a seven-year-old child that her basic needs are not justified and that you do not accept who she is. And the impact of that is long term.*

It is not a game to have a transgender child, Katie. It is not some fun thing for you to speak up in your town about. Imagine if you had a child who had a FIFTY PERCENT CHANCE OF SUICIDE. Imagine if you had a child who was already bullied every single day for her identity, yet still that identity was easier for her than showing up as a boy, because being a boy was so painful and untrue to her core being. Can you fucking imagine what you are doing when you tell that child that she alone, and no other child in the school, needs to walk all the way to the nurse to use the bathroom because adults in her town think there is something strange or sick or scary about her? Something dangerous about her? How do you tell your child that? Tell me how that is ever anything other than bullying a child.

If you want to learn, do some research. Read a fucking book. I know you are in touch with Christopher, and he is a model of how to confront a topic and educate yourself and learn how to be an ally. It is not hard. You do not have to read much. There is so much research out there. Every bit of reliable research ever done on this all says the same thing, Katie. What you and your husband are standing up for is dangerous and destructive and life-threatening to children. Do not ever talk to me again unless you first make a public apology for your actions on behalf of all the students in our district.

Abi

I didn't press send. Instead, the next morning I went to see Christopher. I told him how upset I was by the message he'd forwarded to me. I had my letter printed. "This is how I feel," I said to him, and I handed it over.

He read the first sentence and handed it back. "I don't think you should send that," he said. He asked me if I was taking care of myself.

If I was sleeping, exercising, maybe seeing a therapist. If I was finding things to be grateful for.

"I'm trying," I said.

"Good," he said.

I took his advice, and I kept the letter to myself. I still regret it. I have her email address, and it occurs to me sometimes to go ahead and send it, to maybe include some delightful subject line—*Whoops! Just realized I never pressed send years ago! Letter still accurate!* It's not because I want to attack her. It's because, despite all evidence, I still cannot stop myself from believing that she would understand, if only she bothered to really look. Of course she would.

have always loved November, loved the cold and the early darkness, loved the promise of winter on the horizon. I love the depth the naked trees afford the woods, and that year when I turned my calendar I must have resolved to wake up.

On November 1, 2019, I sent an email to Kasha at the ACLU to tell her about the superintendent's ban on the word *transgender.*

Sending your message on to our lawyer! she responded right away. *Also copying a lawyer from GLAD out of Boston, who we work closely with.* Within two hours, we had a call scheduled for the following week.

That night, I wrote in my journal that I was *starting to notice the crisp air.* That the *night stars are clearer, a low sliver of a moon. Halloween was warm wind, rain gusts.*

It was a Friday. On Monday, we would attend another school board meeting, but I was determined to enjoy the weekend, so while Paul relearned how to get his own water and food, I resolved to leave the house and take Greta to the woods.

On our first day out that weekend, she packed her pink backpack with a notebook, pencil, and bird identification book, and we hiked to the bald top of a mountain in the range across the street from us. We stopped along the way so she could sit down to draw and make notes of her observations.

"When can I go hike alone?" she asked as we walked, and then she just kept pressing. "I want to explore by myself," she said. "What if I just do the short trail behind my school? I could take the walkie-talkie. What do you think is going to happen to me? What, do you think I'm a baby or something?"

She had no idea just how capable I knew she was, nor how every cell in my being was angled toward her protection at every moment. She took the trail map out of her bag and spread it before her, and she explained to me where we were and how much farther we had to go. She showed me where she and her dad used to leave the trail to reach a wide opening of blueberries. They'd gone there every year since she was two. Paul would bring his rake and fill bucket after bucket while she sat in the low bushes for hours, eating berries and giggling as our dog lay down and munched beside her. When Paul missed the west, he would always remember this good blueberry picking in the mountains right across the street.

We could see the lake from the summit. My grandparents had lived in a house with a view of the lake when I was young, and my grandfather used to point to the smallest island in sight and say that it was a canoe with two paddlers in it. As the day went on he would look out and remark on their progress—"Still paddling!" he would say. "My goodness, they're slow." Now I pointed to a small island and told Greta the same tale.

"Oh my god, Mom," she said. "If you think that's a canoe, you are so dumb." I laughed and put my arm around her. She didn't know what was coming in a few days, but in another way she knew much more deeply than anyone.

Before we hiked back down, Greta sat in a stone chair that a long-ago hiker had constructed, leaned back, and rested her head in her intertwined hands. I took her picture, then squeezed in beside her and took another of the two of us. In both photos she looks tired and thirsty, but despite everything she was up against, her smile strikes me. It is soft and easy, the smile of a seven-year-old child at peace.

The following day I took her to the woods again. She wore a pink tutu and hiked ahead of me, her arms swinging, our dog at her side. I have a picture of that day, too—Sunday, November 3, the last photo I would take for the entire month. Later that afternoon, I ran to the local thrift store to look for a pair of ice skates for her. Instead, I found an old wooden labyrinth game like my grandparents had kept for us at their house. As I stood in the long line to buy it, I heard someone say my name. I looked. Katie and her family, off to the side, near the children's clothes. They were staring at me. *Leave,* I told myself. *Put the damn game down and leave.* But also: *Stand your ground, stand your ground.* My name again. Her older daughter was waving to me. I was, after all, her librarian. I ignored her until I couldn't any longer. I turned, looked directly at Katie.

"My daughter wants to say hi," she said almost apologetically.

"Shop somewhere else," my brother Will told me. "Just get out of here. It's too much. Can't you pack a suitcase and move in with Mom or Dad for a while?"

48

....

The November meeting arrived. My husband was on crutches. He was unsteady, slow, and in pain, but he could manage the stairs if forced to do so. He—we—could get out of the building by our own means if necessary, and this simple fact flooded us with relief.

Greta went back to Robin's house to have Eric watch her. My mother came over to pick us up. We drove to the school. Entered. Found a key for the elevator. We walked into a room full of familiar faces. The chair called the meeting to order and opened the floor up to public comment. One person after another after another—fifteen voices in all—went to the podium and urged the board to pass the policy and to provide education to stop the bullying. Interspersed with the support were the same people who had been speaking against the policy for a few months now, but that night they were a small minority. My mind registered that the lights were on. When we got home, my husband and I could sleep.

Before we drifted off, we lay there in bed and looked at each other and made a promise that we would not ever enter that space again. We had said all we could say there, and we were done.

49

Margot told me I had to do something for myself, and she gifted me a visit to a hair salon in Portsmouth, a small New Hampshire city I'd always loved. I dropped Greta at school, then drove the hour and a half. I parked across the street from the ocean, surrounded by the colonial New England buildings that had previously made me feel so at home. Now I looked at them and a bitterness flooded me. What did any of it mean? What was this proud history; who and what, exactly, did it celebrate? I sat there, car running, waiting for my phone to ring because, somehow, I'd scheduled my hair appointment for the same day that I'd scheduled the call with the lawyers.

On the call there were two lawyers—one from the ACLU and one from GLAD, an LGBTQ+ rights organization out of Boston—plus Kasha. I held my phone out before me, speaker on, and told them a short version of my daughter's story, and then what the principal had said: "The superintendent has made a rule that the word *transgender* cannot be used in the classroom setting."

"Start with a meeting," they said. "Go talk to the superintendent." They said it was possible that he didn't know the harm he was causing, didn't know the extent to which my daughter was being bullied. "If we're lucky," they said, "it could all end with a simple conversation."

I thanked them, then got out of my car and walked in a daze to the hair salon. Along the way, I looked in the windows at the holiday decorations. I ducked into one store and bought my daughter an advent calendar. There wasn't a single thread of hope in me that said it would all end with a conversation. I'd had a meeting with the superintendent before, when my daughter was struggling in kindergarten, diagnosed with autism and not receiving support. It had done nothing. Still, talking to the lawyers, scheduling a meeting—it was at least movement. All fall, I'd felt like Greta—banging my head against a wall, backing up, and banging it again because people just would not listen. Now I might be able to get some answers.

The very next day, I walked down the street to sit at the conference table in the superintendent's office. He was a large white man in a crisp suit. I told him why I was there. I said, "The principal of the elementary school told me that you made a rule that the word *transgender* could not be used in the classroom setting. Is that true?"

He sat back in his chair, then leaned forward, adjusted his coat and tie. "I don't remember saying that," he said, "but if someone said I did, it's probably true."

"Excuse me?" I asked.

He got up, walked toward his filing cabinets, then back to me. He sat at the table again, put his hands on it. "I think they're using the word all the time," he said.

"Great!" I told him. "So you're saying I can walk down to the school right now and tell them that this was all a misunderstanding and they are free to use the word *transgender* in the classroom setting?"

He snapped at me then. It was an odd feeling, to be an adult, a parent, and to be snapped at by that man. He said, "Don't you put words into my mouth."

"I'm asking you," I said. "Who uses the word? When is it okay to be used?"

It went back and forth like this until finally I understood precisely what he meant: a teacher could say the word *transgender* when talking privately with my daughter, but never in front of the class. I pressed him, and eventually I learned the source of this ban: a member of the school board, or perhaps an administrator—he would not say who—had brought a children's book with a transgender character to a nonpublic school board meeting over the summer. Surely it had been the meeting when they'd voted on the interim practice of allowing my daughter to use the bathrooms. But where did they get the book? Why did they bring it? *I think a picture book is all it would take,* I remembered telling the teachers as we'd sat in the conference room. Less than a week later, the board—privately, with no public input and no legal right—had decided that such a book could not be used and such a topic could not be discussed.

I asked to see the minutes from that meeting. He said he did not have them. I asked to see the bylaws that outlined when a board could ever decide what books could be used and what words could be said. "When does a school board ever get to decide whose identity can be acknowledged and whose cannot?" I asked. My voice was rising. How was it possible that this stranger could have so much power over my child's well-being?

"If your daughter is being bullied," he said, "then you need to submit a formal bullying investigation." Also: "It is not the school's job to teach about diversity." He suggested I take the topic up at the public library instead.

I left. I remember walking down the sidewalk after that meeting, repeating to myself that I had hit the end of the road. Where else could I go, what could I do? Against this man, I had no voice. It was almost a relief; I would write to the lawyers about the meeting the moment I got home, and from then on, I promised myself, it would be in their hands.

. . .

Just four days later, on a Tuesday morning, I woke up aware that I was about to break the promise I had just made to myself. I tiptoed through the house, showered and got dressed, then walked across the field in the freezing rain to the middle and high school to attend a policy committee meeting, where administrators and two school board representatives would go over the proposed transgender and gender-nonconforming student policy line by line.

I had been to one of these meetings before. They were open to the public but not generally attended. That morning, other than the man in the red hat who recorded all town functions, Katie's husband, Dan, and I were the only members of the public there.

The tables were set up in a rectangle. I sat across from Dan, and I kept my head down, my focus entirely inside the copy of the policy before me. I remember that my hair was soft because I had just been to the hairdresser, and I kept running my fingers through it. The superintendent guided the committee through the policy section by section: a student's right to keep their transgender status private, to be called by their chosen name and pronouns, and to use the bathrooms and locker rooms and play on the sports teams consistent with their gender.

I was right next to the superintendent. He didn't look dissimilar from my father; he was a well-dressed man in his sixties or seventies, and though only days before I had felt such a deep loathing for him, in this setting he suddenly became a comfort to me, an unlikely ally. Dan was objecting to every section of the policy, but the superintendent just wanted to get it passed to comply with the law and be done with it. Both he and the school board members countered each of Dan's arguments, and to my surprise Dan relented easily on pronouns, bathrooms, and locker rooms; he saved his energy for sports.

It was November 2019; we were still four months away from the country's first state ban on transgender youth in sports, which would pass in Idaho to bar transgender girls in kindergarten through college from participating on teams consistent with their gender, even from participating in intramural and club teams. On that morning, I'd heard the topic of trans kids in sports mentioned before, but not much. I hadn't researched it, had scarcely even thought about it. I had no idea that it was about to become a national issue. But now Dan said it was one of his main concerns.

"You're putting my child at risk," he said, "and I do have a problem with that, I— That is a safety issue." He said that once kids hit puberty, there was a difference. He said there was a "possibility of injury" and he had a problem with putting his daughters on the field with someone with a "physical advantage."

I remember looking up across the space between the tables at him, thinking that despite the words coming out of his mouth and the ways they harmed my daughter, he still seemed kind. He was soft-spoken, he listened politely, he seemed to care. I found myself feeling almost bad for him. Here he was, trying so hard to protect his daughters, and he just kept looking in the absolute wrong direction.

A school board member responded to him. I had seen her around town, but I did not know her. She asked Dan what would happen if there was a cisgender girl who had a condition that caused her to grow extremely large. "She has hyper-whatever," she said, "so her hormones have really taken over where she's become a giant."

Dan said that an extremely large cisgender girl would be okay, but with a transgender girl there was a "testosterone level." She pressed him on it, and he said there was a "determination from biology."

I told him he was incorrect. I said that many trans kids—my daughter included—would have access to gender-affirming health care in the form of puberty blockers and grow into bodies indecipherable from their peers'. "My child's body will end up just like mine," I said. I even used his name. "Dan," I said, so calmly. I said that we know that a child's grades would improve if allowed to play on sports teams. I wish I'd said more, wish I'd been able to list all the ways sports help kids: improved physical health and confidence; lower stress, anxiety, and depression; increased work ethic, empathy, and self-control. Instead, I just pointed out that if a transgender child was on the sports team, they, and not his daughters, would be the one truly at risk.

"I understand that," he said. He said he taught his daughters to be nothing but respectful. "It's not about the way somebody looks. To say they only look like a female, they look like a male—there's all kinds of circumstances," he said, and for a moment I thought I'd just watched him realize that there was no substance to his argument. I thought that perhaps I should have had coffee with his wife after all. But then he continued; he said a trans teammate would not be a threat to his daughters, and only an opposing player would. Then he said he could not have his daughters on the field with people who hadn't been through the same puberty as them. A committee member asked him for "evidence of kids being hurt," and he did not have any. Eventually, he said, "If my kid is the first kid cut, are you discriminating against my child?"

I didn't get it. I said, "Your child can still play on the sports team."

"I understand that," Dan said. "But if they take a spot." *They*. He went on to describe who he meant: "If someone takes up a spot on that team that wasn't biologically female, then you are taking an opportunity away from my daughter."

It clicked for me then. We could argue all day, because none of the details actually mattered—not my daughter's size, not her hormones, not the puberty that she would or would not go through. It was just her, the fact of her, a transgender girl. A girl less worthy than his.

The next afternoon, I went out to start my car. The air was biting cold, the sky a stark wintry gray. I had a doctor's appointment on the far side of the lake. It was a drive I had previously loved. Once, when Greta and I had rounded a high corner on the same drive and watched the vast lake appear below, I had told her that looking out at it made me feel something so deep and vital within that I didn't have words for it, couldn't quite touch it. "Is there anything like that in your life?" I had asked her.

"Maybe *Minecraft*?" she'd said, and we had laughed.

Now I didn't want to make the drive. I wanted only to hide. I started my car, then walked to my mailbox. Beneath the pile of junk mail I found a letter from the superintendent. I went to the cold car and tore it open and read. He'd summarized the meeting we'd had. At the end, he'd written: "We do not feel that the subject matter [of being transgender] is age appropriate for 7 and 8 year old children."

The school day was almost done, and for the first time that school year Paul would use his crutches to get down the sidewalk to the elementary school to pick Greta up, because I would be at my appointment. I went back inside, threw the letter at him.

"How is this fucking possible?" I yelled. The letter was marked with the previous day's date. Had he walked directly from that policy committee meeting to his office to sit down and write this letter to me? "Our daughter, her actual self, is not appropriate for her class? He understands what this is doing to her," I yelled. "He fucking understands what happens to these kids, and he just lets it happen so he can keep his comfortable little office in this bigoted fucking town."

I walked toward the back porch. My grandmother's long iron plant holder still sat out there, though it had been empty save for dirt, weeds, and Greta's toys for years. I stepped outside, took a deep breath, then went back in. I could not stop my blood from boiling. Suddenly I had our kitchen chair in my hands, the one that went with the table from my mother's cousin, the one I'd sat in to write my first book. I lifted it above my head and slammed it down. Lifted it up and slammed it again. I had never before known such rage. I let go of the chair, fell to the floor, cried for a moment, then stood up. I looked around, stunned. Paul just stared at me from the couch.

"The car's running," I said hollowly. Who was I? Where was I? "I have to go to my appointment."

"Abi," Paul said. "Just cancel it. What is it for, anyway?"

"Dermatology?" I said. "I don't know. I heard on a podcast that I should have a dermatology check once a year. I never had one before."

"Jesus," Paul said. "Just stay home."

"It's fine," I said. "I'll be back in a few hours." I opened the front door. The middle and high school had just been let out. Kids were walking down the sidewalk across the street.

"Why do they have a fag flag on their house?" one boy yelled across toward us.

I ran out the door, into the yard. "You're talking about human beings!" I yelled at him. "Don't be such a fucking bigot!" Then I got in my car and drove to my appointment, where I sat naked in front of a doctor I'd never met while he ran his light over me to check for skin imperfections. It didn't matter. I wasn't inside my body, anyway. I was far, far away.

50

....

t must have been roughly a year after we visited Noah in Arizona that he returned to New Hampshire for rehab. I remember hearing casually that his DUIs had put him in Tent City, an overflow jail in Phoenix. I also remember that it was said almost comically—imagine Noah, such a queen, forced to live in a tent, never mind a jail. I remember no feeling given with the information.

At the time, my father and stepmother were living in the basement apartment at my grandmother's to help care for her, and Noah stayed with them when his program was through. I was in Montana when he called me, but perhaps because the space where he stood would soon become my home, I see Noah and not myself in my memory of the conversation. I see him looking out the low windows to the backyard that would eventually hold my daughter's wading pool, her sand toys, her makeshift tree fort. I see him looking past it all to the school soccer fields, or over to the pristine lawn next door. He would have been in his early twenties, and Paul and I would have been in our last year in Missoula, in a newly redone second-floor apartment near the railroad tracks. I loved that apartment, and so did Paul. We loved our life there. He baked and I wrote and we rode our bikes all over town, and on weekends we camped in the wilderness with our good friends. But I had an unquenchable sense that none of it was real, that I was floating on the wrong side of the country in a make-believe life. I would lie on the carpet in the sun reading all day, and then I would get up and look out my oversize windows across the sweep of the city that I loved so much and wonder what would happen when the country was on fire or all the water dried up. New Hampshire was so far away, too far to walk. How would I get home when the world crashed?

I see Noah, phone to his ear in the basement of our future house, desperate to get out of his home state, desperate to get back to Arizona, back to his job. I see him pacing back and forth in that small apartment that our brother Will had built so that our grandmother could have someone to care for her in the wake of our grandfather's death. I see him telling me that he wasn't sure he really wanted to continue with his current career. "I don't want to waste my life," I hear him tell me, and I remember how relieved I was to talk to my brother I had so missed in this way, how relieved I was to know that he would still, sometimes, let me in.

Less than a year after that phone call, Paul and I returned east. It rained almost every single day that summer, and it was a wonder that it let up for our wedding. The ceremony was in an old stone church at the top of the highest hill on the island of my childhood, and guests had to hike a short rocky trail from the boat dock to get there. My grandmother was determined to make it up the hill on her own and play the organ for us. She was in her early nineties by then, and at one point she dropped to her knees and crawled on all fours over a rocky incline, but she made it up, and as she played the organ, she belted out the hymns, desperate for others to sing along.

Henry, Will, and Margot walked in a procession ahead of me to begin the ceremony. Courtney was not there, Noah was not there, nor were my two other stepsiblings, whom I scarcely thought of as family anymore; we had all broken so far apart by then. My parents walked me down the aisle, my father on one arm and my mother on the other. There's a picture of me looking at Will and Henry—my only two full siblings—as I walked past them, my face in absolute exclamation that surely they understood: for the first time since I was two years old, our parents were together, right there in the same room, separated only by my body, and no one had been murdered yet. Ingrid stood at my side and Neil stood at Paul's as we took our vows. A Buddhist priest who had been my literature professor in graduate school and a mentor to both Paul and me officiated. At one point, he turned to the pews in that small dark church and asked everyone in attendance to vow to help us hold our marriage up. I hadn't realized that moment was coming, and it struck me then as the entire reason to have a public ceremony. Years later, when Greta transitioned and returned to school, I would rifle through my mental images of our wedding, scanning my memories for who had been there. Where were they now? They had vowed to support us. Why did we feel so alone?

We spent our first months back east on the screened-in porch of the summer house of an old friend. A creek ran below, strong and swift. Its sound, coupled with the pouring rain and bright green ferns, blanket all my memories of that summer. I read two novels a week on the futon on that porch while Paul worked as a baker late into the night. By fall my father and stepmother bought a new home and we moved into the walk-out basement apartment at my grandmother's, into the small house in the center of the village where we knew we didn't fit in from the start.

In those early years, I would sometimes stand at those low windows and look out to the yard of the couple who had been my ski coaches, or to the field and the school beyond. I would think of my childhood self and feel some sense of longing but also of belonging—I knew this place, had deep history here. Now I think of Noah standing there in that same space, looking out to a town and a state that did not want him, would not love him, and describing to me a disdain that I just could not yet fathom.

51

....

My father and stepmother gifted me an appointment to see an acupuncturist I loved to visit. She and I had gone to high school together, and though we had not known each other well, she'd always stood out as someone who'd been kind. I lay down on her treatment table and held out my arm so she could take my pulse.

"Do you want to tell me why you're here?" she asked gently. I looked at her, confused. She'd never asked this before; she'd always just looked at my tongue and taken my pulse and begun her work. Now she said, "Your pulse is a trauma victim's. I've felt this in war vets, but never in you."

I briefly told her what we were going through. She held my hand, then put her needles in and left the room. I lay in silence, finally thinking nothing at all. When she returned, she removed the needles, checked my pulse, then had me turn over so she could grind the knots in my shoulders out. She told me to drink water, to rest. She held my hand again. "You have allies, you know," she said.

I stopped at my mother's house on the way home. I felt stronger, felt my blood surging freshly and powerfully through my body. I felt

I was ready to move forward. I sat at the kitchen table she'd had my entire life while she stood at the stove waiting for the kettle to whistle.

"How can I help?" she asked. "How can my friends help?"

"Boxes," I said.

"Honey," she begged.

"Tell people to leave boxes in my garage so I can empty my goddamn house," I said, and I left before the tea was ready.

52

Bookshelves that my father had built lined the walls of the basement of our small house, and I'd been so grateful for them when we'd moved in. They were the first good bookshelves I'd ever had. Since college, I had moved from Wisconsin to New Hampshire to Idaho to Oregon to Montana to New Hampshire to Michigan to Montana and then, finally, back to New Hampshire, and each time I'd carted my growing collection of books. It drove my husband mad. "You know you can use a library," he would tell me, and "Tell me when you are ever going to reread *Moby-Dick*." But I never let them go. They were what felt like home to me. I used to go down to the basement even after we had bought the house and moved into the main floor, and I'd just stand there looking the shelves over, running my hands along the spines.

Now I stood before those shelves disgusted to see how much time I had wasted. So many hours reading books about straight white men and women who already had rights yet were not fighting for others. I felt nothing as I piled the books into the liquor store boxes that people had dropped off, nothing but physical exhaustion as I carried them up the stairs and to the car, load after load, and left them heartlessly at the donation center.

I got rid of other things, too. Plates, dishes, cooking pots; our daughter's old toys and games; jewelry and art and wall decorations; shovels, rakes, fans, garden equipment. I invited my brother Will over for dinner and told him to bring his truck. In the garage, he looked over the pile as big as two cars in disbelief as I insisted that I didn't want any of it. A true pack rat, he loaded everything up. "Tell me if you ever want your stuff back," he said.

"You don't understand," I told him. I would call him for help again in a few weeks, tell him that there was nothing left of me, that I knew I needed to get out but I couldn't move through the steps. "All I've cared about is this place," I would say. "But it's horrible. This entire place is designed to push people out, and I never even saw it."

"Get out of here," he would say. "Just go. I'll empty your house. I'll sell it. You can't live like this, Abigail. You need to just get the fuck out."

Ingrid said the same thing. Every single day, she called me on her lunch break. It was as if we were teenagers again, just whiling away the hours, talking about nothing at all. But each day, she always managed to work in the same question: "Did you decide to hurry up and get out of that town yet?" she'd say. "You should come to California. Live near us."

I'd tell her we couldn't afford that, that we had to stay for Paul's surgery, that it was all just too much. I'd tell her we would head to Montana in the spring.

"You'd better," she'd say. "But why don't you at least go get an apartment in Concord for a while? It's a nice town. Paul could walk to work." She'd look up listings, send them to me. "You just need to get out of there right now," she'd say.

"I'm not going to Concord," I'd snap at her. "I don't want to move Greta twice. I'm telling you, we're going to Montana in the spring."

"I'm holding you to it," she'd say. "But spring is a long way away."

53

....

Greta came home from school with a flyer for the school's annual Thanksgiving celebration, "Lunch with a Loved One."

"I'll go with her," Paul said. I stared at him. "What?" he asked. "Boxed mashed potatoes, canned cranberry sauce—it will be great."

For days I asked him if he was sure. But he didn't get it. "What's the big deal?" he'd ask.

"Everyone will be there?" I would say. "You'll have to sit in the cafeteria with the whole town?" But he'd never gone before; he'd always been at work. He said he was excited to finally be the one to show up for Greta.

On the day of the event, Robin and Eric met Paul at our house.

"You're not coming?" Robin asked me.

"Are you kidding?" I said.

The three of them walked down the street slowly, Paul on crutches. I watched out the window. Behind them, I could see the low rise of the mountains. In those days, I kept looking at that view, studying it, trying to prepare myself to not see it anymore. To accept that it was not enough to hold me up.

Paul returned less than an hour later. He slammed the door open, threw a crutch across the room, and hopped to the couch. His mouth was pressed in so tightly it looked like his jaw had locked. I hovered around him until he spoke. He told me that just behind Greta, at the next table, was Keith. The entire meal, he'd been in Paul's line of vision. "To be sitting there trying to make her laugh," he said, "and at the same time to be imagining smashing that guy's head into the wall until it bleeds." He lay down, covered his head with a pillow. "There's something wrong with me," he said. "I'm going fucking crazy."

On the Tuesday before Thanksgiving, the lawyers from the ACLU and GLAD emailed a letter to the superintendent. *We are deeply concerned that the Superintendent's recent directive that school personnel not provide information on transgender people and gender transition to students has left faculty and staff unable to educate students in Greta's class on these matters, leaving Greta more vulnerable to harassment, bullying, and discrimination at school,* they wrote. They listed the bullying Greta had experienced, and they reported that I'd gone to the school for help. *But school personnel informed the Maxwells that they had been directed not to educate the children on gender transition and, disturbingly, not to use the word "transgender" in front of students other than Greta . . . This position was memorialized in a letter from the superintendent.* They pointed out that the school was *implicitly condoning bullying by other students* and failing to meet one of its core obligations: *to provide all students, including Greta, a safe learning environment, free from discrimination and harassment.*

At the end of their letter, they reiterated their point: the school was in violation of the state's anti-bullying law and nondiscrimination law. In addition, the district's failure to make the school board meeting minutes available to the public was in violation of the state's law that granted access to governmental records and meetings. Also, *This letter should be viewed as a formal bullying complaint, and we request the commencement of an immediate investigation,* the lawyers said.

I imagined the superintendent receiving the letter just before the holiday break, printing it out, reading it. I imagined him standing at his marble countertops, a tumbler of whiskey sweating in his hand, knowing he'd been caught. I hoped the letter ruined his holiday.

Paul, Greta, and I attended the annual Thanksgiving on my father's side of the family. When I was a child, the get-together had been large, some fifty people, but now it was less than half that. I'd reached out to relatives before the celebration, told them of Greta's new name and pronouns. Everyone had been kind, and it had filled me with love for my family; we might have been an unhealthy mess, but at least we could accept people.

The celebration was held on the far side of the lake, in the large farmhouse of my father's cousin. He'd raised his sons in Gilford, right at the base of the mountains. I didn't know him well, but I saw him around town sometimes, and he had a soft, easy presence and a clear familial resemblance that I found calming. Just that year, he'd lost one of his sons to suicide, and that day a soft cloud of sadness wrapped around him so tangibly I felt I could reach out and push on it.

A fire burned in the large open fireplace, and an oversize oil painting of our shared patriarch hung on the wall. There were built-in floor-to-ceiling bookshelves with very few books on them, but one was my first. It made me feel at ease, this care and attention. I stayed at Greta's side as I reintroduced her to family, and then I watched her from a distance as she played with the children of her generation. They put their coats on and ran outside, jumped off stone walls, explored the cemetery across the field. It felt good in a way I had not expected. When the time came, we made our plates and sat down. I sat across from a distant cousin I'd always adored. She asked me about Greta.

"Maybe your child just thinks the boy clothes are boring?" she asked.

I was trying to enjoy my stuffing and cranberry sauce and the strange marshmallow fruit salad that was my family's tradition. Where was Greta? Where was Paul?

"Did you ever think that your child just likes brighter colors and doesn't know how to ask for that? I just worry that it's such a fad," she said. "I worry about people not loving their bodies as they are."

"It's not like that," I began. I started to tell the story I told everyone, the memorized script that I kept folded in the corner of my mouth. I wanted to cry, or scream. I hadn't expected this, hadn't been prepared to defend our daughter's life in this way. Why couldn't we talk about books? Television? Even the upcoming presidential election? Or anything else about my daughter; there were so many other things about her. Her love of the lake, the mountains. Her love of books. Her uncanny similarity to my brother Will, the way the two of them would sit together for hours, entirely entranced as they disassembled a broken windup toy that someone had probably won at an arcade a decade ago, repaired it, and put it all back together again.

Will's partner sat next to me as I struggled to explain. She was the only one listening in. For some reason, she and I had never gotten along easily, but now she jumped in, interrupted me, and took over. "It's not about the clothes," she said forcefully to my cousin. She said she wasn't quite clear why people had such a hard time understanding it. "I swear my parents thought Abi's daughter was being sent to the surgeon today," she said, and laughed. I looked at her, let out a long breath. I had never before felt so grateful to her.

"Excuse me," I said, and I stood up, took my plate, and went to the small table behind me to sit next to my outcast cousin with a drinking problem who cast no judgment, not an ounce of it. We talked about the days of skiing when we were young. My brother Will and his partner joined us, and I stayed at their side for the rest of the night.

It was dark when we left. We had to pull over on the way home, because we got a message from my father that he had a bag of ours that we'd forgotten. My father pulled over behind us, and we each got out of our cars. I walked to him and we stood together for a moment on the roadside beneath the bare trees, the lake so close I could smell it. I had already shed so much. My books, heaping piles of my possessions.

My attachment to some dream future of my daughter growing up on this lake, in these mountains. I started to say something to my father, then stopped, and instead simply gave him a hug and told him to have a good night. I didn't want to disappoint him, to make him sad. But I knew on that day that I would never again attend another family Thanksgiving. I had learned to shed people. It occurs to me now that this is what Noah must have learned, too.

54

....

December. We received a letter from the principal saying that she'd conducted a formal bullying investigation: she'd asked Greta for names of the students who had bullied her, and Greta had been unable to respond. *Based on the information I gained from the investigation,* she wrote, *I could not determine at this point that any particular student bullied or discriminated against Greta based on her gender identity.*

One week later, parents of the graduating class of 2030—Greta's class—formed a group and advertised their meetings in the local paper and on the community Facebook page. They said they were getting together to discuss *Transgender Rights in Schools,* and they invited a reporter to join them. In their advertisements, they said their group would offer a place to speak openly, to discuss a *common ground* proposal that would be *safe for all children.* To find out the location of the group's meeting, you had to contact them.

Robin tried. They wouldn't give her the information. The group, it turned out, was only for those against transgender rights in schools.

People are afraid to say how they feel in fear of losing their jobs, customers, friends, and being labeled, the group wrote online. This space would offer them a chance to speak freely, without fear, and to plan.

"So you've formed a hate group?" Robin asked.

I wrote to the principal and teachers to inform them about the group. I said they had even invited children to join them. I said I wanted to know what could be done to ensure Greta would be safe from bullying by these people. *I want to be assured that there are extra eyes on her in the hallway, bathroom, lunchroom, recess,* I wrote. *I want to know that if parents in this group are volunteers in the school, they are not allowed to interact with my child.*

The teachers promised they would keep an eye on Greta, would keep her safe. The principal said she was aware of the group, and that she would try to limit interactions with volunteers, though that would be difficult during classroom parties.

Paul finally got up from the couch one afternoon and approached the kitchen. He wanted to cook a treat for Greta—caramel popcorn, which until this year we'd made every October of her life. It took all his focus to pop the corn while leaning on his crutches, to measure the molasses, the brown sugar, the butter. He poured the hot, foamy mixture over the pan of popped corn and put it in the oven. When the fifteen-minute timer went off to alert him that it was time to stir, he opened the oven and smoke poured out. Something had gone wrong with the heating element—the temperature just kept rising. The popcorn was on fire. He dropped one crutch, leaned down over the other, grabbed the pan, and hobbled to the porch door. He threw the whole blackened, smoking tray into the snow.

I called the real estate agent. "Do you think having no stove or oven will affect the sale of the house?" I asked.

"No," he said. "But that doesn't seem like the right question. We have no date set to put the house on the market. I'm just thinking you might need to eat between now and then?" he asked gently.

Christopher hosted another panel discussion at his church. Once again, Eric watched Greta while my mother, Paul, Robin, and I attended together. This time we sat in the sanctuary, squeezed into the hard pews. An endocrinologist who specialized in transgender care was there to speak alongside one of his patients, a police officer in her fifties who had transitioned in adulthood. They talked about the science, the lived experience. They talked about the need for a community to be inclusive, to make sure the transgender children knew they were safe.

When they opened the floor to questions, I turned to rearrange my jacket behind me and noticed the superintendent at the back of the room. I faced forward again. I took a deep breath. My heart pounded. I raised my hand. They came right to me with their microphone.

"My daughter is transgender," I said. I told them that she was seven, that she had socially transitioned over the summer, and that she'd been so excited to go back to school and tell her peers her new name, to explain to them who she is. "But our school will not teach the word *transgender*," I said. I announced to the entire room that the superintendent had made a rule against it, and that it was having detrimental effects on my child. I said that we heard the word *inclusive* tossed around a lot, but I wanted to hear their opinion about what that really meant.

"It is damaging to your kid," the woman on the panel said, her voice so forceful. "It is damaging to your kid," she repeated. "It's going to be damaging to any kid to be told, 'Oh, yes, there's a word for you, and your teachers aren't allowed to use that word.' The bottom line is, you're telling your kid that the word that they are is unspeakable. That's a damaging thing."

Paul and I stood up and pushed through the crowd, heads down, the moment the panel ended. I noticed Maggie, the school board member, in the audience. People I hardly knew tried to stop us on the way out, to shake our hands, to give us a hug, but we just kept moving forward. We made it to the foyer ahead of everyone.

"Abi!" I suddenly heard someone shout, just before I left the building. It was Christopher. "There's someone I want you to meet," he said.

A woman stepped out from behind him, wrapped up tightly in her coat. She walked toward me and grasped my hands with her soft ones. She was small and old and well dressed, shorter than me, and somehow warm. She leaned in. "I'm transgender," she whispered. "Your daughter is going to be okay. *You* will make it so."

"Thank you," I said, looking into her eyes. I let out a breath. For the first time in what felt like months, I let my shoulders fall.

I had messages when I got home. They were from three different friends, but they all said the same thing: Maggie had stayed after the panel to talk with people. My question had come up—my claim about the superintendent. She'd told a circle of people that it wasn't true. But also, she'd told them that if children were taught about being transgender, then what would the district say to a parent who wanted creationism taught? Where would they draw the line?

"What are these people even thinking?" I said to Paul. "Greta's not a fucking religion, she's a human being. And also, obviously if a student is being bullied because of their religion, the class should be educated."

"Abi," Paul said firmly. "Stop. Stop engaging, stop trying. They won't get it because they don't want to. You just need to stop."

"Easy for you to say," I snapped. "Why don't you try being the one the teachers email. Why don't you try going to talk to the school."

"I will," he snapped back, and then he slept on the couch.

For Christmas Day I said no to all invitations from family and instead I had only my mother over—though why didn't we go to her comfortable house with a working stove instead? We heated frozen donuts in the toaster oven for brunch, and we made veggie burgers and frozen French fries for dinner. I found an old puzzle of the lake in my newest heap of belongings to get rid of, and I brought it up from the basement. My mother extended our table with cardboard boxes, and we focused all our energy on that puzzle until, at ten at night, it was complete.

After that, every day, Paul and Greta and I filled our lives with puzzles, card games, board games, video games. It was a place we could be in together. This focus and joy—it was something no one could take from us.

January, February. With the stove broken, I cooked on the grill on the back porch, grateful to be forced to look up, to take in the fresh air. On nights when school board meetings took place, I looked across at the lights in the school library.

"I wonder if anyone's speaking up," I would sometimes say. Paul would tell me to stop torturing myself, to sit down with him, to listen to music or watch a show.

My husband returned to work. Each day, he had to drive by the woodstove shop owned by one of the men who kept speaking out. When he got home, he'd tell me what he'd imagined: throwing bricks through the windows, setting the building on fire, spray-painting *BIGOT* across the front. After that, he'd go to the bedroom, lie down, and disappear into his phone. Sometimes I would ask him to get up, to be with us. "You realize your entire life is spent in bed?" I would say.

"Can you get off my fucking back?" he would snap.

I went to my boss's office. I told her I was officially putting my notice in. My last day at the library would be at the end of February. In March, we would put our house on the market, pack what we'd kept into a moving van, and drive across the country, back to that western valley tucked into the center of the mountains we loved.

....

55

When the snow had begun to fall in early December, my husband had told me to use my small savings account to finally buy season passes and ski equipment for Greta and me, which I'd dreamed of for years. Because of the writing life I'd chosen—which meant a generally low, unstable income—it had been nearly two decades since I'd downhill skied. Now I told him it was too much money. "We need to save for our move," I said.

"It doesn't matter," he'd said. "You have to do something. We need you to not lose your mind, too."

Greta learned to downhill ski quickly, thanks to years of cross-country skiing and ice skating. We spent only a few days on the beginner chairlift, and then we went all over the mountain together.

"This is the trail Aunt Courtney and I used to race on," I would tell her, and I would see visions of my father—who had sometimes volunteered as a gatekeeper for my races—standing off to the side with his clipboard, keeping notes on each skier that passed.

"You have to turn," I would tell Greta when I'd catch her at the bottom. "Good skiers turn," I would say.

"That makes no sense," she would insist. "If the point is to go from the top of the hill to the bottom, why would I bother turning?"

I kept taking pictures of the two of us and sending them to Paul. I kept thanking him for making me do this. Sometimes, like a child, I would ask him to drive to the mountain and stand at the bottom of the trail to watch us come down. "Skiing is basically my best skill," I'd tell him, "and you've never even seen me do it." I wanted him to watch because I couldn't explain what I felt: out there, I clicked back into myself. It was the push of my legs against the snow and ice, the cold wind against my face. It was the rhythm, the speed. This motion on this mountain—as a child, and still now, it was the way I knew how to be inside my body. It was where I knew I was whole.

"Skiing is my favorite thing in the world," Greta began to say that winter. "It's even better than video games."

"It sure is," I would answer. We'd stand together at the top of the lift and look out at the breathtaking view, the entire lake spread before us, the White Mountains beyond.

"It's so beautiful," she would say. We'd point to our island and I would wonder if she felt what I did—such longing, such sadness. We loved this place, and we knew we had to leave. Here, on the mountain, we could be alone and silent together, but we'd always see at least one person who'd fought against her rights. We'd always see at least one person who'd bullied her. We were surrounded, even in this place of such escape.

One night a nor'easter hit, and school was called off for the next day. Greta and I got up, looked through the packet of work that had been sent home, and then we dropped the worksheets in the recycling bin and loaded our car with our ski gear. I shoveled us out, then hovered over the steering wheel as I drove the few miles up the road to the ski area. It was nearly deserted, the snow falling heavy and fast. Greta had never been up the summit chair before, and she was desperate to try. She called out in awe at the rocky outcroppings beneath us on the ride

up, and the swift change in trees, the way the evergreens became scraggly and windblown.

"These are my favorite trees in the world!" she called through the
snow. "It's so beautiful!" she called as she skied down in front of me,
her skis slicing through the powder, the snow-laden trees tenting us in.
"It's so magical!"

We stopped for a break. We went to the small ski lodge. Once,
when I was a child, after the mountain had closed for the day, a worker
had come out the back with a plate of leftover donuts for the wild pack
of us—my siblings, cousin, and I. It happened only that once, but after
that, each time I walked by the lodge on the way to the parking lot at
the end of the day, hungry and cold, I would look at that building and
wish desperately for someone to come out and feed us again.

In the lodge, I let Greta get multiple snacks and drinks. I always
thought of my own want in that same space and I said yes to everything. Cookie, sure. French fries, hot chocolate, Gatorade, yes, yes, yes.
She could convince me of anything but to quit for the day. When she
wanted that, I would think of all the childhood discomfort I'd skied
through—all the hunger and cold, the exhaustion—and still, the way
I had been so thankful to just be skiing, and I'd become unfairly disappointed and annoyed with my daughter. It bewildered her.

That day, we took our break, then bundled back up. Outside, as
Greta struggled to get her skis on in the ever deepening snow, I heard
someone call her name.

Katie.

"How are you?" she asked my daughter. "Are you enjoying your
snow day? Isn't it so beautiful?"

I stood looking on a few feet away, too stunned to speak. What
was she thinking, interfering with our perfect day? Greta finally
clicked her boots into her bindings and I called to her, told her to
hurry up. When I could reach her, I held her arm and maneuvered us
back to the summit chair without a word. I was flooded with relief
when I looked up through the falling snow to see some of my family

there before me. My cousin—the one I'd skied with as a child and sat with at Thanksgiving—and his children; and Ingrid's older brother and his children, also family to me. I stayed glued to them for the rest of the day. Later, I texted them, told them what had happened in the moment before we'd run into each other. For the rest of the winter, every single snowstorm, they contacted me before going to the mountain, asked me where and when I wanted to meet.

That night, I sent an email.

From: Abi Maxwell
To: Katie Blake
Subject: (no subject)

Katie,

The way that you speak to my child so casually suggests to me that you believe that the actions of you and your husband have not affected her. Let me be clear in telling you that your actions have directly and severely affected her in an exceedingly negative way. The clearest example of this is the fact that because of voices like yours, the school made a rule that the word transgender *could not be used in the classroom setting. This made my child's transition EXTREMELY difficult, and has transformed her former pride to shame and fear. So, moving forward, for the remainder of the time that my family has to be in this town, I would appreciate it if you would not speak to her. The chances of her noticing you are extremely slim. If she happens to notice you and say hi, great, say hi back. I am and always will be happy to say hi to your children if they notice me, and of course I am happy to have your children reach out to Greta. But if you or your husband sees us, please do not approach us. You and your husband do not have the right to speak to my daughter, who you are doing everything in your power to hurt. Furthermore, my daughter does not need to learn that the people who are actively trying to harm her will also make themselves feel better by saying hi*

and being pleasant to her in public. That said, I do, however, assume
that you are a good person, and that you just need to educate yourself.
I hope you will do so (with reliable sources, including many books at
the public library) for the sake of all LGBTQ+ kids in our district,
for the future ones, and particularly for the ones living in hiding
because of voices like yours.

She never responded. I had wanted her to. I had even expected it.
If I had been her, I would have begged for forgiveness.

56

Late one January night my mother texted me from inside the high school library. *You did it, honey. The policy passed.*

I stood in the cold dark on the back porch and looked across the field to the lights of the school. Now transgender and gender-nonconforming students in the district were protected; their right to privacy, to chosen name and pronouns, to bathrooms and locker rooms and sports teams—it was all official policy.

But what did it add up to? I never could have imagined the wave our voices had brought forth. I thought of families like mine, searching for a school for their transgender child. What if they saw that our district had passed a policy and they took that to mean that this place would be supportive? It felt like such a false promise. It felt like they would be unknowingly throwing their child to the wolves.

Once the policy was passed, the superintendent responded to the lawyers. He wrote that his words were being *misconstrued,* that he *did not direct school personnel to not provide information on transgender people and gender identity.* He was lying—it seemed so clear that he was. But also, he was saying what I needed him to say: *The District takes the civil rights of all its students seriously and wants to make all students and adults feel safe in its schools.* It was a written promise that what had happened to my daughter had not happened, would not happen.

The next day, a crack of light came through. Greta had been standing in the lunch line when a classmate who'd repeatedly bullied her pointed at her and called her a boy. She corrected him, got her lunch, and sat down to eat. The guidance counselor pulled the classmate aside. Later, she wrote to me about it: *I told the child that Greta is transgender and explained that her head and her heart do not match her assigned body at birth and the importance of being respectful of her individuality.* It was the first time a teacher had ever taught this boy the word *transgender,* the first time they'd ever taught him that people like my daughter exist. Also, it was the last time he ever bullied her.

57

One February morning Paul and I skipped work and Greta skipped school and we all put our nice clothes on to go together to the county courthouse to have her name officially changed. It was the same courthouse where my parents had spent countless years in custody battles. My great-uncle had been a judge there, and a large portrait of him hung on one of the walls. But that day I didn't bother finding it to point it out to Greta. We just sat nervously in the hall, awaiting our turn. A library patron I'd seen for years sat on the bench across from me. We pretended not to recognize each other. I wondered why he was there, and why he thought I was there. Paul and I held Greta's hands.

"The judge will have to say your old name," we told her.

"Will it be gone after that?" she asked, as if the name itself were some physical entity we were about to drop off a cliff.

"It will be gone," we promised her.

When the judge called us in, we sat at the table and answered all the questions. Yes, this was our daughter; yes, we were sure she should change her name.

"Yes," Greta said when it was her turn. "I am sure I want to change my name."

A paper was stamped and it was done. We walked downtown, past the old movie theater, past the shoe store. I didn't reminisce. I didn't care for my memories, not anymore. We bought coffee, juice, and waffles, and we clinked our glasses together. We took a picture of Greta and a picture of the three of us. We were all so happy.

Later that night, I sat down at my computer to work on plans for our move. I'd contacted a few apartment complexes, and now I had to fill out applications. Paul had contacted former coworkers, and he had a few calls scheduled for a job. At school, Greta had announced that she was moving to Montana. Often, we'd look at the calendar—our countdown.

"Next comes March," I would say to Greta, "when we will put a *For Sale* sign in front of our house and people will come in to see it."

"We'll show them our house?"

"We won't," I said. "Someone called a real estate agent will. We'll leave for a few hours while they look."

She seemed satisfied enough. She was sad, but she was excited. She wanted to be close to her cousins and the mountains of the west. She wanted a fresh start.

Greta was asleep in her room that February night. She was just on the other side of the wall from me, beneath the glow-in-the-dark stars that she and Paul had covered her ceiling with. LEGOs were spread across her floor. Paul was on the couch. I was at my computer, suddenly pulling up a list of rights our daughter would not have in Montana. I sat there in the cushioned office chair my mother had gifted me when I was pregnant, and I stared at the terrible screen.

Housing: The state does not prohibit housing discrimination
based on sexual orientation and gender identity.

Employment: The state does not prohibit employment discrimination based on sexual orientation and gender identity.

Hate Crimes: The state does not have a law that addresses hate or bias crimes based on sexual orientation and gender identity.

Public Accommodations: The state does not prohibit discrimination in public accommodations based on sexual orientation and gender identity.

School Anti-Bullying: The state does not have a law that addresses harassment and/or bullying of students based on sexual orientation and gender identity.

Education: The state does not have a law that addresses discrimination against students based on sexual orientation and gender identity.

Anti–Conversion Therapy: This state does not protect youth from so-called conversion therapy.

How could I have failed so colossally in my planning? After all we'd been through just to get her rights at her school, how could I have failed to understand that our country has no federal laws to protect my daughter? Had I not heard the members of my PFLAG group when they talked about how hard they'd worked just to pass nondiscrimination laws in our state one year earlier?

I sent the list to Paul. And then I sat there, immobilized, waiting for him to respond. To call out to me, to walk down the hall and join me. Instead, silence. Our daughter could be discriminated against in school with no legal recourse. She could be kicked out of a bathroom or locker room, but she could also be denied housing, kicked out of a restaurant, a theme park, a store, anything.

I lay down in bed and stared at the ceiling. I thought of my grandmother lying in this same place, staring at this same ceiling, and then I watched as the future we'd created in that western city we loved disappeared. I watched the bike paths vanish, the mountains, the rivers. I watched the carousel in the park disappear, our favorite tea shop, bakery, ice cream shop. Weekends and holidays with her cousins—gone.

I got back up, went to the living room. Paul looked up at me. I could see in his eyes that he knew what I did.

"She'd still be okay in Missoula, though," I told him gently, half-heartedly.

He had the iPad in front of him. I saw that he'd already pulled up a map. It was early 2020, and we had begun to understand that what we'd seen in our town was on the rise in state governments across the country. That year, a record number of anti-LGBTQ+ bills would be introduced in state legislatures; and then, each year after that, the record would be surpassed until, by 2022, the number of anti-LGBTQ+ bills—most of them targeting transgender youth—would have increased by 800 percent in just four years. From there, the number would just keep rising; by 2023, more than 340 anti-LGBTQ+ bills would be introduced across the country.

Paul followed the news like a hawk. We knew it wasn't only bathroom bills, and it wasn't only sports bans. That year alone, fifteen states would introduce legislation to ban and, in some cases, criminalize our daughter's gender-affirming health care. If such a measure passed, it would not only mean that our daughter would lose access to the puberty blockers that every major medical association in our country recommended; it could also mean that Greta's therapist would not be allowed to affirm her gender, to recognize her as a girl. It could mean that her primary-care doctor would not. In some cases, it would mean that if we still sought the care she needed—perhaps by leaving the state for treatment—we could be criminalized, and she could be removed from our home.

Paul and I had already learned that nondiscrimination and equality laws did not necessarily equal a culture in which our daughter could thrive. But without the laws, what ground did we have to stand on?

"We're not going," Paul said firmly, without even looking at me.

"Paul," I said.

"I have to write to my brother," he said. He was moving so quickly.

"Paul," I pleaded.

"Forget it, Abi," he said. "I don't fucking care. I'm not moving my daughter to a state where she has no fucking rights."

He never came to bed that night. In the morning, he asked me to read the letter he'd written, which he would send to his whole family:

I've done well. I didn't lose my mind. I didn't hurt anybody. I healed and now I am able to see clearly enough to know what to do. I am able to be pragmatic and calculating and calm. What I see is a world that needs to be navigated carefully, especially for Greta. I see that I have to make the decisions that put her in the safest possible place. There is a war coming against transgender youth if Trump gets reelected. It might happen even if he doesn't win, and in some states it has already happened. I know it sounds crazy. It is crazy. But it's real. We can't move to Montana.

I handed his letter back to him silently. He was right; everything he'd written was true. What else was there to say? He was so closed off. His mouth was tight, his eyes were darting away from me. What good would it do to tell him that I didn't recognize the person who was speaking here, that I didn't know the man who said words like *pragmatic* and *calculating*? There was no helpful way to tell him that, no matter where we landed, I just wanted that other person back. I wanted the man I'd married, the one who loved to ride his bike aimlessly around town, to fly kites, to spend an entire afternoon trying to start a fire with just two sticks and friction.

This man on the couch, I hardly recognized him.

58

....

n the last week of February, I took Greta skiing for what would turn out to be our final trip ever to that mountain. We had heard of this new virus, even heard that it was in New Hampshire, but it still felt like a vague threat. We rode the chairlift I had spent my childhood on, and as I looked back at the race below, I saw Katie cheering for her daughter.

I'd researched trans girls in sports by then, and I'd learned that there were two trans high school athletes—only two, out of hundreds of thousands of athletes across the entire country—whom legislators repeatedly cited. They were the only two who had ever even won anything. What must it feel like to be them, just girls trying to live? Parents would bully them from the sidelines, yell that they were boys. If Greta raced one day, would Katie and her husband yell out that she was a *biological male* as she sped by?

I told myself to focus, to stay present. I skied behind Greta, who was already so steady and fearless on her skis. We cut across the mountain, rode to the summit. At the top, I bought her a cookie and a Gatorade and we sat at the picnic table and took in the magnificent spread below. I sent a picture to my father, told him that as a child I had never quite realized how stunning the view was. Looking at the lake was like looking into the snow globe of my escape.

Maybe we can do this, I thought. Maybe the superintendent's written promise to not discriminate could really matter. Or maybe I could homeschool Greta, sell our house in the center of town and move to the woods—hidden from view but still so close to the lake and mountains. Maybe, I thought as I sat at the top of the mountain of my childhood and looked at the lake below, maybe I could keep my daughter safe and remain on this land that held my heart.

March arrived. It was my hardest month, that stretch of time when the land is stuck between winter and spring and I spiral, unsure what to do with myself. March, the month I'd gotten drunk one college night and learned to fly farther from my body than I ever had before—so far that, when I reentered, nothing had felt real, nothing solid.

Town elections were coming up. Keith was running for the open seat on the school board. His campaign focused on "protecting girls' sports" from transgender girls.

"I'll be damned if he gets to make decisions for my child," Robin said, and she went to the town hall to register as his opponent. The county Democrats paid for campaign signs to be made. We propped one for her in our dirty snowbank and distributed the rest around town. We told everyone we knew to vote for her. We believed it would work.

When election day arrived, Paul and I took turns walking to the community center to cast our votes so that Greta could stay home. He went first. On his way into the building, he walked by Keith, who looked at Paul and—in the moment before recognition hit—waved his campaign sign and said, "Vote Keith for School Board!"

"Eat shit," my husband responded.

I looked out the window and watched as Paul walked home. From a distance he looked almost happy. He loved voting. He was off his crutches now, and he could finally walk without pain. He came in the house, told me what had happened at the polls.

I laughed and told him he shouldn't have said that, and then I left to vote. People whispered and pointed as I walked by.

"That's her, that's the mom," I heard one woman say. I stopped, turned around, and looked straight at the woman. I didn't know her, had never seen her before.

"Yes," I said to her. "I am that mother of the seven-year-old girl you are all so terrified of."

I voted, walked home. Paul met me in the doorway. He said that the police had just left. They'd come to issue him a verbal warning. There had been a report that my husband had said "fuck" while children were present. It wasn't true, but also, what did it matter? How was it possible that the police could show up at my house when my husband swore at a grown man, but they could do nothing when that grown man's father had announced publicly that he wanted to find and take my child?

That night, I got a text from Robin: *I lost.*

A neighbor a few houses down contacted me to let me know they'd heard we might be leaving, and they wanted to look at our house. It wasn't officially on the market, and if it sold we had no idea where we would go, but our town had just elected a school board member who'd run on an anti-trans platform; we knew we had to get out. We cleaned the house, and on Saturday morning we left so that our real estate agent could give his first showing. We went to the lake, walked in a daze along the shore. All the snow had melted and the ice had broken on the water, forming a jigsaw of relief across the surface, still thick with freeze but too weak to cross. Had my husband and I ever wintered the island—as we'd dreamed of in our early days together—this would have been the hardest month, because there would be no crossing over. The bob houses were gone. The sun was bright and the sand underfoot was hard with freeze. I looked in the direction of our island and wondered where we would end up. How far from the lake would it be?

Eventually, we got the call that we could return home. Our house was empty and clean and our voices echoed in it. We ran Clorox wipes over all the surfaces as we reentered. When an offer came in a few hours later, we said no. We knew it was a low offer, but we also knew that the virus was knocking at our door. That night, we got the message that school would shut down.

59

Greta and I closed in while Paul drove the ghostlike highways back and forth to work in the surreal early days of the pandemic, because his job at the food cooperative meant that he was an "essential worker," exempt from lockdown but not eligible for increased benefits. One morning, he got pulled over for driving 95 miles per hour. I didn't know what to say to him. He was so afraid, and so angry at so much. Every day became a tick mark on the way to an ever moving target; if he doesn't get sick fourteen days from today, he's safe. From today. Always fourteen days from every day.

Yet a new form of safety had also fallen over us. Our daughter was free from the bullying; no one passed our house on the way to school; I did not have to go out and see people. Instead, I took Greta to the woods. We hiked up to where the snow had not yet melted and then we went farther, to the place where the trees became scraggly and windblown and wide swaths of rock outcroppings afforded views below. We walked to the top of a mountain road to watch the sun set. Mornings, we attempted schoolwork, but usually we would just give up and go outside. On weekends we'd beg Paul to come with us to the woods, to see the world. Sometimes he would, but more often he just stayed huddled up at home.

With the town silenced, I began to look at our little house, our little plot of land, and say to myself, *This is ours.* I bought a new oven. I made raised beds for vegetable gardens in the backyard. I had an old friend come over to give me an estimate for re-siding the house. I started to read novels again; I sat in the sun on the back porch and read novel after novel, and when it got too hot I brought Greta to the lake to cool off. I thought of how perfect our spot was, tucked between the mountains and the lake.

A family I knew passed their children's old play structure on to Greta. It had a high fort, a slide, and a rope ladder. My mother got her neighbor to move it to our backyard on his trailer in trade for tutoring his girls in math. His family came to help. We all stood at an awkward distance from each other, unsure if we should be masked, unsure if we should wear gloves. The structure was so heavy, so hard to move, such an ordeal. When it finally sat in our yard, it felt like a promise. We would stay.

Or would we?

Sometimes, I called my mother crying. "I got stuck here," I'd tell her, repeating back words she had said to me my entire life.

It was the summer of George Floyd's murder. A young woman in town hand-painted *Black Lives Matter* signs and posted them on all the telephone poles in the village, but each night they got torn down or vandalized. Eventually she and her mother—whose grandparents had been some of my grandparents' closest friends—went door to door asking if they could post the signs in front yards. Almost every household agreed. But one house across the street from us said no, and they posted their thoughts about the signs on Facebook: *Are there any white people out there that are sick or [sic] this crap. We live in Gilford because we don't want this bull crap.*

Robin sent me a screenshot of the comment. I could not stop reading it. I could not stop thinking that, in just one quick post, these people had proven everything I'd come to feel about our town, about the way it was designed to push people out.

I had a new garden now, and the front yard was looking a little better, but if we were actually staying, we knew we needed to invest in home repairs before irreversible damage occurred. One afternoon while Greta lay in her new play structure drinking lemonade and reading, I sat down at my computer. My plan was to figure out what kind of home equity loan we could get.

"Jesus Christ, don't do that—just get out of there," my mother-in-law had said. "I don't understand why you don't at least go to Concord."

Ingrid was more straightforward: "You're being an idiot," she told me.

I told her that once all the meetings had stopped and Greta was home from school, I'd been able to love this place again. That I loved the mountains, the lake, that I didn't want to leave. "I don't want to be run out of my own home," I said.

"Sorry, you already were," she said. "Did you not notice their pitchforks?"

While Greta dozed in the sun, I began to search for the bank's web page, but then I pulled up a map of voting records instead. Had the lake really been drawn on it? And was the map itself really in color, or did my mind just add the red? I still see that color pulsing, surrounding my daughter and closing in. We were in the center of the reddest county in the entire state, surrounded two towns deep in every direction. Her rights had become a focus of their political party. What was I doing, trying to raise her here?

60

But the lake, the lake. I could say goodbye to the mountains, but I knew that it would always hurt to leave the lake. For the one-year anniversary of the day Greta had sat on the beach in front of our cabin and said she was transgender, I ordered cupcakes decorated in the pink, blue, and white of the trans pride flag and the three of us went to the island together. It was the first time since the pandemic had hit that we'd left our house for the night. Paul woke us before sunrise and we paddled out early, the water still as glass. We spent the day swimming, reading, walking the island trails. We dove to the spot where we could reach our hands down beneath the lake moss and come up with handfuls of clay to rub on our bodies in the sun, a makeshift spa to draw the toxins out. We grilled on the fire for dinner, and then we sat on the porch to toast our drinks and eat our celebration cupcakes. We took pictures of our proud, strong daughter. Paul even hiked all the way across the island to the spring to fill our water jugs, his hip healed and his anger buried, for the time being, beneath the peace of the island.

· · ·

The following weekend, Paul said he wanted to return to the lake. I agreed. I called my father and asked if we could have the cabin, and then we once again paddled out in the early hours of morning. It was a clear-skied, hot blue day, the kind my grandmother called an "Island Day." The cabin had become a work zone thanks to my brother Will's efforts to save it from collapsing, but we hardly ever used it anyway. We just set up our tent off to the side of the construction, and we cooked over the fire on the beach.

The three of us were sitting on the beach, clay from below the water drying on our bodies, when Will approached on his work boat. I hadn't known he was coming out, and we hadn't seen each other since that pre-pandemic winter day when he'd come over with his truck to clear my belongings from my house. I ran to the edge of the water and waved, but I quickly realized that he was yelling at me. His boat was loaded with lumber. When he got close enough for me to hear, I understood that he was dropping the wood off, then heading for more, and because of the pandemic, he felt that he could not do his work since we were there.

"But my family doesn't even need to go inside," I told him. "We have a cooler, we cook on the fire. We sleep in a tent." Also: "You didn't tell me you would be here either."

It didn't matter. He was furious with me for not telling him I would be there, for sitting there relaxing in the sun while he worked so hard to rebuild the place. It wasn't new, this fight we had about the cabin; it kept coming up, and it kept eroding our relationship.

Will threw his lumber onto the beach and sped off to get more. I walked in circles while he was gone, anxious about whether he would calm down. When I finally saw him reemerge on the horizon, I was relieved; it was a beautiful day, I had missed my brother, and we would fix this. But when he pulled up, he was still furious.

I remember standing on the roots of a tall old pine just to the side of the cabin while he yelled at me, and gazing out at the crystal-blue water, the mountains to the north, and the two small islands across the way. There wasn't a view I knew more than this one. There wasn't a place—no place at all—that could remove me in this way from the troubles of the world.

Will and I argued for over an hour. I'd cried, but now, as Will drilled new boards on the porch, I shored myself up and called to Paul. I told him to get Greta, to help me pack our stuff up.

"You don't have to go," Will said. "I'm really sorry, Ab."

"It's fine," I said, "it's not your fault," and I think I meant it. We'd had a stupid fight. I was still angry, and still so sad that after the year my family had just been through, my brother had failed to give us more kindness. But what were Paul and I even doing there in the first place?

The previous summer, on my thirty-ninth birthday, just days before Greta changed her name and pronouns but after she'd started wearing dresses, I'd asked Paul and Greta to go with me to Weirs Beach, an old, run-down lakeside boardwalk with arcades, bumper cars, fried dough, saltwater taffy, and cheap souvenirs. As a young teenager, I would get my mother to drop me there with a friend, and we would walk up and down the crowded boardwalk talking about our crushes and feeling like we lived in a city. Later, before we were parents, I would convince Paul to go there with me. We'd get our fortunes from the fortune teller machine, play pinball, and he'd impress me with his perfect aim in the antique rifle shooting gallery. We would walk the boardwalk holding hands. Sometimes I would think of my childhood self there and feel such deep happiness to be so loved and secure now.

There had been a sudden thundershower the afternoon we were there for my birthday, and beneath it the lake transformed to wide, whitecapped swaths of blue to black, so demarcated by section it was like each was fed from a separate source. The rain came down hard and fast, blowing sideways. We put our arms up in the storm and breathed the wild world in, and then suddenly it cleared just as quickly as it had arrived. The lake returned to its steady color, the waves quieted, and people came out to crowd the boardwalk. Paul and Greta and I began our walk up, stopping first at the fortune teller, and then straight to the back of the oldest arcade for the shooting gallery. As always, Paul hit every shot, which awoke all the figures—a slumped piano player sat up and began to play; cans fell; birds flapped their wings; beavers and squirrels appeared. Greta and I laughed in joy at this strange hidden talent of our sweet Paul, who would never hold a real gun. We played some more games, won a prize for Greta, and returned to the boardwalk. We walked up toward the lake's famous cruise ship, which docked there. Its daily route passed by our camp on the island, and Greta was the third generation of children in our family to run into the cabin each time she spotted the ship, reach up to the top bookshelf behind the old door, grab the megaphone, and run back to the beach to call out "Ahoy, *Mount Washington*!" as it lumbered past.

Our plan on my birthday had been to buy candy and ice cream, look at the boat, and play some more games. But as we walked, I'd suddenly noticed all the souvenirs with slogans about guns and freedom, tough men and hypersexualized women, and I became afraid. Greta— her pronoun still *he* on that June day—wore her rainbow dress. I put my arm around her, held her close, and after a few minutes I told my husband to forget it. I said I didn't want to be there, I just wanted to go home. He understood.

As Paul drove, I'd texted my father, who loved the lake as deeply as I did. I told him that I finally saw why Noah never returned. I told him I was so sorry, so ashamed that I hadn't understood this before. I said that if my daughter grew up and never returned here, I would understand.

Yet here we still were, one year and an entire lifetime later. Maybe Will had just given us the push we needed.

The lake was still as glass as we paddled off the island that evening. I remember thinking that the stillness in that season, at that time of day, was a rare miracle, because it allowed us to paddle slowly, mindfully, and say goodbye.

That night, I lay in our bed alone crying, heaving. Paul kept coming to me with water, tea, trays of food. "Do you want a back massage?" he'd ask. "Do you want ice cream?" He'd sit down next to me and run his hand over my forehead. I didn't have to explain any of it to him; he understood. I had made a decision. I'd finally gone ahead and let my heart break clear through, and I'd let go. I wouldn't be going out to the island again.

It was a kind of freedom. Without the lake, we had not one single reason left to stay.

PART THREE

On our first night in our new house, after we've emptied the moving vans and stacked all our possessions in the middle of the big coral living room, we sit in camp chairs on the back porch, whose railing is about to fall over, beneath the towering white pines that we know will have to come down, and we order a pizza. We drink cans of seltzer because we have a dug well that needs a filtration system. My mother is with us, and while our daughter runs back and forth through the rooms, calling out that the house is so big, that she can't find us, the three of us just look at each other in awe.

"You did it," my mother says, tearing up as she speaks.

I look up at this big old house that, through a stroke of wild real estate luck brought on by the pandemic, is now ours. I'd found a listing for it one July evening just weeks after we'd left the island. That day, Paul had returned home from work to say that he'd been offered a promotion; the kitchen manager had left, and now, in addition to overseeing the bakery and its staff, Paul would run the entire prepared-foods department. It meant a significant raise, a way to get a new mortgage. I'd called Ingrid.

"Do it," she'd said. "Remember when we went to that open mic in

Concord in high school? If it was that cool back then, it's got to be good now."

"Ingrid," I'd said. "I'm not basing my life on some stupid open mic when we were sixteen." But then I listened, because what else could I do?

The house was within Concord city limits but just outside the city, in the area that had been home to the dairy farms a century before. It was surrounded by conservation land. There were no other houses in sight. Our therapist had told us about one particular elementary school in Concord that she knew did well for all types of kids, and it happened to be the one that house was zoned for. The house was big—an old-style cape attached to a 1970s barnlike addition. It was also out of our price range, even with Paul's promotion. But the rental market was impossible, and there were no other houses in the school district I wanted Greta to attend. I called our real estate agent.

"That house is already under contract," he'd said. But the next day, he called me back; the house's contract had fallen through. I called Paul at work. Within hours, our family was walking through the strange former home of a man who'd passed away a year before. It sat at the top of a steep hill, and a creek ran below. Huge windows looked out to the woods. A field lay just beyond.

"It's going to be a labor of love," our real estate agent remarked. It was his kind way to say that the place had been let go and was now a disaster waiting to happen.

I looked out all the windows, opened all the cupboards and closets. I stood in the yard with Paul and I said, "What's the worst that could happen?"

He understood my point. Our cells had been recalibrated. I'd looked up Concord city voting records and I'd read Concord school board minutes and I knew that what had happened to Greta in Gilford could not happen here. Here, it seemed that worst-case scenario meant sleeping in a tent in the backyard, shitting in a bucket, and cooking on a camp stove because suddenly the house needed such major work that it had become unlivable. That scenario didn't scare us.

I found the real estate agent on the back porch and told him we wanted to list our house and put in an offer for this one immediately.

That weekend, while our real estate agent opened our doors and led people through our rooms, we went up to Henry's in Maine. We had no cell service, so we had no idea what was transpiring. Our offer for the new house had been so low and the listing price for our own so high—could any of it work?

We swam in the cold ocean, we lay on the rocks in the sun, we cooked on the fire. Greta took a picture of Paul and me posing on the shore—our eleventh wedding anniversary. We smiled and held each other close. When we returned home three days later, we discovered that it had all worked; someone had put an offer in on our house and our offer for a new one had been accepted. We were getting out.

A few days after we moved in, Greta began her year of remote third grade. I took her first-day picture—my almost-eight-year-old standing on our new front step in her favorite dress, the one decorated in video game controllers.

"Do you know what console this one is for?" she'd ask people, pointing. "What about this one?"

In the afternoons, I'd drive her to her new school for her daily hour of one-on-one instruction. I'd walk our dog through the neighborhood while she was in the building, and I'd call Ingrid.

"There's pride flags everywhere," I'd tell her. "In almost every yard. What happened to her there could not possibly happen here."

It was our first season in our new city. The country was still mostly shut down, but after school we'd go out—I'd take Greta to a park or walking trail, or I'd put a mask on and run in to get us croissants at a bakery. Sometimes we'd park downtown and have Paul come outside to say hi to us, or we'd just sit on the city benches and point out all the pride flags in all the businesses. On weekends, our family would drive an hour to the ocean to walk the shore and play in the waves. We felt so good, so free. The forces that had threatened us were far enough away. Greta's school had shocked us with its support, offering more than we would have known to ask for, even contracting an LGBTQ+ consultant to be on her team.

Yet something had happened to us. Our fear encased us—all of us—like a layer of ice, though we wouldn't notice it on Greta until months and months later, when it was time for her to return to in-person school.

But on Paul and me, it was so immediately obvious. I suddenly had an office lined with bookshelves, a window to each side of my desk. By June the mountain laurel outside my windows would erupt in an astounding pink bloom. I could see trees out there, and beyond that an open field. There were no neighbors in view, but they lived just up the hill, and they'd stop by with gifts: pastries, fresh eggs, cards to welcome us to the neighborhood. It felt like a trick of the universe. I began to scan our ceilings for cracks and send photos of them to my father, my carpenter friends: "Is my roof going to cave in?" I'd ask. "Is my foundation sinking?" I'd walk the perimeter of each room and press my hand against the wood, searching for a wall that had rotted through. I sneezed and looked black mold up online.

"Should I buy a mold test kit?" I would constantly ask Paul. "I feel kind of stuffy. Should we get the air tested?"

"You need to stop," Paul would tell me. "You need to calm down."

But what about him?

"How are you doing?" I would ask. "You seem so quiet."

"Fine," he would say, and nothing more. Sometimes I'd push and we'd argue; other times, I'd retreat. It would be months before I'd learn what had been going through his mind: Our new house had more doors than he'd ever thought possible. Three sliding doors, two Dutch doors, one odd unused door without a step that opened into a holly bush, plus the basement slider. None of the doors locked well; there were long pieces of wood to drop into place to keep the sliding doors closed, and the top half of the Dutch doors could just swing open in the wind if we weren't careful. At night, instead of sleeping, my husband once again searched his mind for ways to barricade every entrance.

But I didn't know that then. At the time, all I knew was that we would lie down in our new bedroom surrounded by the greens of the bright fern wallpaper, each of us on our separate side of the bed, so distant after nearly twenty years. I'd look out the windows and scan the line of trees at the end of the yard, memorizing their shape on the horizon, and I would wonder if maybe our perfect landing place was cursed, if maybe in trade for this space our marriage would fall apart.

62

A few weeks after we moved, we celebrated Greta's eighth birthday. We strung cardboard birthday cats from the curtain rods, draped Christmas lights on the doorframes. We put flowers and presents on the table, and we carried in a cake of a smiling pink kitten. She held her long hair back and leaned over, made her wish, and blew out her candles.

The following Saturday, the three of us got up early, got dressed, and drove to the post office in our new city for an appointment I'd scheduled. We were getting Greta a passport, one with her correct name and gender. It was something Ingrid had told me to do.

"I keep looking out the window and feeling like I want to stay here," I'd told her, "and now I'm sick with the fact that I might have to leave again."

It was September 2020, two months from the upcoming presidential election. I'd been so immersed in our immediate surroundings that I hadn't allowed myself to think of that outer layer of safety. But now, it would be stupid to not recognize that Greta's rights were on the ballot. Already, her right to gender-affirming health care was being challenged in state after state; what would happen if a nationwide ban was put in place?

"You can worry," Ingrid had said, "but you could also just do something logical."

I'd asked her what would be logical.

"Get her a passport," she'd said. In case the election was bad. In case Greta lost all her rights. In case we had to leave.

I'd always loved post offices, loved letters and stamps, and I'd spent time in them in every town I'd lived in. Before we used the internet much, I'd gone there with stacks of my printed writing submissions, paper-clipped and tucked carefully into manila envelopes. Our old post office had been downtown, in Laconia, in a building across the street from the castle-like structure of my childhood library. There was a large painting of the lake's famous ship on the wall above the postal clerks' desk, and I'd felt such satisfaction as I stood there looking at it, like I'd finally landed back in my place in the world.

Our new post office was in a strip mall with T.J. Maxx on one side and a hardware store on the other. Paul waited with Greta at the back of the room, near the PO boxes, while I prepped the clerk with my folder of paperwork—legal name change, updated birth certificate, attestation of gender from her doctor. Paul and I had printed all the rules, tirelessly gone over this right she had to get a passport with her gender, but we were both still so nervous. We were handing a stranger a piece of paper with her name change, meaning that her former name was there, too—what if he decided to use it? What if he misgendered her?

"Don't worry," the clerk said as I quietly overexplained all the paperwork. "We've done this before. Why don't you call your daughter over for a picture?"

I looked up at him. He was bald, probably older than me, tall. He had an almost stern manner—almost. I had the sense that he was in charge at that office. As my life moves forward and I return to the post office now and then, I will see him. Of course he won't recognize me, but I will remember this moment when I had wanted to hug him, to cry, to fall over onto his desk and say, *Thank you. You have no idea what we've been through.*

Paul and Greta went into the hardware store when we were done. I stood outside in the sun, waiting. I thought of what the appointment could have looked like in our old town, of how bad it could have been. I thought of that painting of the lake that had comforted me in my former post office, and my disappointment at the strip mall location of this new one, and it occurred to me once again that I'd spent my life caring about all the wrong things.

Soon Greta's passport arrived in the mail. She held it up next to her smiling face and we took pictures, sent them around to family. We were all so unprepared for the relief we felt to see her true name and that correct gender marker, *F*, on this official document from the U.S. government.

63

I t rained on the first Thanksgiving in our new house. I put my jacket on and walked up the hill to visit our neighbor Hope. She'd begun stopping by almost daily. She'd ask me if I wanted to walk the dogs in the field, if I wanted fresh eggs, if I wanted some honey from the bees she kept.

"If you need anything at all, tell me," she would insist.

She was in her eighties, and when her hands and eyes had still been good enough, she'd been a photographer who specialized in gum prints. Now the equipment was strewn around her yard amid the chickens, quail, and sheep, and her strange, ethereal photography decorated her walls.

We walked out to the end of her field together, past the halfway mark with its line of trees, where she had two headstones for old friends and a crumbling piano that was easing its way into the earth, all its veins exposed.

"Don't you just love that piano?" she asked. I told her I did. She wanted to know why we'd moved to Concord. As the rain soaked us, I unexpectedly found myself telling her a short version of what we'd endured. She grabbed my arm. "No," she said. "What is wrong with people?" My jacket was orange, hers red. I thought of the bright spots of us in the gloomy November field.

Back home, I hung my wet clothes up and settled in with Greta. We played a game, worked on a puzzle. Paul went upstairs to lie in bed. I joined a Zoom call with my father's family, and I saw Noah on the screen. His teeth were bright white and his skin was glowing. He'd become a lap swimmer, and he looked so handsome and strong. He'd moved from New York to London, but was figuring out how to relocate to Paris, and just now, while we were all holed up, he was in the Canary Islands for a holiday. He was happy.

After we hung up, I yelled up to Paul, told him that Greta and I wanted to watch a movie. He didn't join us. He came down only when it was time to eat; and in another few weeks, on Christmas Eve, he would barely even manage that. We'd made fondue, decorated the table with candles and gnomes and glistening oranges, and I had to beg him to sit down.

"I hate this chair," he said after a few minutes. "This table makes me claustrophobic." He stood abruptly and left for the couch. After Greta went to bed, we bickered as I wrapped presents, but then it escalated into a blowout fight that we'd kept at bay for months. I don't even know what it was about. His sadness, mine, our longing, our distance.

"You've let them squeeze your heart out," I snapped cruelly, imagining that vine wrapped tightly in his chest, those thorns pressing in. The election was through, and a president who supported trans rights had won. Foolishly, I'd believed this would bring Paul back. "Wake up," I yelled at him. "Look around at all we have."

I went to our bedroom, but then I heard a loud crash. I reemerged to see he'd thrown my blooming Christmas cactus at the living room wall.

"I can't do this anymore," I said. "I can't live like this."

"Fine," he said. "I'll just fucking leave. I don't even want to exist anyway."

"Paul," I said softly, as he collapsed in tears.

Two days later, he called me from an outdoor Covid testing site. We were still months ahead of a vaccine, and he had tested positive. I told him to come home, to not worry. I told him I loved him. I set the bedroom up for his return, and I made a bed for myself on the couch. I made dinner. When he got home, I had him enter through the back door, away from us.

Paul shut himself into our room and stayed there for the next fourteen days, coughing, taking his temperature and oxygen levels. I delivered food, liquids, medicines on a tray outside the door. In the late afternoons, while Greta played a video game, I went out to the field to walk our dog across the frozen ground.

One cold day, I stood in the wind at the crest of the hill and I called Ingrid. "I'm afraid for when he's better," I told her. "He's so angry at so much. He can't even function anymore."

"You have to call a doctor for him," she said. "It's not fair that you've had to do so much for so long, but you have to do this one more thing."

I promised I would, and then I walked a slow circle around the field, my dog running ahead. A red-tailed hawk circled above; I'd seen it nearly every day for the past few weeks. I could see our home in the distance. It felt so impossible that we should get to land here, so unexpected and so good.

When I got home, I called Paul over video from the kitchen while I waited for pasta water to boil.

"I'm going to call your doctor," I told him.

"I'm getting better," he said in his raspy voice.

"I mean your mental health," I said gently. "I'm going to make an appointment for you to talk to her, and I'm going to find you a therapist. Is that okay?"

"That's okay," he said, and hung up.

64

·····················

Greta and I got passes at the local ski area. It wasn't as big as our former one, and the view from the summit wasn't as beautiful, but we preferred it so much. No one knew us. When we went to the bathroom, we never worried about who we might see.

Often we would ski at night, under the lights, while school ski teams practiced. I'd point to them from the chairlift, tell Greta that I used to race like them, sometimes even on that very same trail.

"Can I be a racer when I'm older?" she'd ask.

"Of course," I would say. "Of course you can." But it was January by then, meaning that the year's legislative session had begun—a fact I'd had the immense privilege of never really noticing before. Even that year, while headline after headline proved that the letter Paul had written to his family had been right—*There is a war coming against transgender youth*—I'd still believed we were exempt because our state had a nondiscrimination law. I was wrong.

That year, two bills that threatened our new life had been filed in our state—one to block gender-affirming health care and to criminalize the doctors and parents; and the other to block transgender girls from joining sports teams with all the other girls. As Greta flew down the trail ahead of me, arms held high in joy, I'd follow behind, rehearsing what I would say when, in a few weeks, I would testify in front of the legislative committees. The bill to ban her health care was so terrifying that it felt almost absurd, the product of a dystopian novel, but it at least felt simple to defend; obviously my daughter—like all children—required access to the lifesaving treatments recommended by her doctors and every major medical association in the country. But sports—that somehow seemed murkier to people.

It was Greta's second winter downhill skiing. She'd joined a school ski group, and that winter she'd also joined a roller derby team. I'd been nervous about signing her up for both sports; she was so hard on herself, so prone to explode when she messed up. But she shocked me. She fell down in both sports—of course she did—but instead of slamming her poles against the snow or kicking her skates on the floor while repeating that she hated herself, she just looked at the other kids around her and got right back up and tried again.

I told Ingrid. I said that I thought the effect of sports was seeping into her life—she was becoming calmer, and kinder to herself.

"Duh," Ingrid said. "We obviously know as a country the benefit of sports."

But it shocks me every time I think of it. Such a simple thing—an activity with a group, one where you have to try together and learn and fail and try again. That winter, my husband would text me while at roller derby practice: *She just had a bad fall and I watched her slam her fists a minute and then she just looked around and got up.* I got emails from her teachers. *She's so excited about the ski club! She did a great job on the playground building a snow fort with a peer today!* Which is to say, the benefit of sports to my daughter—to her confidence, her frustration tolerance, her general life skill of being able to show up and try—was fast and extreme.

Greta and I would ski until late at night. I'd beg her to stop going straight down the hill, to practice her turns.

"I'm already good at them," she'd say.

"Prove it," I'd tell her, and she would—suddenly, she'd be carving her skis fast and hard, back and forth across the trail.

"Told you," she'd say at the bottom, and again I would think of her racing one day. Ostensibly, the reason our country had latched onto the idea of blocking her was because she might win. But even in the Olympics, transgender women have been allowed to participate with their gender since 2004, and it wasn't until 2021 that one single transgender female athlete in the entire world even qualified. She went on to place last in her group.

Yet the bills sweeping the country aren't aimed at professional athletes or collegiate ones, both of whom already abide by strict hormone regulations. They're aimed at children, and a categorical ban would mean that my daughter—having never gone through male puberty and living inside a body indecipherable from her cisgender peers—would not be allowed to join for the simple fact of who she comes to the world as. It would be the very definition of discrimination.

Still, my daughter could win, if she decided she wanted to. She is strong and determined, single-minded in her goals. But her winning would have nothing—absolutely nothing—to do with what a doctor identified her as at birth. It would have to do with the way she feels on skis, whole and sure and unafraid.

One night that winter, Paul and I got word from a friend that the bill to ban gender-affirming care for minors had passed through the Montana House. They'd already voted to ban trans girls from sports. Paul and I lay in the dark of our bedroom. We shouted about the bills, about the way they kept being introduced together—one to ban trans girls from sports because there was a supposed fear that they would be too large or have too much testosterone to play; but then the other to ban the very medical care that would spare them such a fate. We shook and cried. We closed our eyes, opened them again. We looked at news reports, then snapped at each other not to look. Eventually, we huddled together in the center of our bed, brokenhearted, terrified by a future we'd almost walked into.

Soon Paul and I would watch the health care ban pass in Arkansas, where my husband had lived in middle school. By 2022, we would watch it move forward in Ohio, Kansas, Missouri, South Carolina, Wisconsin, Louisiana, Idaho, Utah, Mississippi, Arizona, Oklahoma, Florida, and Tennessee; and we'd watch it pass in Alabama and—by executive order—in Texas. We'd watch the sports ban move forward in some thirty-seven states and go into effect in eighteen. By the following year, we would no longer have the strength to keep track, because nearly half our country would ban the medical care that our child requires.

That first winter in our new home, the bills were stopped in New Hampshire, and I was still ignorant enough to believe we were done. Instead, with each passing year, the bills only multiply, transforming our beloved winters to a strange landscape of snow, blue skies, and fear of the legislative session. We spend weekends skiing, or sledding in the field just through the woods, and we return home to sit by the fire and remark that we are so thankful to be here, so completely awed by how it all turned out. My husband and I look at each other. We know what we're holding in, what we're smothering. We know that since we've already fled once, that outcome will always be a reality.

....

O n an afternoon in January of our first winter in Concord, I took Greta to one of the city's large medical complexes for an appointment. I pulled into a parking spot and looked forward. There before me was Katie's car, recognizable by her vanity plate.

I took a picture, sent it to Robin.

Guess you didn't move far enough, Robin responded.

We're here for allergy shots, I told her, *but the endocrinologist's office is also here. Imagine if one of her daughters started precocious puberty and she's here to get the exact same puberty blockers that she wants to outlaw for my kid.*

As Greta and I walked through the doors, that familiar sense encased me—I was on guard, scanning every direction, preparing to defend my daughter. I was running through scripts and scenarios, trying to decide if I would speak up or hide when I ran into Katie. Thankfully I didn't see her, and I resolved to not tell Paul about it; I didn't need him to get that same old feeling, too.

The appointment was Greta's first in a five-year series of shots to combat what we now knew was a life-threatening allergy to stinging insects. When we got home, she pulled up her sleeves to show Paul where each shot had gone, and she described how each had stung just like a bee. Then she said that the doctor had told her to rest for a few hours, and she asked to go watch TV.

"Katie was there," I suddenly said, once Greta had left the room. I couldn't hold it in. "I didn't see her, but I saw her car."

Paul got up, walked away. Every time we talked about our old town, or Montana, or all the bills moving across the country, it was like he stepped inside a new skin. I could see it, I could feel it—a seething rage. I knew I should probably stay away. But I followed him to the kitchen. I loved that odd new room of ours, loved the gas range and unmatched counters, loved the lime-green 1950s feel. Paul looked at me, defeated. He said, "I really didn't realize how much that bee sting affected me."

It had been six months before, when we were still in Gilford. Our house had been under contract and empty save for our air mattresses, my computer, some food and cookware, an old couch, and a few duffel bags of clothes. It was a Saturday, and I was scheduled to teach an online writing class, so Paul decided to take Greta up north to hike and fish. It was special, a big event; because of his hip, it had been so long since he'd been able to hike with his daughter. He packed a big lunch, full of all the things Greta always wanted and never got: cheese puffs, store-bought cookies, Gatorade. They drove to the White Mountains, parked, ate a snack and set their rods up, then headed to the trail. Before entering, they cut down under a small bridge to feel the cold creek. A bee stung Greta, but she didn't care much. It had happened many times before. They walked back up to the trail.

"Dad," she said. "I feel really weird."

Paul looked at her—lips white as snow, face so swollen her eyes were nearly closed.

"You're okay," he said. "We just have to go find a doctor. Hurry, let's get in the car, no big deal."

They were out of phone service, some thirty minutes from the nearest town. Paul drove the winding road as fast as he could. He kept talking to Greta as he drove, making jokes, singing, using every bit of strength he had to keep her calm while he glanced constantly in the rearview mirror to make sure she was alive. When he saw a clinic, he pulled up to its door, jumped out, and left the car running while he ran inside.

"My daughter is in anaphylactic shock!" he yelled. Doctors or nurses or both ran out with EpiPens. They gave her two that day, then sent her to the emergency room at the hospital on the other side of town.

That evening, I tucked Greta beneath blankets on the couch and put *Scooby-Doo* on for her. She was still swollen, her body still flushed. Paul followed me into our tiny box of a kitchen. I'd gone to the grocery store, wandered the aisles for something easy and comforting that we could all eat, and after years of being vegan, I gave up right then. I came home with two frozen pizzas and two tubs of ice cream. Paul watched me put the pizzas on their trays.

"To protect her so constantly from so many angles," he kept saying. It was like he was in a trance. "And then she almost dies from a fucking bee sting."

I haven't seen Katie's car since that day at the doctor's office. I think often of the wild chance of seeing it then, at our first appointment for bee shots. I think of the way her presence collided with our routine care for our daughter, and how, after two impossibly dark years, the collision helped my husband to peer up and out from inside his storm of fear and rage and begin to arrange the pieces into some kind of map, and in that way to claw himself free.

He began therapy. He went on medication. Slowly, he quelled his fear of people, of bees, of anything at all that might harm his daughter. He emerged from the cocoon he'd made for himself in our bed, and he sat by the fire and played board games with us. He cooked. He watched movies. He rode his bike. He signed up for a pottery class.

One night at dinner he put his fork down and looked at Greta and said, "I got so sad and mad and scared for so long. Could you tell?"

"Um, obviously," she said.

"I'm taking medication now to try to help me get back to myself. I'm doing lots of things. I'm trying. I'm sorry I was gone for so long."

"Are you going to play *Zelda* with me again?" she asked plainly.

"I've missed you so much," I found myself saying to him, over and over again. I didn't say that I'd nearly forgotten who he even was.

In summer, when we had been in our new city for nearly a year, Greta went away to a sleepover camp for the first time in her life. The camp is like any other—swimming and boating and archery, songs, campfires, nights in a cabin with cabinmates and counselors. But this camp is different in that it exists for transgender and gender-nonconforming kids. Also, for the children's safety, the location is undisclosed and shared only with families upon final confirmation of drop-off plans. I look at pictures from the camp—kids jumping off the docks into the water, kids stretching a bow back in preparation to shoot an arrow—and I am overcome by the beauty of the existence of such a place and the wreckage that has necessitated it.

On the morning that we prepared to drop Greta off, I was so nervous that my hands shook too much to even braid her hair. I'd spent weeks packing for her, labeling her clothes, writing notes in a journal I'd send with her. *Brush your teeth! Carry your EpiPen everywhere!!!! Get your clean clothes from the pink bag and put your dirty clothes in the green one. Remember how amazing you are! Be strong! Be proud! Do not get mad at yourself if you have a hard time. If you lose your temper, do not get mad at yourself. Just forgive yourself, apologize if you need to, and move on. If you can't sleep, don't worry. Just lie there and listen to the sounds of the night and remember that it's only one little night in so many, and just be thankful to be there sleeping in a cabin by a lake. Be kind to yourself. I love you, I love you, I love you.*

We were the first family to arrive for camp drop-off, and soon a long line of cars wove up the dirt road behind us. Greta unbuckled to turn around in her seat and search for children like her. I looked in the rearview mirror—car after car after car, license plates from all over the country. I put my sunglasses on to hide my tears. So many families behind us, so many people who might not have lived through our specific hell but had just survived an unprecedented year of legislative bills that attacked their children's lives and bodies. How many in that line behind us had fled their town or state? Which parents were counting the entrances to their homes when they should have been sleeping? Which children were too afraid to sleep alone because they'd heard on the radio—as Greta had one morning while I scraped the ice off the windshield—that a state governor in our country wanted transgender children removed from their homes?

The night before we dropped Greta off at camp, I got a text message from Robin with a link to a news article. It showed the mug shot of the superintendent of Gilford, arrested on one charge of simple assault and one charge of domestic violence simple assault. I looked at his face and something toxic sprang back up within me. I zoomed in on his photo, scanned the scratches on his neck. They did not seem like shaving wounds.

Paul wanted to make copies of the photo, put it on his archery target, and post it around the man's neighborhood, the word *BIGOT* scrawled across it. I wanted to find more news about it, more information. I wanted to know if anyone in Gilford would bother to call for his removal.

Instead, Paul and I promised each other to try to stop the noise. To not water the wrong seeds. To think instead of joy, of that pure, precious seed inside our family that fought back against the dark, thorny vine.

We sent a letter to Greta every day she was gone. I took walks with our neighbor Hope, and I swam with her in the nearby pond. When Paul got home from work, we basked in hours of uninterrupted TV time, too exhausted for anything else.

On the last night of camp, the director sent parents an audio file of everyone singing the camp song together. *I promise I'll call you, I promise you'll call me.* I listened three times. Tears streamed down my face. I thought of Noah, of what that song might have meant to him if only he'd had it, of who he might have decided to call in the moments before swallowing the pills that left him intubated for days.

At the end of the week, when I returned to pick Greta up from camp, I had to pull over before I entered the grounds to wipe the tears from my face so as not to embarrass myself or her. Paul was at work. I put my sunglasses on and then I drove through the camp slowly, down the hill and toward the lake, then back up to my daughter's cabin. I rolled down the window and said I was there for Greta and the counselors hollered her name. Out she walked in her long dress and visor hat, her headlamp on and every bit of her wonderfully dirty from a week in the woods. She hugged her friends goodbye and she got in the back seat and it seemed to me that there was something different about her. Once we were out of sight of everyone, I pulled over again and turned around to really look at her. She seemed somehow taller, or her shoulders were set back more, or her chin was turned up higher. Something powerful that I could not name.

"My old school basically ruined my life," she said the next morning as we walked up the hill to say hello to Hope and her animals.

"How?" I asked her gently. I had no idea why she was bringing this up now. She never had, not once before.

"Ohhhhhhh," she said in a cruel sneer. She gesticulated in imitation of an adult. "Don't make noise, don't make anyone ever notice you, you have to be quiet and perfect and just like everyone else."

"They said that to you?" I asked. It was a dumb question; of course that was the message she had received, and of course the words they had used didn't matter. "Do you miss camp?" I asked instead.

"I probably would have missed it more if we still lived in our old town," she said.

I understood, in my own way. In Greta's first weeks of school in her new city, just days after we'd moved into our new house, the school board had introduced and passed a transgender and gender-nonconforming policy almost identical to the one we'd fought so hard for in Gilford. Before their vote, they invited families of transgender students to a meeting to share their concerns. They invited Kasha, the trans justice advocate from the ACLU, along with a lawyer she worked with, to attend the meeting and help guide the process. Then, in a city of 43,000 people, they passed the policy without one single person speaking publicly against it.

This is the story in my mind now, this gravitational pull between how good it can be and how horrifically bad. What if we hadn't been able to leave that town that refused to accept and include our daughter? It's not exactly a question. I can look to the statistics, or I can look to my little brother, to find the answer.

Summer ended, and Greta began fourth grade. It was her first year back to full, in-person school since the shutdown a year and a half earlier. A few weeks in, she told us she wanted to come out to her class.

School was going well enough at that point, though she struggled, that old faith she'd had—the one that had allowed her to march into the cafeteria at seven years old and announce, "I have a new name!"— now gone. We hadn't realized it during the shutdown. But now we saw it—our daughter, always on guard, always sure that threats were everywhere. Her dad and I had spent the last year unraveling ourselves from that consciousness. We would spend the next two unraveling her.

But she was still herself, of course she was. She was grounded and proud. She looked at the world and she said firmly what she thought.

Now she told us that she would just feel better if she came out. It was such a part of her—she didn't want to keep holding it alone. I contacted the teacher.

Great! the teacher wrote back. *She and I can talk about it and make a plan tomorrow.*

The next morning, Greta went to our shelf of art supplies and found the roll of trans flag stickers. She put one on her shirt.

"What will you say if people ask what it is?" I pressed her on the drive to school.

"God, Mom, would you chill out?" she said. "I can handle it myself."

She could. Two classmates asked. She explained, and she told them she was transgender. At lunch, she sat down with the teacher to plan. The next day, the teacher read a book about diversity to the class, then gave each student an opportunity to share one way they were unique. When it was Greta's turn, she said that she was transgender. The teacher defined the word. One classmate said she had a transgender brother. Another said her grandmother was trans. In art class, a girl sat next to Greta and asked her to explain more.

"That is so cool," the girl said.

It was the last thing anyone in the school ever said to her about her gender.

67

....

That winter—the second in our new home—Greta and I began a tradition: one day each year, she skips school and I skip work and we drive up north to go to a big ski area. On the morning of our first trip, I woke her up early and surprised her with the plan.

"What?" she said, staring at me, her head still on her pillow. "Am I dreaming right now?"

We drove an hour north, to a mountain I'd been to once in childhood. It was far bigger than anywhere Greta had ever skied before. The snow was fresh and soft, and national forest land stretched in every direction—endless woods and peaks and cliffs and valleys. We could see a mountain lake in the distance. Greta kept a map of the area in her pocket, and she'd chart our course, trying to make each run as long and winding as possible. When we took her first gondola ride up, she laughed the whole way. We skied from nine a.m. until four p.m. that day, and we stopped for a treat at every lodge on the mountain. We were deliriously happy.

Then, on the drive home, she said quietly from the back seat, "I'm sad." And after a few minutes of silence: "Why didn't you let me transition earlier?"

I don't know why she asked me that right then. My guess is it was because she'd just felt such pure joy, a joy she hadn't really been able to access before transition. But she'd asked me the same question many times before. My answer never satisfies her. I tell her everything I can think of to explain why her dad and I forced her to go on living miserably as a boy for so long: ignorance, fear, doubt, social pressure. I say that at least she got to transition when she was six, unlike so many others, but I know as I speak the words that they are not enough. There is nothing I can say to get back those years when my daughter could have been herself.

When we got home, we ate heaping bowls of chili that Paul had made for us, and we huddled in together by the warmth of the fireplace to show him our photos from the day. I sent a few to my mother. Greta was nine that winter—the age that had floated on my horizon for so long. How old had I been, that year we went to that ski area? I asked my mother, because I'd had a few memories of my childhood while there: sitting by the window in the lodge, my mother's bad fall. None of the memories were very significant, other than the fact that my memory before age nine is a near-total void. Yet here these snippets were, and something deep told me they'd occurred before that time. My mother, precise in all things, looked through her yearly records, stored chronologically in her kitchen filing cabinet. I had been eight, meaning I would have had roughly six months left of a childhood fully within my body.

But, as the years went on, I would also have ski racing, and it would allow me to access myself, my strength. What if legislators had decided to pass a law to ban me from the sport?

n our new home, Greta, Paul, and I took to standing in our backyard on clear, cold nights and looking up at the stars. The routine had started in winter, after Greta spent months consumed by Gary Paulsen novels and the reality survival show *Alone*. She'd begun to long for a life in the far reaches of Alaska; and without the mountains we'd formerly lived across from, we all longed for a sense of wilderness. I'd decided that perhaps the wilds of the sky could fill such a void.

One winter night as we stood out there together and looked up at the stars, she said, "Do you ever feel that you just don't belong in civilization?"

I put my arm around her and held her close. I love our new home, I love our new city, I love her new school. Yet often, as I fight for her rights, I do have that feeling.

"Yes," I said to Greta as we all stood under the stars. Yes, it does sometimes occur to me to just pack it all up and go to my brother Henry's land in the far reaches of Maine, to remove her and us from everything but the pine trees and sea. "Yes, I understand what you mean," I said again, and then we went inside and put another survival documentary on. I sat on the floor by the fire and stretched. The man on the screen huddled by a fire in the cold wilderness and listed the stages of grief.

"Wait," I said, and looked up at my family. "What were the stages?"

Greta pressed pause. Her memory is a steel trap. She repeated the stages back to me: "Denial, anger, bargaining, depression, acceptance."

"Okay," I said to Paul. "I think maybe we're teetering between the final two now."

"Yup," he said. "Press play, Greta."

On my forty-second birthday, I swam laps at the public pool and then we drove to Portsmouth to walk around town, look at the ocean, and see a play in the park.

"This is exactly where I parked when I first talked to the lawyers," I told Paul as he pulled into a spot on the side of the road.

"What?" he said. "Why were you here?"

My bag was filled with special Swedish candy I'd bought for my birthday. Greta kept reaching into it and I kept swatting her hand away. We walked the city, and we wandered into a strange little shop filled with crystals and herbs, tarot cards, spell books. Greta chose an amulet and we each chose a stone—Paul's to overcome anger from past trauma, mine to ease an overload of emotional stress, and Greta's to ignite the power of her third eye. It felt silly and fun and also like we were ready to do anything, try anything. We were ready to reenter the world, alive, whole, together.

"Paul," I'd said gently, late one night while we sat up in bed, the moon so bright we could see the ferns of our bedroom walls. "I'm still kind of angry at you for how much you disappeared over the past few years. I don't really know how to let go of it all."

I didn't exactly expect an answer. What could he possibly say? He'd fallen apart, but he'd also kept functioning just enough to keep our family afloat and to get us out of our town. He didn't really deserve my anger, and it wasn't his job to help me get over it. Still, I didn't know how to do it on my own.

"Maybe we should get married again?" he asked plainly, shocking me. "We're completely different people now."

"Yes," I'd said. "Let's do that."

"We could go back to the magic shop sometime," I told Greta that night on my birthday. "You could come up with a wish and we can go back and have them cast a spell for you."

"But does it work?" she asked. "It probably won't."

"Who knows," I said.

"It's not like you believe in magic, Mom."

"Maybe," I said.

"Well, do you?" she asked.

"I don't know. I guess I believe anything is possible."

"But magic?" she pressed.

I didn't know what to say. I've been run out of my town, not by strangers voting for laws and policies while blind to the harm they cause, but by people who knew us, who spoke with us, who witnessed our suffering. I've attended countless hearings to testify for my daughter's rights to medical care, to sports, to bathrooms and locker rooms, to simply being recognized and affirmed at school—and I know I will have to attend countless more. I've watched in horror as an elected official announced that she wanted to hang the skeletons of trans girls from the ceiling. I've woken on nights before testimony terrified, electrical volts radiating from my chest, sure that I was having a heart attack. *If the stress of fighting for her literally kills me,* I've wondered, *how will Paul protect her alone?* I miss the mountains of my former home, miss the lake—I miss that land so much it still hurts to even think of. I have a recurring dream: my body curled around Greta's like a wolf curling around its young, while outside strangers shovel through a snow embankment to get in and find her.

And still—still—there's a small voice in me that I just cannot quiet. No matter what happens, it just keeps reaching upward for the light, keeps saying that if people really saw my daughter, if they really bothered to look, they'd understand. I suppose I wouldn't call that voice magic. But I know that nothing logical can possibly account for it.

And I also know this: My daughter is only a girl. She's a ten-year-old girl who likes skiing and nature, Taylor Swift, reading, and video games. But her path to getting people to let her just be a girl is astoundingly difficult; and her power at only six years old to refuse to have herself silenced, because otherwise she knew she would not have a fighting chance in this world, that feels magical to me. When my daughter, a six-year-old in a beautiful mountain and lake town whose bigotry is an open secret and a plague, had the force and drive to stand up, to say simply, "I can wear my pink shoes, those other people should just disappear," that feels magical.

I see her walking our old street in her dress, staring down a centuries-old culture made in part by her own ancestors, looking it in the eye and saying, *This is possible, I am possible.*

To this day, people keep trying to stop her. They keep standing at their podiums and casting their votes to say that she either does not or should not exist. And she keeps going. She keeps telling the world, *I am here. I exist. You can, too.*

Magic: the power of apparently influencing the course of events by using mysterious or supernatural forces.

I look at my daughter, and I just see a little girl. But also, I see a deep, magical power.

ACKNOWLEDGMENTS

The promise that I would one day sit down to write these acknowledgments truly kept me going on some of the hardest days of this project. I have so many people to thank.

This book would not exist without the faith, wisdom, patience, and support of Eleanor Jackson and Jenny Jackson. They took a pile of angry pages and saw something beautiful within, and they spent literal years gently guiding me toward what this book could be. I am so enormously grateful. Thank you also to everyone else at Knopf who read drafts and helped bring this book into being: Kathleen Cook, Maris Dyer, Casey Hampton, Janet Hansen, Claire Leonard, Clare McCarthy, Tiara Sharma, and the entire Knopf team.

Writing a memoir was not something I ever expected or wanted to do, and this book would also not exist if not for the writers whose memoirs gave me a path and the courage to write my own: Stephanie Danler, Chanel Miller, Dani Shapiro, Susan Straight, Michelle Zauner. Thank you also to Noah Grigni, whose art shows me how to do this work with light.

And then to the people who held my family up during the experiences in this book: Aaron, Amber, Betty, Caroline, Claire, Jason,

Jennifer, Jessie, Jon, Josiah, Kerstin, Maria, Melissa, Sean, Seth, Zelda. Thank you for showing me in your own ways what it means to show up for a friend. Thank you to Michael and everyone else in our old town who stood up to publicly support transgender rights. Thank you to PFLAG NH and its members—Christine, Erica, Jenn, Jennifer, Jess, Paul, Skylar—for the early support you gave our family. Thank you to Hope for appearing at my door and restoring my faith in humanity. Thank you to Paul and the Lake Superior Zendo. Thank you to my entire big, messy family for being the kind of people who can love and accept each other, and for graciously allowing me to write about our mess.

It's not ideal to be a kid whose life is made public in order to convince voters and lawmakers of your humanity. Thank you to all the trans youth and families who share your stories for change—I would not have the courage to publish this book without you. Thank you also to so many people doing the hard work of trying to make this state safe for LGBTQ+ youth: Palana Belken, Gilles Bissonnette, Chris Erchull, Jess Goff, Linds Jakows, Amy Rock, and everyone else at 603 Equality, the ACLU, GLAD, and Seacoast Outright.

Thank you to my husband, who has spent years working jobs he'd prefer not to work so that I can write, who continuously rearranges our life in any way possible so that I can keep writing, who has retraumatized himself countless times to read this book, and who lived through this and came out the other side with me.

Finally, thank you to my little brother and my daughter for trusting me with your stories. I am a better person because of you.

I finished the final draft of this book at a time when I knew that leaving my home would always be a possibility, but when I also had deep faith in the state's nondiscrimination laws. However, we are now in April 2024, and we have lived through yet another relentless season of unprecedented anti-trans legislation that is rapidly moving forward in our state, which means that my family is once again packing our bags. This time we will move out of the state. We continue to love our new community and the refuge of our house, but that is not enough in the face of legislation that seeks to remove our daughter from every aspect of public life and take away her medical care. If you live in a state where these laws are moving forward, I urge you to speak up.

A NOTE ABOUT THE AUTHOR

Abi Maxwell is the author of the novels *Lake People* and *The Den*. After graduating from the writing program at the University of Montana, she spent many years working in public libraries, and she now works as a high school librarian. She is a dedicated advocate for the rights of transgender youth in her state and frequently testifies in front of the legislature on their behalf.

A NOTE ON THE TYPE

This book was set in Adobe Garamond. Designed for the Adobe Corporation by Robert Slimbach, the fonts are based on types first cut by Claude Garamond (ca. 1480–1561). Garamond was a pupil of Geoffroy Tory and is believed to have followed the Venetian models, although he introduced a number of important differences, and it is to him that we owe the letter we now know as "old style." He gave to his letters a certain elegance and feeling of movement that won their creator an immediate reputation and the patronage of Francis I of France.

Typeset by Scribe
Philadelphia, Pennsylvania

Printed and bound by Berryville Graphics
Berryville, Virginia

Designed by Casey Hampton